FIELD&
STREAM

THE TOTAL
FLY FISHING
MANUAL

FIELD & STREAM

JOE CERMELE
and the Editors of
FIELD & STREAM

THE TOTAL FLY FISHING MANUAL

weldon**owen**

CONTENTS

TOOLS

TYING

TECHNIQUES

TACTICS

YOU CAN SPEND YOUR WHOLE LIFE TRYING

to master flyfishing, and no matter how proficient you become, there will always be more for you to learn. Or, you can enjoy a lazy afternoon on a creek bank trout fishing with your kid. The key to becoming a truly great angler, and to getting the most out of this book, is to recognize that these two ends of the spectrum are not mutually exclusive. If you pursue both with the same zeal, the sport of flyfishing can make you happy your entire life. That's the goal of the book you're holding in your hands. *Field & Stream* magazine's experts want to make sure that you have the knowledge, skills, and attitude to have a blast every time you're on the water.

For me, the key is to try new things while not forgetting about what you've loved in the past. Lately I've been obsessed with hiking to small mountain streams to cast tiny flies to small trout that spook as soon as I make a mistake. I'm catching a few, but more important, I'm learning a lot and loving the challenge.

Joe Cermele, *Field & Stream*'s fishing editor and the author of this book, is the ideal guide for this lesson. Cermele has traveled around the world fishing, and he is one of the most talented anglers I've ever met. He shares a wealth of tactics, tips, and techniques. Now it's up to you to go out on the water and find your fun. Go for it.

ANTHONY LICATA
Editor-in-Chief, *Field & Stream*

THE FIRST FISH I EVER CAUGHT ON A FLY ROD

was a bluegill when I was 10 years old. I had no idea what I was doing, but somehow that summer afternoon, one of my wild flails got a little Wooly Bugger—one of six flies I owned—just far enough off the bank to get eaten. I was instantly in love with flyfishing,  and 22 years later, I've come to realize that no matter your skill level, the excitement of a hooking a fish on fly mirrors the first time again and again.

I believe that's because flyfishing makes you think. Every aspect—from where you stand, to how your fly lands, to how you'll fight a fish—requires calculation. Is it more work than casting and retrieving a lure? Absolutely, but it's this challenge that makes every fish caught on fly a little sweeter.

What I don't believe is that flyfishing is superior to any other form of the sport. To me, a fly rod is another tool in my arsenal, and just as a good golfer needs to know how to putt and drive, all anglers should have a basic understanding of flyfishing. Fish long enough and I guarantee a scenario will arise when a well-presented fly will hook a fish faster than any lure or bait. And whether you are a life-long flycaster or thinking about buying your first outfit, I promise this book will ready you for any situation you face with a fly rod in hand.

JOE CERMELE
Fishing Editor, *Field & Stream*

OF ALL THE FLY SHOPS I'VE VISITED

over the years, none has stuck with me more than Trout Brook Fly Shop in Trout Brook, New Brunswick, Canada. It's just a tiny shack off a quiet country road in the middle of nowhere that caters to local Atlantic salmon fishermen. The folks who own Trout Brook don't stock flasks, T-shirts, reels worth a thousand dollars, or titanium nippers. They have only what you need. Their 50-dollar reels will land salmon just fine, and their 99-cent nippers will cut your line perfectly. They do, however, have an exceptional assortment of hand-tied salmon flies and, even more important, years of tips and tricks to share about getting finicky Atlantics to hit those flies.

My hope is that your take-away from this chapter matches what I took from Trout Brook: a clear understanding of what you need to be effective on the water without all the "add-on sales." Here you will find the basic breakdowns of the gear that matters most, backed up with insider tips, tricks, and tweaks to get the most out of all your equipment—your rod, your net, your flies, and even the soles of your wading boots.

1 BUILD A PRO TROUT KIT

Flyfishing guide Pat Dorsey is a hot-stick guide on some of America's toughest trout waters. Over the years, he's gotten gear organization down to a science. Here, he shares the stuff that he can't fish without.

A MULTITOOL The Tie-Fast knot-tying multitool is always handy and speeds the knot-tying process.

B NIPPERS & HEMOS These are the tools he uses most. Absolutely essential.

C TIPPETS & LEADERS Dorsey uses mono Rio Powerflex leaders, sizes 2X through 6X, and organizes them in a Rio Leader Wallet. He separates his spools of mono and fluoro tippet onto two Tippet-T holders. "I use mono 80 percent of the time, and save the fluoro for clear water and really spooky fish," he says.

D STRIKE INDICATORS Here is a Dorsey hallmark: He makes his indicators from Holly Twist brown craft yarn— pre-cut in 1½-inch strips—that he gets at a crafts store. He fastens the yarn to leaders with orthodontic rubber bands. "Yarn is most sensitive in detecting strikes," Dorsey says.

E SHARPENER "Too many anglers fish with dull hooks and wonder why they don't catch more trout. I check my hook points when I tie on any fly."

F FLUFFING TOOL To fluff out the yarn of his indicators, Dorsey carries this homemade tool. To make one, wrap a strip of Velcro tape (the "teeth" half) around one end of a wooden dowel. Fluff the yarn by brushing it with the Velcro.

G HEADLAMP "Not many other guides I know carry a headlamp, but I don't ever want to be caught hiking out of a dark canyon or trying to fish an evening hatch without one."

H WEIGHT Dorsey carries two types of sinkers: Mojo Mud, a soft tungsten-based weight; and Orvis nontoxic split shot. "I use split shot as a base, and then form Mojo Mud around it. I can add or remove Mojo Mud to adjust my nymph rig weight from run to run, which is important because I'll change weight a few times before I even think about switching flies."

I STOMACH PUMP "Sometimes it pays to discover what the trout are actually eating," Dorsey says of this handy tool. "You might hook a fish on a midge fly but discover they're also eating mayfly nymphs. The pump has often led me to switch fly patterns."

J SUN PROTECTION Dorsey is never without Simms lip balm, 50-SPF sunscreen, and Off! bug spray.

K FLY BOXES Dorsey organizes his dry-fly boxes by hatch, and arranges his nymphs in rows by theme: small tailwater flies, beadheads, attractor nymphs, and so on. "Being organized with your flies is critical," Dorsey says. "Most people have the stuff they need. They just don't know how to find it."

2 SEINE TO MATCH THE HATCH

Instead of grabbing a fly and hoping that you're close, get some inside information by seining a stream before you fish it. First, wade out to where fish typically hold. Firmly grasp a small hand seine downstream from your feet on the creekbottom and turn over a dozen rocks or so. Bring up the net and look closely. Also check the surface flow in the current below if fish are actively feeding around you. You should pick up hatching insects, as well as any terrestrials that have the fish turned on. You don't have to be an entomologist to figure out how to match what you seine.

MAYFLY NYMPHS come in many forms, depending on the particular species: crawling, swimming, or burrowing. Try to match the general size, color, and profile of the insect.

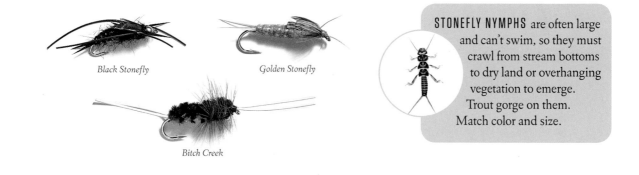

Gold Ribbed Hare's Ear

March Brown

Prince Nymph

Pheasant Tail Nymph

Black Stonefly

Golden Stonefly

Bitch Creek

STONEFLY NYMPHS are often large and can't swim, so they must crawl from stream bottoms to dry land or overhanging vegetation to emerge. Trout gorge on them. Match color and size.

CADDISFLY NYMPHS have two aquatic life stages. The larva lives in a tiny tube made of twigs and sand grains. It then seals itself into a case to pupate and grow legs and wing pads before emerging.

Sparkle Pupa

Pulsating Caddis

Squirrel Nymph

3 KNOW WHAT YOU'RE CASTING

There are hundreds of thousand of trout flies on the market, and the specific pattern you need to hook up will change from season to season and region to region. But before diving into the details, it's important to first have a basic understanding of common fly styles so you know what they represent and when to put them in play on the river.

(A) STREAMERS These big flies represent large forage like small baitfish, leeches, and crayfish. While dry-fly and nymph techniques use the current to impart natural action to the flies, streamers require the angler to work them with the rod and line to bring them to life. Cast one just above a likely trout hiding spot, and strip the streamer back with pops and pauses as it moves with the current. Quite often, the more frantic and erratic you make the fly's swimming, the more strikes it draws. Many streamers have weighted cores or heads to help them get down faster in moving water, but depending on the depth, hardcore streamer junkies often lean on sink-tip lines to up their drop rate even more. Regardless of what streamer pattern you buy, it's smart to grab some in white, black, and bright chartreuse. Use white on sunny days, black on overcast days, and the bright colors when the water's stained.

(B) NYMPHS Nymphs represent aquatic insects in their larval stage, during which they live on the bottom of rivers and lakes before moving to the surface and hatching into adults. How you fish nymphs will depend largely on water speed and depth. As they don't float on the surface, you commonly drift nymphs with a few lead split shot crimped to the leader to get them ticking over the bottom. However, in shallow water, you can fish nymphs with no added weight. You can also go weightless when trying to represent an emerging insect, which would be rising in the water column. To create this illusion, cast a nymph upstream, mend your line to help it sink, and then let it swing tight as it rides the current. If you are fishing nymphs close to the bottom, a strike indicator connected to the top end of your leader and floating on the surface can help you detect subtle bites. If the indicator stutters as it drifts, set the hook. Like dry flies, nymphs are available in nearly endless patterns, but having an array of basic nymph colors is often more useful than a variety of sizes. If you have nymphs in tan, black, and olive, you're usually all set for any situation.

(C) DRY FLIES Dry flies represent adult aquatic insects. As the name suggests, these patterns float on the surface and prompt feeding trout to rise for the take, resulting in some of the most memorable eats you'll ever experience on the water. Flyfishing as a sport is rooted in the use of dry flies. They were the beginning from which new tactics and fly styles evolved. Dries come in a huge range of sizes, and fly size is arguably the most important element when choosing one of these bugs. Suppose you're watching trout rise to sulfurs, which are pale yellow. In your box you have dries that match the color but are larger than the live bugs. You also have flies that are gray but match the size perfectly. The fish are likely to hit the size match before they go for the color match. Most of the time, this rule will keep the line tight even when you don't have the perfect representation of the hatching bugs.

4 DRESS APPROPRIATELY

Drifting a dry fly is all about creating a natural presentation. Most of that comes from your ability to cast in the right feeding lane and manage your line so the fly never drags. But having a fly that looks as good as possible and floats high doesn't hurt either. Here's how to dress your dries for maximum success.

1 PREP YOUR FLY Before you tie on your fly pattern, use a toothpick (or another pointed object) to tease the wings and tail into shape—spread out the hackle fibers and separate the wings. Clip off any loose threads or feathers, check the sharpness of your hook, and bend down the barb if you plan to catch and release.

2 USE FLOATANT Work a bit of liquid floatant between your fingers, and then massage just enough on the fly to darken the fur and feathers. Next, re-tease the wings and tail with your toothpick. Coating foam-bodied flies, such as Chernobyl Ants, in liquid floatant works, but you will want to air-dry the bug before that first cast.

3 MAINTAIN THE DRESSING If the fly drowns in the current or gets eaten by a trout, use a powder floatant to wick away moisture and recondition the materials. No-hackle patterns and those with CDC accents don't benefit from liquids and greases. Simply shake the fly before fishing it.

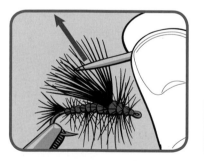

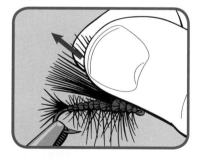

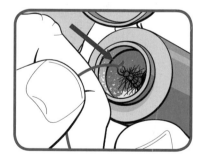

5 BEWARE OF BARGAIN BUGS

Lots of online retailers these days sell flies by the dozen for cheap—but consider that super-cheap flies are often tied on super-cheap hooks. And when the trout of a lifetime straightens the hook of your tiny discount dry fly, you'll wish you had spent a few dollars more for a quality bug.

6 HANDLE TINY FLIES

To hold small flies that you're tying onto fine-diameter leaders, use an X-Acto hobby knife handle, which is about the size of a ballpoint pen. Insert the barb into the jaws, where the blade would go, and tighten.

7 GET VERSED IN THE MIGHTY MUDDLER MINNOW

If I'm asked to name the most versatile fly ever tied, it's an easy choice: the Muddler Minnow. You can fish this fly (and its cousins) several ways, and it imitates a wide range of things trout love to eat. Greased up, it floats like a grasshopper. Stripped through deep pools, it resembles a juicy sculpin. Skated at night, it's a mouse. The more creative you are, the more you appreciate this classic.

TOP SPIN The more densely spun and tightly clipped the deer hair, the more buoyant the Muddler, and the more water it displaces when ripped below the surface as a streamer.

ORIGINAL RECIPE The typical Muddler features a spun deer-hair head, a turkey feather underwing and tail, and a tinsel-wrapped body.

There are plenty of variants. The original Gapen Muddler (A), created in 1937 by Don Gapen, has a sparser head section and is ideal for clear sculpin-laden waters. A Marabou Muddler (B) has a softer marabou underwing, which pulsates in the water; it's a solid leech imitation when dead-drifted. The weighted Tunghead Muddler (C) dives quickly. Fish it by swinging it through swift currents, or dredge it through deep pools The Black Muddler (D) is best for tinted water, in low-light, or on the surface as a cicada or cricket mimic.

8 MOD YOUR MUDDLER (AND MORE)

Another great thing about the Muddler Minnow is that with its multiple personalities, you can fish it in different ways to cover a variety of situations.

Its primary role is that of a streamer. Pulled below the surface, it looks like a sculpin or other baitfish. If you grease the deer hair on a Muddler, however, and either dead-drift it on the surface or twitch it slightly under a cutbank, it looks a lot like a grasshopper.

The Muddler offers a prime example of the fact that all flies can assume very different traits if an angler understands how to adapt its presentations. Clip the wings and hackles on an Adams dry fly, for example, and you've just made an RS2 emerger.

The point is to adapt your flies to different situations. You don't need to use 50 patterns for 50 scenarios. You're better off with 10 flies, knowing how to fish each one five different ways.

9 MAKE A DRY RUN

Although waders and wading boots are designed to get wet, that doesn't mean water can't do long-term damage to them. When a trip is over, proper drying of boots and waders is critical for many reasons. Prolonged dampness breeds bacteria that can cause boots and waders to smell pretty gamey. It can also foster mold growth, which over time can cause these items to deteriorate. Though it might seem counterintuitive, you should turn waders inside out and hang them to dry. This helps any interior moisture from sweat or pinhole leaks evaporate. After they've dried inside out for a day, reverse them and let the exterior dry. If you store wet boots in a dank basement or garage, they probably won't dry as quickly as they should. Leave them outside, preferably in a sunny spot, where they can get plenty of air circulation. If you've got a heated garage or basement, however, they may actually dry faster close to the heat source than they would outside, especially during colder times of year.

ESSENTIAL FLIES: PARACHUTE ADAMS

TYPE: Dry Fly
PRIMARY SPECIES: Trout

Most dry flies mimic a specific bug; the Adams represents absolutely nothing in particular and is one of the most—if not *the* most—potent dry flies ever tied. When in doubt, or if you can't decipher exactly what bug is drifting on the surface, try an Adams. Its neutral colors and generic profile make the play more often than not, provided you match the live bug's size. It is available with multiple wing types, but the parachute wing is the most buoyant and easiest for the angler to see during the drift.

10 SAVE YOUR EYES TWO WAYS

Not only are polarized sunglasses one of the most important tools for fly casting because they help you spot fish, discern depth, and pick out bottom structure; they protect your eyes. If you're whipping a fly through the air, it doesn't take much more than a little gust of wind to botch a cast and send a bug screaming at your face. That fly could be tied to your buddy's line, or just as easily to yours during a solo outing. If you're flyfishing, your sunglasses should stay on regardless of the weather or light conditions. In low light, try yellow lenses. I've learned this the hard way, as you can see in the photo.

11 GET THE LIGHT STUFF

A headlamp is a must for nighttime trout hunters, and lens color is key. Here's what to use when . . . if ever.

GREEN LENS COLOR
ALWAYS
Great for tying knots, won't hurt your night vision, and won't spook fish

RED LENS COLOR
SOMETIMES
O.K. for tying knots up close, but won't light anything more than a few feet away.

WHITE LENS COLOR
NEVER
It's the brightest, but it will hamper your night vision and scare fish.

12 STRING 'EM UP

Looking for a better way to transport fly rods without breaking them down every time you change spots? All you need are two lengths of cheap ¼-inch rope. Connect the ends of one length to the hanger hooks found in the back of most SUVs. You want the rope high enough that it allows you to stow other gear beneath, but don't pull it too tight. A little slack forces all the heavy butt ends with reels to rest in the middle so that they don't bounce around. Loop a second shorter length of rope around your rearview mirror. The rope in the back of the truck will cradle the butts, and the small loop in front will hold all the rod tips so they don't knock against the windshield.

13 MIND YOUR GRIP

Fly rod blanks are built first and foremost to deliver anglers the best possible cast based on line and fly weight. What they're *not* typically designed for is winching a fish to the net at warp speed. Unlike spinning and conventional rods with tapers that can accommodate a heavy-handed approach to fighting fish, there is no faster way to break a fly rod than to grip the blank above the cork during a battle. By gripping the rod ahead of the cork, you are moving the rear flex point to a spot not intended to carry that load. Some rods built for large gamefish feature a second "fighting grip" above the handle to provide extra power, but these rods are designed to flex at the fighting grip. If you remember to only grab cork during the fight, you will greatly extended the life of your fly rods.

14 PLAY WITH FATAL ATTRACTION

Absent an obvious hatch, you want a fly pattern that's buggy enough to earn interest, gaudy enough to cause a reaction strike, or just plain meaty-looking enough that the trout cannot let it float by. You want an attractor, and it's hard to beat these four.

	Rubber Legged Stimulator	Autumn Splendor	Twenty Incher	Mercer's Lemming
THE PATTERN				
WHY IT WORKS	This fly replicates a wide range of natural insects, from stoneflies to caddisflies to hoppers.	The brown body gives it crayfish appeal, and the rubber legs can drive trout wild.	It's a Prince Nymph on steroids, with soft hackle wing accents that oscillate in the water.	No natural food packs more protein power than mice. This imitator signals a big meal for big fish.
WHEN TO FISH IT	Spring through fall, especially midsummer.	It's not a fall-only pattern. Fish it year-round.	Year-round, but it's most deadly in spring and summer.	Summer nights when big trout are on the prowl.
HOW TO WORK IT	Dead-drift the fly tight to banks. The seductive legs will do the rest.	Bang the banks, and then retrieve the fly with fast, erratic strips.	Make it the lead fly on a double rig, and dead-drift it through deep runs.	Make short, erratic strips toward the shore, above runs, and around cover.
TYING TWEAK	In dirty water, increase the flash with a sparkle dubbing body.	Remove the conehead weight for softer presentations to lake fish.	Mix and match head dubbing colors to find the money mix.	Dab a spot of glow-in-the-dark paint on the head so you can see it at night.

ESSENTIAL FLIES: WOOLLY BUGGER

TYPE: Streamer/Nymph
PRIMARY SPECIES: Trout, Bass, Panfish, Carp

Not only is the Woolly Bugger an easy fly to tie, it's one of the most versatile in freshwater. Depending on size and color, this fly can represent almost anything. A black one drifting down a smallmouth river is a spot-on hellgrammite copy. Stripped deep and fast, an olive-green bugger will fool brown trout feeding on sculpins. Slow-hop a rusty orange one in front of a carp rooting for crayfish, and it will get slurped. Don't hit a lake or river without your Woolly Buggers. They'll score when fish refuse all other flies.

15 MINT A MINI FLY BOX

Aside from sparing your fishing buddies your early-morning coffee breath, there's another reason to eat Altoids: The empty tin makes an ideal fly box. And if one of those pals who's suffered your horrible breath before is new to flyfishing, you can apologize with one of these. It's the perfect beginner's fly box.

STEP 1 First clean out the mint dust from the tin. Cut the following from a shoebox: one 3½x¾-inch strip to fit lengthwise inside the tin, and two 2⅛x¾-inch strips to fit widthwise.

STEP 2 Cut two notches halfway through the longer strip. Do the same down the center of each shorter strip. Insert those shorter strips into the longer piece at the notches you have made.

STEP 3 Wrap the cardboard with duct tape. The tape strengthens the cardboard, protects it from water damage, and gives the grid a snugger fit inside the tin. If you don't need compartments, stick sheets of magnet or foam inside the tin.

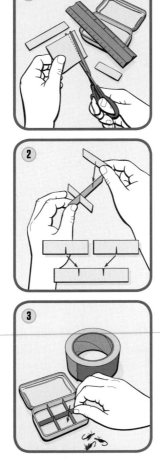

16 FLOAT BIG WHEN THE GOING'S TOUGH

One of the lessons I learned from scuba diving with trout came from watching them react to attractor flies. To set the scene, I had a buddy fishing a two-fly dry-fly rig. The lead fly was a size 12 Stimulator—a big bug that might look like a terrestrial or a stonefly, although its basic mission is to stimulate a rise. The second fly, trailed 18 inches off the bend of the first, was a size 18 Bluewing Olive, meant to match natural Baetis flies.

As I watched the fish from below the surface, I noticed they'd swim up to check the larger fly, then catch sight of the smaller fly and go eat it. The lesson is that if you are fishing two small dries, you will not draw the fishes' attention as consistently as you would with an attractor.

The attractor fly really works when you are out prospecting and when there isn't a consistent hatch coming off. When you're fishing a prolific hatch, don't mess around with attractors.

17 CHECK YOUR ROD SPEED

"Fast" and "slow" are adjectives you'll hear often when describing the action of a fly rod. But what do they mean? It's all about how much or how little a rod flexes when you cast. Here are the advantages of slow and fast.

FAST These days, the majority of fly rods on the market are considered fast, which ultimately means they're stiff. While that might seem counterproductive, a rod that flexes quickly and more rigidly increases casting distances and actually makes casting easier on the arm. This is especially true when using heavier fly rods for big game, or when casting sink tip lines and weighted flies. Modern graphite rods are also very light. Combine the weight with a fast action, and you have a rod that delivers far and accurately and won't kill you when you're casting all day.

SLOW Before graphite came along, most fly rods were considered slow. That's because materials such as fiberglass and bamboo were naturally "softer," and therefore had more flex. These materials also made rods much heavier, but plenty of casters still prefer the action of fiberglass and split cane, especially for delivering bulky flies like deer hair bass bugs. Slow rods can be cast just as accurately as fast rods, but they force you to think a bit more about each stroke and take your time.

Many casting instructors prefer that beginners learn on slow rods for that very reason. Many anglers also prefer the soft action for hard-fighting fish such as salmon and steelhead, because a mushier rod better absorbs the sudden line jolts that happen when these fish run, theoretically resulting in fewer break-offs.

18 AVOID GETTING LOST

On a summer evening, you may very well wade-fish a river until after the sun has set and the path back to your vehicle is no longer clear. Bankside brush all looks pretty much the same in darkness; bushwhacking out is too often the result. But the solution is easy: When you first enter the river, tie a white handkerchief or paper towel to a branch to make your return path easy to find. Just be sure to remove the marker as you exit.

19 GET A BEAD ON THE BIG BUGS

There are thousands of hatches that occur across the U.S., many of which involve relatively small bugs. Then there are those special hatches where the insects are monstrous and the trout that rise to them to them are massive. The key to cashing in on these big-trout feeding frenzies is knowing when and where these jumbo bugs are going to show up.

	BROWN DRAKE (*Ephemera Simulans*)	GREEN DRAKE (*Ephemera Guttulata*)	MICHIGAN CADDIS, HEX (*Hexagina Limbata*)	GIANT SALMONFLY (*Pteronarcyidae*)	GOLDEN STONE (*Ephemera Guttulata*)
COMMON NAME (*Latin Name*)					
COLOR	Speckled brown	Green, olive, brown	Yellow and brown	Salmon-orange body, dark wings	Gold and brown
SIZE	3/4 inch	1 inch	1 1/2 inches	2 1/2 inches	1 1/2 inches
HABITAT	Silt, fine gravel: riffles and pools	Silt, fine gravel: riffles and pools	Silt: slow water	Rocky, fast water	Rocky, fast water
TIME OF YEAR	Late spring, early summer	Late spring, early summer	Early spring, midsummer	Late spring, midsummer	Late spring, midsummer
TIME OF DAY	Late afternoon, evening	Late afternoon, evening	Evening, twilight, dark	All day	All day
REGIONS	Midwest, West, East	East, West	Midwest, Northeast, Northwest	West, Midwest, East	West, Midwest, East
ALL-AROUND FLY	BROWN DRAKE WULFF	EXTENDED BODY GREEN DRAKE	HEXAGENIA	ROGUE FOAM STONE	YELLOW STIMULATOR

20 DIP SOME RUBBER

Studies show that nets with rubber bags are ideal for all species of gamefish. Nylon nets (especially those with knots) and mesh cloth nets have been proven to damage fins and remove a fish's protective slime coating, leaving it prone to disease and infection until the coating re-forms. Rubber nets are far gentler, which is especially important with the more delicate species such as trout. Over the last few years, rubber "ghost nets" have become very popular. They cause minimal damage to the catch and fishermen also widely believe the translucent color further reduces stress, as it blends better with the water than a traditional black or green bag. As a bonus, flies won't tangle in a rubber net nearly as easily as they will in a cloth net.

21 ANTE UP WITH ANTS

Ants of various types are numerous along the shores of all trout streams. They also fall in the water often, so trout are accustomed to seeing them. The best imitation by far is a simple Fur Ant, which you can fish either dry or wet.

Black and cinnamon are common ant colors, and it's easy to carry both imitations in sizes 10 to 20. Fishing slow water behind a logjam might call for a size 10 to imitate the larger carpenter ants that most likely live among the logs above water. At the other extreme, I often use a size 20 Fur Ant to fool trout that I find making intermittent sipping rises in the slow-moving water of larger pools. For general searching in the absence of rises—and for fishing wet—I'll use a size 16. In all cases, you should dead-drift the fly to simulate how trout encounter any of the natural ones.

One special—and also potentially frustrating—ant situation usually happens in summertime: Vast flights of winged ants sometimes appear—often the day after a rainstorm—and accidentally fall on trout streams, quickly covering the surface with thousands of dead and dying insects.

Trout go crazy over these fallen swarms. But because the natural bugs are all identical in size and color, the trout also become extremely selective. You must have the right size (usually 14 to 20) and color (usually black) parachute ant pattern in your fly box. Without it, you may as well sit there and just watch all the rising trout.

Fur Ant (black)

Fur Ant (cinnamon)

Schroeder's Parachute Ant

22 GET THE DIRT ON HOPPERS

Forget everything you've heard about dry-fly fishing with grasshopper patterns—all that crazy stuff about so-called hopper plagues or how monster browns will smash these things like largemouths hammering a bass bug. Chances are, it's not going to happen.

Instead, you'll see selective brown trout gently, almost imperceptibly, sipping a small hopper dry as it dead-drifts along a bank. On heavily fished rivers, such as Montana's Madison or Yellowstone, many flyfishermen cast hopper patterns all day—and the fish have wised up. Yes, there are still rare times and places when a size 8 high-floating hopper will draw a heart-stopping rise. More often, though, you'll do much better by carefully fishing a smaller, lower-floating pattern such as a Henry's Fork Hopper in size 12 or 14.

Now, forget the hopper-and-dropper combination that is so popular these days. The addition of a small, trailing nymph behind your hopper dry can make things worse instead of better. You'll be trying to cast and dead-drift your little hopper tight to the edges of stream-bank cover where the trout are; if there's a trailing nymph extending beyond the hopper, it will likely hook and tangle on that cover as the flies land.

Finally—and this pertains to all terrestrial fishing—at the end of the day, you'll need to chill out. No, I don't mean relax. I mean quit fishing terrestrials. As the sun goes down and the air cools, terrestrials naturally become less active and less available to trout. Switch to a caddis dry, or maybe a streamer fly, and your hot-streak day will continue into evening.

Henry's Fork Hopper

23 LET YOUR BUGS BREATHE

Small nymphs and dry flies don't hold on to much water, but large streamers—especially those tied with rabbit strips or marabou—act like sponges. A meaty streamer dunked on Saturday will still be soggy the next weekend if you left it sealed up in your fly box, and will leave condensation that gets the rest of your flies damp. Given that you use flies in the water it seems counterintuitive, but moisture is the enemy. Prolonged wetness can actually cause the materials to rot and stink. It can also cause feathers and synthetic fibers to get matted, hindering them from wiggling the way they should the next time you fish the flies. At the end of a day of streamer fishing, I always leave my box open in the garage or on the deck overnight to let air circulate around the bugs for proper drying.

ESSENTIAL FLIES: HARE'S EAR

TYPE: Nymph
PRIMARY SPECIES: Trout

Available in many colors and sizes, the Hare's Ear is a go-to nymph when you're just not sure what to go to. It can represent almost anything small—a stonefly emerger, an emerging caddis, a tiny crayfish—based on how you fish it. If you're not seeing any surface activity on a trout stream, and streamers just aren't turning fish, it's hard to go wrong bouncing a Hare's Ear across the bottom on a weighted rig, or swinging it just below the surface unweighted. It's almost guaranteed to match some aquatic larvae present in the river that the trout want to eat. As a loose rule, I like black Hare's Ears in stained water, and tan or olive in clear water.

24 TACKLE TOOTHY FISH

Over the last few years, flyfishing for pike and muskies has become very en vogue. And why not? These species are big and mean, and when they explode on a streamer, it can stop your heart. Thing is, pike and muskies have lots of teeth, so you can't just tie on a big fly and start casting with traditional leaders, unless, of course, you're really into losing flies. Before you set out for toothy targets, consider adding these tools to your arsenal.

BITE TIPPET A bite tippet is critical for thwarting pike and muskie chompers. You can buy a cheap pack of pre-tied steel leaders at the sporting goods store, but I don't recommend it. These leaders are designed for use with hard lures and bait hooks in saltwater, where the species being targeted don't often require much finesse. They're very stiff, and a fly needs to move seductively and naturally in the water. Tie-able steel leader, such as Cortland's Toothy Critter Tie-able, is soft, and you can knot it to the end of your main leader with a simple Albright knot. It's also very limp, so your flies will maintain their action. Try losing the steel leader all together and using a piece of 80-pound fluorocarbon if you're dealing with extra-finicky pike and muskies. It's invisible underwater, and their teeth won't cut through it most of the time.

JAW SPREADERS Pike and muskies have a bad habit crushing a fly so hard that they literally inhale it into the back of their throat. Problem is, these fish are also notorious for not unclenching their jaws, even after they're in the net. A set of jaw spreaders shouldn't set you back more than $15, and they're one of the best investments you can make. This simple tool will keep the mouth pried open wide so you can control the fish with one hand and remove the hook with the other hand, using long pliers. Not only will a jaw spreader make life easier and save your fingers, it'll help ensure more fish swim away healthy.

HOOK SHARPENER In most flyfishing scenarios you'll probably never take the time to sharpen a hook, and that's okay because you'll probably never regret that decision. But that's not the case in the pike and muskie game. Their mouths are very bony, making it more difficult than you might think to stick the hook in their jaw. Your best offense against those rock-hard mouths is a razor-sharp hook. Even if you're not catching any fish, check the hook frequently. It only takes one bump of a log to dull a point, and, considering you might only get one shot at a muskie all day, you don't want to blow it because you were too lazy to quickly run a sharpening file over the hook.

25 PICK A COLD REMEDY

Trout feeding patterns change when temperatures drop and insect life cycles slow down, so you'll have to alter your tactics a bit. One of these three approaches should coax a few fish from their icy lies.

SMALL & SLIM On most winter trout streams, tiny mosquito-like midges are the most active and available food form. Standard midge pupa patterns—such as Brassies and Serendipities—can be effective. So can slim-bodied nymphs, such as the Flashback Pheasant Tail. But size is often more important than the specific fly. Think small, and go for patterns in sizes 18 to 22 on 5X to 7X tippets.

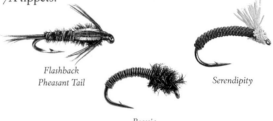

Flashback Pheasant Tail

Serendipity

Brassie

HIGH & DRY Rising fish are a bonus rather than a mainstay of winter fishing, but it's worth it to be prepared. A size 18 or 20 Parachute Adams or Parachute Black Gnat, or a Griffith's Gnat in sizes 18 to 22, will cover the occasional hatch of midges or, on some rivers, bluewing olive mayflies. Low, clear winter water can make rising fish ultracautious. Keep a low profile and use long, fine leaders.

Parachute Black Gnat

Parachute Adams

BIG & GAUDY If the microflies aren't bringing them in, you might try the other extreme—big leeches and streamers down to size 4 or so. I hooked my largest winter trout on an ordinary No. 8 black woolly bugger. Fish near the bottom, and dead-drift with short twitches.

Bunny Leech

Woolly Bugger

26 GET STEAMY

To restore mashed flies to their original operating condition, all you need to do is boil water. Just put a teakettle on, and crank up the heat to produce a healthy jet of steam. Grip the fly you need to revive at the hook bend with a pair of pliers and hold it in the vapor stream, rotating slowly so that the mist penetrates the fly's wings, tails, and hackles. Heat and moisture will relax the kinks, massage out the crimps, and return the fly to fishable shape. As soon as it looks refreshed, shake off excess moisture and lay it on a paper towel to dry.

27 EGG STEELHEAD ON

If the river stains in winter, open your fly box and reach for a Meth Egg. Slowly drift the pattern under a strike indicator through areas of soft current, or high-stick it with plenty of lead in the fast runs that steelhead use to make their way upriver. This flashy material reflects even low amounts of sunlight and gets chromers hyper.

28 MATCHBOOK YOUR MIDGES

Tiny midge and mayfly patterns give you great results when used in the fall and winter months, but putting one of these flies on a strand of tippet can be a serious nightmare, especially with cold fingers after a cup of coffee or two. Of course, before you can even tie one on, you've got to remove one of these micros from your fly box. Drop it, and there's a good chance you won't find it again. To help get the frustration out of the midge game, try this trick from legendary Wisconsin fly tyer John Gribb. His "midge matchbook" does away with the need for tweezers to extract a fly from your box, and makes tying a midge on your line a cinch.

STEP 1 Slice a sheet of foam with scissors to create a series of matchstick-sized sections.

STEP 2 Staple the foam to a tab of cardboard or heavy card-stock paper.

STEP 3 Stick the midge (or small mayfly, caddis, or other) flies to the ends of your "matches" to protect the flies when you fold the cardboard like a matchbook and tuck the tab under the stapled end. This packet easily fits in your shirt pocket, vest, or pack.

STEP 4 When you're ready to fish, thread the tippet through the eye with the fly still on the foam (you can either tear off the individual tab, or twist the whole booklet to help you tie your knot). Then simply detach the fly from the foam and maybe add a dab of floatant—and you are good to go.

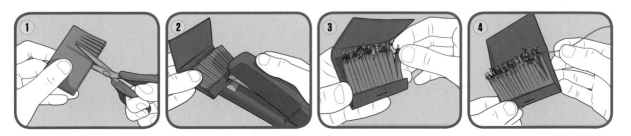

29 GET CRABBY IN WINTER

Your local river may be frigid, but if you can get to (or live in) one of the warmer coastal areas from South Carolina to Florida to Texas, winter offers some of the year's best shots at skinny-water redfish that are quick to eat a crab. When temps dip, these crustaceans can be more abundant than shrimp, but the trick to hooking up is picking the right one. Here's why you should give Simon's Hover Crab a shot.

RIPPLE EFFECT Fish this fly on a mono leader dressed with a smear of floatant, and you can swim the crab right across the surface. Make the tasty morsel ripple and wake, and any redfish looking up to feed will crush it with the same conviction as a summer largemouth smashing a foam popper.

HOVER CRAFT Lightly belly weighted and created with foam, Simon's HoverCrab is designed to suspend in the strike zone. This makes it a deadly choice when reds are rooting in weeds or submerged grass that is too thick for a dumbbell-weighted fly. Get this pattern hovering just above the grass tops with sink help from a fluorocarbon leader, and get ready for the slurp.

30 MAKE LIKE BIGFOOT TO STAY WARM

If you plan to wade in a cold winter trout stream, you'll want to opt for boot-foot neoprene waders with boots that are a half size to a full size larger than you normally wear. The bigger the boot, the more dead air space inside; by giving your feet extra wiggle room, you'll keep blood flowing to your toes all day. The extra space also means your foot is farther away from the thick rubber material that's making direct contact with the water. Stocking-foot waders worn with wading shoes allow the icy water to surround your feet, and when that happens, even the best wool or battery-operated socks will offer little long-term defense against the chill.

31 WADE OVER TO THE HOCKEY SECTION

A lot of really expensive wading boots seem to come with absolutely lousy laces. We're talking $200 boots with laces that break after being soaked in a river four or five times. That, to me, is plain cheap and stupid.

I've worn fancy boots from all over, and they all claim to be the next best thing. Some of them fit great and grip great on the bottom of the river, but after a few trips, when I go to tie them, the laces break. Do yourself a favor. Don't trust any of the mainstream boot companies.

Oh sure, go find a pair that fit you just so, have a good tread and all of that. But if those boots don't come with a set of wire laces, go ahead and punt the laces that they come with.

Instead, go to the nearest sporting goods store, buy some hockey skate laces, and swap those in. Ice hockey skates see plenty of moisture and wear and tear. While not perfect, their laces are far better than the cheap import stuff that comes standard on most wading boots.

32 JOIN THE BASS BUG REVOLUTION

Compared with the drabness of many trout patterns, flies for bass are a carnival freak show come to life. Garish colors and outlandish names, such as Meat Whistle and Chubby Gummy, highlight the bass fishing midway these days, where high-tech glitter promises plenty of low-tech fun.

The essence of flyfishing for bass is a kind of laid-back antidote to trout fishing's match-the-hatch intensity. Bass bugs are fanciful rather than factual, full of wanton wiggles as they pop, slide, or slither among the lily pads of summer. New materials and tying techniques are making bass flies more diverse and more effective than ever.

Poppers and sliders are both essential patterns for topwater fishing. The styles are classic, but modern bodies of painted, dense foam float better and last longer than the cork versions. Soft silicone-rubber legs, meanwhile, add lifelike movement that drives bass nuts. Cup-faced poppers like the Umpqua Bass Popper make lots of surface noise when twitched, thereby stirring up

lethargic fish. As much fun as poppers are to fish, I often use a subtler floating slider, such as Murray's Shenandoah Sunfish Slider. Sliders make a slow and quiet surface wake when stripped with intermittent pauses. Perhaps imitating a wounded bluegill, sliders are the answer for pressured bass in clear water.

Newer developments in trout flies also have some application in bass fishing, notably various popular and large foam-bodied dries. Patterns like Mercer's Flush Floater Stone work as well for smallmouth bass as for trout—or even better.

Not all modern bass bugs are high floating. Polk's Dirty Rat swims with only its nose above water when retrieved—just like a mouse. Then there's Chocklett's Chubby Gummy Minnow, a fly-casting version of the soft-plastic jerkbaits used by conventional bass anglers. Its soft, reflective body is a great imitation of the threadfin shad that are common forage in many lakes.

33 THROW THE NEW BASS CLASSICS

Looking to fool big largemouths? Sure, hair bugs are classics, but these new-school patterns must find a home in your arsenal. Whether you're looking for blow-ups in the lily pads, or have to dredge a bass off a deep rock pile, these ties have you covered.

Hare Jig

Polk's Dirty Rat

Chocklett's Chubby Gummy Minnow

Murray's Shenandoah Sunfish Slider

Gulley Ultra Craw

Barr's Meat Whistle

Mercer's Flush Floater Stone

Umpqua Bass Popper

Messinger's Frog

34 FISH LURE-INSPIRED FLIES

Fly anglers are now imitating bass lures, and the results can be terrific. Barr's Meat Whistle, and the Gulley Ultra Craw from Orvis, are similar to skirted bass jigs, but with a key difference: They have even more fish-appealing wiggle—thanks to the combination of flexible furs and feathers and comparatively little weight. They're heavy enough to sink, but won't rocket to the bottom. Because bass often hit while the fly is sinking, a slow drop is a good thing.

There are equivalents for soft-plastic worms, too. The Hare Jig is based on a long, flexible strip of wiggly rabbit fur. That soft fur has more bass-tempting wiggle than even the softest of plastics. The fly also has a lightly weighted head to give a jiglike action when retrieved.

Rabbit-fur flies do raise one critical point: Fur soaks up water, and the weight can become very difficult to cast with lighter gear. Although lighter bugs can easily be cast with trout tackle, bigger flies require a heavier line and rod. Eight- to 10-weight rods are not too big for larger bugs, and they're best coupled with a bass-taper fly line. Heavy rods may seem intimidating, but the latest graphite models, like the Bass series from Sage, feel quite light and do a superlative job of casting big bugs 40 to 50 feet away.

This is not dainty stuff. When a 6-pound bass smashes your bug, those heavier rods have enough power to keep the fish from diving back into cover. So not only will you have awesome surface strikes, you might land the fish, too.

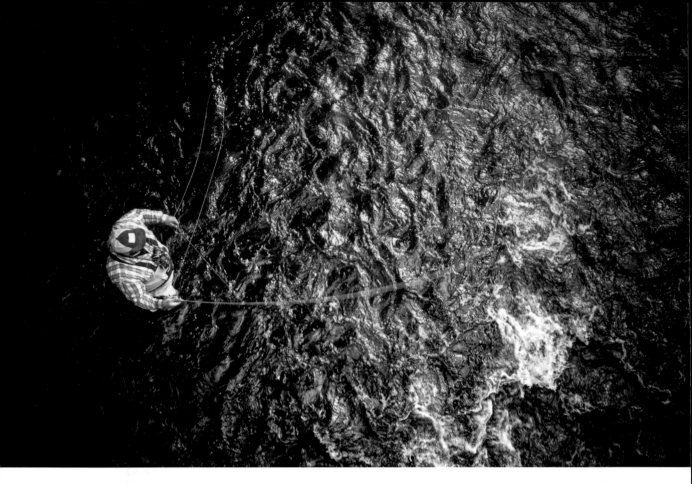

35 CARRY EVERYTHING YOU NEED AROUND YOUR NECK

Why weigh yourself down when all you want to do is blitz a local creek for a few hours? Flyfishermen have a nasty habit of carrying too much gear when, in reality, quick jaunts require very little. A neck lanyard, like the Neckvest Lanyard 5 from Loon Outdoors, is a great option for a "get in, hook a few, and get out" trip. The trick is making sure you have exactly what you need. Load your lanyard with these tools, and you're all set.

Ⓐ FORCEPS Clip them anywhere on your lanyard and forget about them.

Ⓑ NIPPERS If your lanyard doesn't come with this handy tool, buy an inexpensive pair that always stays with your neck gear.

Ⓒ FLOATANT Necessary for that whole critical "keeping your dry flies on the surface" thing.

Ⓓ TOP FLIES You should really hope to have a bead on your specific local hatches, but if not, a few Adams, buggers, caddis, and hare's ears should have you well covered.

Ⓔ TIPPET Don't worry so much about carrying extra leaders. Just bring a spool of tippet in the size you'll use most.

36 DUNK SOME WOOL

The StrikeIndicator tool was developed in New Zealand (famous for its fickle trophy trout). It's pretty simple: Small tubing pieces are threaded on a tool that grabs the leader like a crochet hook. Pull the leader, slide the tube in place, and form a loop through which you place chunks of colored wool. Then cinch the loop tight, and the wool stays put—you can slide it up and down the leader on a whim. You choose how much wool forms the indicator, depending on the currents you're fishing. You can use orange-dyed wool, but I like white—it looks like the bubbles on the water.

To me, the wool is the real attraction. We like wool sweaters and socks because they wick water. In the case of this indicator, a dab will do. It rides high, but sinks quick on the tug, so it's super-responsive. Casting-wise, it cleanly slices through the air and lands on the surface with barely a splat.

In addition, you can shape the wool. I like to make it stand up in a tapered "flame" shape. That post stands straight up when the weight and flies drop into the zone. Any hitch or bobble prompts me to set the hook. When the flies are grabbed hard, it plunges. Don't lean on the indicator as the end-all, be-all solution for catching trout with flies. But if you're going the strike indicator route—and most of us do, sooner or later—this option is worth a look.

37 PAINT IT BLACK

A black Sharpie is a permanent fixture in my trout pack. It has been ever since I traveled to western Colorado last year and caught a 32-inch rainbow—the biggest trout of my life. After a solid morning with streamers and dries, my guide had me switch to a tan hopper for the afternoon. But before I tied the fly on, he colored the body black with a Sharpie he kept in his vest, explaining that when fish see the same pattern over and over, a little change can make a big difference. Sure enough, the fish hammered the black bug, and I caught my best trout ever. And that was enough to convince me to carry a Sharpie from then on.

38 GO WEEDLESS

Not all bass flies come with integral weedguards, but it's easy to add your own. One trick involves stretching a small rubber band between the hook eye and the barb. The rubber band deflects weeds as you retrieve but pops free when a bass grabs your fly.

In some cases, you'll be better off using a weedguard made for crappie jigs by Southern Pro Tackle (shown below). The soft-plastic device has a small eyelet that slips over the hook eye before you tie a bug to your leader. A slim cylinder trails the eyelet; stick the end over your hook point. This commercial weedguard might be too small for some larger hook sizes, but once you get the idea, it's very simple to make larger versions. All you need is sharp scissors and a soft-plastic worm.

39 PLAY THE ULTRAVIOLET CARD

While we can debate whether fly colors really matter all that much compared to other factors such as size, profile, and so forth, I don't think it hurts to add a little eye-grabbing detail, particularly when you're fishing attractor patterns, and especially when you plan to be fishing nymphs in deeper runs when the water is off-color. As a rule of thumb, it's best to mimic natural bugs as closely as possible when you know fish are keyed on a specific food source. But when you're prospecting, any and all "attention-getters" are worth a shot.

Spectrum Response UV spray is designed to make all of the colors pop on your flies. Squirt it on a surface, such as fur or feathers, and it will cause any of those materials to absorb radiation in the ultraviolet range of the electromagnetic spectrum, and then emit that radiation as light. In simplest terms, it makes flies appear brighter when the water is darker. The theory is pretty simple: Fish sees fly better; fish is more apt to eat said fly.

The spray is nontoxic and hydrophobic, meaning it doesn't wash off of treated surfaces (so you want to be careful not to spray your tippet if you don't want that to shine). It doesn't involve resins that will gum up your flies. One tube of spray goes a long way; it only takes a squirt or two to treat a fly.

If you're looking for a bit of an advantage but you're not willing to go so far as to scent your flies (that would be a low-down dirty trick, after all), this bottle might be $20 well spent.

40 STOCK THE EXTRAS

Other than the usual stuff, here are four key items to carry in your flyfishing vest.

BINOCULARS I use my Swarovski 8x20s to better see what the trout are doing, not to mention for spying on the other guys.

IBUPROFEN The best antidote for long sessions of casting and stripping heavy flies.

SAFETY PINS Fix your wader suspenders, make an emergency line guide or tip-top guide, untangle knots, or clear the eye of a hook. Pinned to your vest, this is the ultimate inexpensive field tool.

CHEAP STOGIES Perfect for sitting on the stream bank waiting for rises; also repels insects and other nosy anglers.

41 BUILD A THROWBACK FLY BOX

If you can find a videocassette case—maybe at a flea market or yard sale—it's easy to turn it into a cheap fly box.

Line the case with foam weatherproofing tape, which works well because it's already cut to the perfect size and the adhesive backing makes it easy to install. This box is packed with 109 flies, and ridiculously easy to carry in any vest or pack. For a bonus, find an old box for *Jaws*. Or maybe *A River Runs Through It*. How about *The Fly*?

42 CHECK THE AIRWAYS

Unlike Bob Dylan, fishermen do need a weatherman to know which way the wind blows. A small portable radio designed to receive NOAA weather forecasts should be an essential part of your fishing gear. Mine lives in the glove box of my truck, along with spare batteries. If I'm wade fishing, I listen to the latest forecast while suiting up streamside. When I head out in a boat, I take my radio along and tune in periodically. Aside from the obvious safety advantage, the short-term wind forecasts allow me to pick a protected river bend or stretch of canyon, or to find the lee and windward shores of a lake. If this technology seems archaic, you'll thank me when you're in a remote spot where your cell phone is worthless but the radio is still getting a signal.

ESSENTIAL FLIES: STIMULATOR

TYPE: Dry Fly
PRIMARY SPECIES: Trout, Bass

A stimulator is designed to do exactly what its name suggests; stimulate a fish into rising. A favorite pattern on Western waters where fish tend to be looking up even without a major hatch occurring, this fly simply gives trout a large target that looks like a juicy meal. While the "stimmy" may not represent anything specific, it is a perfect match for certain large bugs such as salmon flies and grasshoppers. As stimulators are very buoyant, they are ideal for fishing in tandem with a heavier nymph riding below, or as a marker fly ahead of a smaller dry that's not as easy to see. Though stimulators are mostly associated with trout, I've caught many fine smallmouth bass drifting them in summer on East Coast rivers.

43 WAX ON

Waxed cotton is a great option for waterproof clothing, but the coating eventually wears thin. Here's how to rewax that old-school wading jacket without spending big bucks.

STEP 1 Warm up your garment in the sun, on a heater, or, if you're vigilant, in an oven. It's easier to wax warm cloth.

STEP 2 Create a handy applicator by cutting a 10x15-inch piece from an old T-shirt, folding it in half lengthwise, and rolling it up. Tie it off with a string so it doesn't unravel. It's easy to hold, covers a large area if you lay it down flat, and gets into tight spots if you hold it upright.

STEP 3 Heat water in a pan and add the can of wax to melt it. If the molten wax starts to solidify while you are using it, reheat it in the pan until it's easy to work with again.

STEP 4 Apply the wax to your garment's exterior, but judiciously. Resist the temptation to just slather it on, even if you haven't waxed your gear in a while. Lighter, regular applications are best. Cotton can only absorb so much wax, and the excess stays on the surface, gunking up anything it comes into contact with.

STEP 5 When you're finished with the rewaxing process, you'll want to either hang the garment in the sun or place it over a radiator or furnace (and keep an eye on it). For extra credit, you can warm it with a blow-dryer. This will really help draw the wax into the cotton.

44 REPAIR WADERS IN THE FIELD

PATCH KIT MATERIALS

Small pouch or zip-seal bag for storage
Aquaseal • Cotol-240 • Alcohol swabs
Coffee stirrers • Nylon stockings • Craft knife
Latex gloves • Athletic tape • Wader patches

Don't let a leaky boot be the end of your day. Canvas, rubber, or breathable waders usually require 24 hours to repair, but toss this emergency patch kit in your vest and you'll be back on the water after lunch. Note that this fix won't allow moisture to escape—but will a square inch of nonbreathable material kill you?

First, clean the area around the hole with an alcohol swab, then tape the tear closed from the inside of your waders. Cut a patch from the nylons big enough to cover the hole. Mix 1 part Cotol-240 accelerator with 3 to 4 parts Aquaseal using a coffee stirrer or brush (this speeds up the glue's drying time). Spread the mixture around the tear, extending the glue $1/3$ inch beyond the patch size. Place the patch in the mixture and lay it flat over the tear. Finally, apply a light coat of Aquaseal on top, and lay the waders flat to dry for one hour.

45 SPIKE IT

When I fall, I fall hard, so you won't find me wading a rocky river without spike-sole boots. Goat Head Sole Spikes have saved my hide on some seriously snot-slick rivers. These $1/4$-inch cold-forged, heat-hardened steel spikes, which have 28 biting edges per head and a serrated base to stop them from backing out, install easily in soles with or without pre-drilled holes.

46 FIND A HOLE WITH ALCOHOL

Gore-Tex is a common material for waders and rain gear because it'll keep you dry without becoming clammy . . . until you poke a hole in it. Here's a simple trick to find all those pesky pinhole leaks. Simply turn the waders, jacket, or rain pants inside out and spray the garment with rubbing alcohol. Any spot with a hole will darken when the alcohol is applied. Dab the dark spot with sealant, and you're back to dry.

47 PROTECT YOUR BOOTLACES

You may find that hooking your gravel guards onto the end of your wading-boot laces will result in torn laces after a while. To solve this problem, cut a couple of thick rubber bands crosswise from a bicycle inner tube (they're stronger than regular rubber bands). Loop the bands around the first wrap of the bootlaces and hook the gravel guards into them instead. This saves your shoelaces, and gives flexibility as you bend and move.

48 GET WIRED (OR NOT)

You don't see a lot of innovation in shoelaces, but the Boa closure system for wading boots counts for sure. Boa laces are wire and they crank tight by turning a knob at the top of the boot. Pull the knob, the wire loosens, and you step right out of the boot. If you ski or snowboard, you're familiar with the idea. But are these laces a good idea? It's usually a matter of personal preference. Some people swear by the Boa system, and some hate it.

The biggest problem with this system is that there's no bailout or quick fix if it breaks when you're on the river. You can't splice the wire and most anglers don't carry a repair kit. So if you're three miles into the back country, or if you're in the middle of a river float, and that thing gives way, you basically have a flat tire you can't fix. For that reason, I would never hike-in fish with Boa boots and I would never make Boa boots my dedicated pair for taking on a long trip, especially to somewhere like Alaska.

Having said that, they are comfortable and convenient. I like being able to immediately loosen them and kick my boots off at the end of a long day, especially when the weather is cold enough to make laces icy.

If you have a place where you normally fish that's not too far off the beaten path, and you don't like bending over and lacing up your boots. (Some people have flexibility issues.) I say go for it. Boa is great, especially if you don't go fishing very many times per year.

If you're whacking out 100 river days a year or more, if you hike a lot or travel a lot, and especially if you are hard on your gear, I'd suggest you take a pass.

49 GET IN LINE

Unlike a spinning or conventional outfit, where the reel and weight of the lure or bait you're using dictate how far or how accurately you can cast, when it comes to flyfishing, things are a bit different. The reel won't help you gain distance, and what's tied to the end of the line makes no difference. What you're actually casting is the line, and the weight of the fly

you choose simply makes it more or less difficult to cast that line properly. Different styles of water, proper presentation of certain styles of fly, and the pursuit of different species of fish sometimes call for specialty fly lines. These are the four most commonly used, and picking the right one will up your success with the long rod.

A FLOATING LINE The vast majority of flyfishing situations call for a fully floating line. Whether you're presenting dry flies on a trout stream or bass bugs on a lake, floating lines cast the easiest and most accurately. Even if you need to fish a wet fly or nymph below the surface, most fly anglers aren't fishing areas deeper than 6 feet or so, or are targeting fish holding higher in the water column. The 7- to 12-foot leader you'd use with a floating line is typically long enough to allow your flies to reach the proper depth. Floating line also acts as its own strike indicator; when swinging a fly below the surface, keep an eye on the point where the fly line meets the water and watch for ticks and stops. It's important to occasionally treat floating lines with dressing to keep them supple and slick for good castability. If they crack or lose their coating, they may not float as well. You can also find specialty floating lines that perform best in warm or cold water.

B SINK-TIP LINE Sink-tip lines offer the ease of casting of a full-floating line, but with the addition of a 5- to 12-foot tip section that sinks. They are popular with anglers who lean heavily on streamers that have to be stripped back to mimic baitfish in the water. You can also use a sink-tip line to fish nymphs and wet flies in deeper rivers and lakes. A sink-tip line is ideal for water in the 5- to 10-foot depth range, but you can also use it to increase your success in shallower water when you need to get a fly in the zone quickly. As an example, if you are floating in a drift boat and want to strip your streamer through a deep pocket, that fly may take longer to sink if you fish it on a floating line, and by the time it reaches the proper depth, you might only get a strip or two in the zone. A sink-tip line will let the fly sink into the same pocket fast, thus giving your fly maximum time in the strike zone when you only have a few seconds to make your presentation.

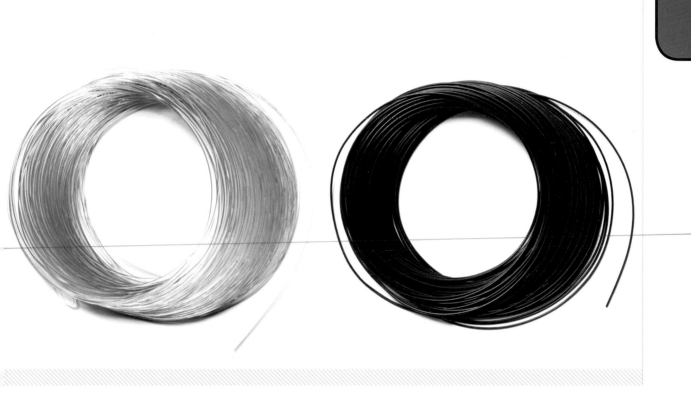

C INTERMEDIATE LINE Often clear or light colored, intermediate line is heavier than floating line, but as you'd imagine from the name, lighter than a full-sink line. This weight is designed to sink slowly, allowing you to present flies to fish holding in the middle of the water column. The coloring helps this line blend into the surroundings underwater. Saltwater flyfishermen use it for chasing wary species like striped bass; It's also used by freshwater anglers who strip streamers in clear lakes and deeper rivers for everything from trout to smallmouth bass to muskies. Though you can use an intermediate line to present trout flies in streams, one disadvantage is that it's harder to see the line in the water, which can make detecting subtle strikes tricky. Intermediate lines shine when the target species is going to crush a fly that you are stripping, as opposed to gently nipping a fly that's drifting in the current.

D FULL-SINK LINE Though it's not very fun to cast, full-sink line exists for special situations and for the anglers who like to push the limits of flyfishing. In saltwater, a full-sink line might be in order to get a fly down 20 feet or more in a hurry to a school of bluefin tuna. In freshwater, anglers use full-sink lines to get streamers to the deepest, darkest holes in lakes and rivers, where monster trout and bass live. Sinking lines are generally configured by grain, which translates to weight, thus telling you how many feet or inches per second the line will sink. One drawback to a full-sink line is that it has no versatility, so, while one hole in the river may call for it, you'll likely be hanging flies in the rocks all day in areas of shallower depths. But if you think there is a huge pike on the bottom in 25 feet of water at your favorite lake and you insist on catching it on the fly, a full-sink might be the only way to get a streamer in front of its face.

50 TAKE THE LEAD

Leaders are among the basic elements of fly tackle, but the essentials of leader design and performance get the least attention from most anglers. Modern knotless leaders are designed for the law of averages: average casters casting average-size flies to an average distance. But most fly anglers constantly change fly sizes and casting distances, so no leader is perfect all the time. When your fly is landing off target, or you can't get a drag-free drift, don't automatically blame your casting—it could be your leader.

TWEAK THE TIPPET If your dry fly is falling back on the leader when you make a presentation, shorten the tippet by a foot, use a tippet one size larger, or both. This is often a problem when you're switching from a small dry fly to one that is larger and less aerodynamic. The same remedy will also help you punch a dry fly into the wind. If you can't get a drag-free drift, on the other hand, lengthen your tippet by 1 or 2 feet, which will create a bit of slack leader near the fly when it lands.

Changing a tippet section takes just a few minutes on the water. Granted, it's another thing to keep track of while you're fishing, but paying attention to those sorts of details will definitely catch you more fish.

GET A HEAVY REAR END In both bass and saltwater fishing, where I will be using larger lines and flies, I solve most leader problems by using a heavier butt section with 9-weight lines and above. That might mean about 3 feet of 50-pound mono (.030 inch diameter) at the end of the fly line, to which I attach a knotless, tapered leader after cutting a couple of feet off the leader's smaller-diameter butt. The added mass helps extend heavier flies at the end of the cast.

ESSENTIAL FLIES: COPPER JOHN

TYPE: Nymph
PRIMARY SPECIES: Trout

Introduced by legendary fly tyer John Barr in 1996, this nymph has a reputation of scoring trout when nothing else will. Part of its magic stems from its weight. The combination of a lead-wrapped core, wire-wrapped body, and bead head get the fly down faster than nymphs of similar size. Though you can find Copper Johns tied with many different body colors, the traditional copper is hailed as the most effective. It's neutral, so it matches a wide variety of aquatic insects, yet it provides some eye-catching flash. The Flashabou wing case coated in epoxy also allows the fly to glint like a natural aquatic insect as it rides the current.

51 CHECK YOUR LEADER

Knotless leaders of nylon monofilament are a common sight these days, but the basic taper designs are the same as ever. The flyfishing pioneer and French hotelier Charles Ritz worked out the basic 60-20-20 leader formula in the early days of mono after World War II. By his design, 60 percent of a leader's length is a level, large-diameter butt; 20 percent is a steeply tapered transition; and the last 20 percent is a fine-diameter tippet to which his fly is tied.

The leader-butt diameter should be two-thirds the diameter of the end of the fly line for best performance. The 5-weight fly line you may use for fishing small dry flies has a tip diameter of about .030 inch. The 9-foot, 6X leader you attach to it should then have a butt diameter of about .020 inch. Most light trout leaders conform to that standard.

Problems may occur when you start switching line, leader, or fly sizes. The leader taper that works for small dry flies on a 5-weight won't work for big steelhead dries on an 8-weight, and vice versa. The tip diameter of an 8-weight floating line is about .040 inch, which requires a larger .026-inch-diameter leader butt to get the leader to turn a large fly over properly in casting.

You don't need a micrometer in your vest to keep track of all the numbers, because many manufacturers label their packaging with both the butt and tippet diameters. Some companies even distinguish their leaders by species, such as trout or bass. In this case, trout should mean a small-butt, small-fly leader; and bass, the opposite.

52 CHANGE ON THE FLY

Moving from a shallow riffle to a deep pool will sometimes mean switching from a floating line to a sink-tip line. This will involve changing your spool, restringing, and rerigging—a time-gobbling task, especially when fish are rising. Avoid the hassle and get up and running in seconds by using an interchangeable sink-tip. Here's how to make one.

STEP 1 Cut a piece of running line from an old sinking line. A good rule of thumb is 5 feet for shallow water, 10 feet for middle depths, and 15 feet for deep water. Vary the length for individual streams or current speeds.

STEP 2 Take a braided loop and work the Chinese finger-lock over the line as far as it will go. Slide a piece of the included tubing over the braid.

STEP 3 Apply a drop of instant glue to seal the deal [A].

STEP 4 Use a loop-to-loop connection to attach the sink tip to the fly line, and then the leader to the sink tip [B].

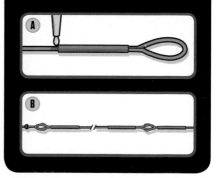

53 HIT THE BAR BEFORE YOU STRIP

You can use stripping baskets when wading in deep or rough water to prevent loose line from getting tangled at your feet or blowing in the wind. But stripping baskets are a hassle to travel with. Luckily, if you're ever in a pinch, making one isn't that difficult.

STEP 1 Head to the local watering hole. If you're vacationing somewhere tropical that doesn't have a bar (if that's even possible), find the closest grocery store.

STEP 2 Ask the bartender for an empty case from bottled beer (or a full case that you'll empty later). Tip the mixologist a dollar or two and find the local hardware store.

STEP 3 Shop for yarn, string, or rope by the foot. You'll need 10 feet max to do the trick. Remember, this will be hanging around your neck for a decent period of time. Make sure the material is wide and soft enough that it won't rub your skin raw. If you can't find a hardware store, use the thickest piece of monofilament in your gear bag and apply a length of tape where it contacts your neck.

STEP 4 Punch a hole 3 inches from the top on both sides of the box. Attach the string so that the box comes to your waist. If you want to get fancy, hit up the closest restaurant and ask for two large egg trays. Cut to size and thrown in the bottom of the case, they make cone spacers that help keep the line snarl-free.

ESSENTIAL FLIES: ELK HAIR CADDIS

TYPE: Dry Fly
PRIMARY SPECIES: Trout

There are few trout streams in the world that don't experience a caddis hatch at some point during the season. Although these insects vary in color, a simple elk hair caddis with a neutral tan or cream underbelly will match most hatches anywhere in the world. Elk hair does the best job of capturing the elongated wing profile of a live caddis, and also allows the flies to float very high on the surface, barely making a dimple, just like the real deal. This extra-buoyant material is tough to sink when dressed properly, which makes it easier for the angler to "skate" or "skitter" the fly, mimicking the action of a real caddis hopping and dancing across the water's surface.

54 DUCK TANGLED LINES

The problem? A rat's nest of floating, sinking, and intermediate fly lines in various weights. Wind them on reels for storage, and line memory sets in, setting you up for coil-snared casts in spring. Dump them in a shoebox, and they end up as tangled as Medusa's tresses on a bad hair day. The solution? A permanent marker and an old duck mount. Trust me.

STEP 1 Clean each line by soaking in warm water with a few drops of mild dish soap. Pull the line through a clean cloth, and apply fly-line dressing. Let the lines dry.

STEP 2 Mark each butt end. Using Lefty Kreh's smart system, make one long dash to represent a 5-weight. Add or subtract dots in front or behind to delineate line weight. (For example, a dot in front of the long dash means 1 subtracted from 5, branding the line as a 4 weight.) Use different colors for various tapers and sink rates.

STEP 3 Coil each line in long loops and hang the loops from your duck (or a board studded with nails). My ancient canvasback holds eight lines. Hang the duck in a cool, dry place away from direct sunlight.

55 REDUCE FLY-LINE MEMORY WITH A COFFEE CAN

If I know I won't be flyfishing for a straight month or so, I store my flyline by wrapping the first 40 feet around a large coffee can. The diameter of the can prevents tight curls from forming in the line, which helps it lie straight on the water the next time you go fishing.

56 UNDERSTAND YOUR FLY REEL

A fly reel has three purposes: to store line and backing, to provide a smooth drag against running fish, and to balance your rod's weight and leverage. Even the most complex flyfishing reels are simpler than an average spinning reel, but it still behooves you to understand and utilize this vital gear. Flyfishing reels don't revolve during a cast, since fly anglers strip line from the reel and let it pay out during the back-and-forth motion called "false casting." In the past, fly reels have served largely as line-storage devices with simple mechanical drags. Advancing technology and an increase in flyfishing for big, strong-fighting fish have led to strong drag systems that can stop fish as large as tarpon. Other recent developments include warp- and corrosion-resistant materials and larger arbors (the spindles around which the line is wrapped) that reduce coils and help maintain consistent drag pressure.

FRAME Holds the spool. A weak frame will warp, causing friction as the spool revolves.

DRAG KNOB Adjusts drag tension. Some smaller reels have click-pawl drags, while reels for larger fish sport strong cork and composite disc braking systems.

SPOOL Many reels are fitted with removable spools. Having different fly lines ready on a number of spools allows an angler to switch tactics more quickly.

ARBOR The spindle around which the fly line is wrapped. Many modern reels have larger arbors that help recover line quickly when a fish swims toward the angler.

HANDLE Unlike with spinning and baitcasting reels, rotating the handle of a fly reel typically turns the spool a single revolution.

57 GET THE INSIDE SCOOP ON FLY REELS

A spinning reel that costs $30 is going to mechanically function the same as one that costs $1,000. The expensive reel may have a stronger drag system and be constructed of better quality components, but in the end, the inner workings aren't much different from the budget model. This, however, isn't the case with fly reels, so if you're in the market for a new one, understanding the advantages and disadvantages to the two most common styles of internal gears can help you determine how much to spend and which reel is best for you. It ultimately boils down to what species of fish you intend to hook, and how hard that fish is going to fight.

Ⓐ CLICK-PAWL DRAG In the early days of flyfishing, all reels featured a click-pawl drag. In a simple setup, a gear fixed to the back side of the spool locks into triangle-shaped clickers held in place with tension on the inside of the reel frame. When the spool turns, the clickers keep up tension to stop the line from overrunning, and also prevent the spool from moving in reverse. Some click-pawl reels feature adjustment knobs that allow the angler to change the amount of pressure on the clickers, thus making it easier to reduce tension when stripping line off to cast, and making it easier to increase tension when a fish is pulling against the reel. Click-pawl drags are still popular today, but they are mostly found on inexpensive reels. Click-pawls are also typically reserved for chasing smaller fish, such as stream trout and pond bass. Species such as these aren't likely to peel all the line off the reel and get into the backing, and that's important because a click-pawl isn't designed to handle smoking runs from big, fast fish. In fact, most of the time while trout or bass fishing, the fish won't pull much line at all, and the angler often does not even use the reel to retrieve the catch. That said, it doesn't make much sense to spend a ton of money on a click pawl for small-water applications, as the reel is little more than a line holder.

ESSENTIAL FLIES: FLASHBACK PHEASANT TAIL

TYPE: Nymph
PRIMARY SPECIES: Trout

Another generic imitator of a wide range of aquatic insects, the pheasant tail might be tiny, but it packs a wallop. Most anglers don't fish this nymph solo, instead incorporating it into a double nymph rig aimed at giving trout a choice of meal sizes. The flashback version of this fly actually makes a great add-on to almost any rig, as it doesn't increase the overall weight. Drifting a dry fly? Hang a flashback pheasant tail under it. Stripping a streamer? Get a flashback in tow. Working in this little bonus fly certainly never hurts, and quite often, the wee flashy morsel gets eaten faster than the main course.

Ⓑ DISC DRAG Disc-drag reels use a series of stacked washers sandwiched between plates covered in materials such as cork or carbon-fiber that can be compressed or decompressed via a drag adjustment knob to increase or decrease tension. Disc-drag systems factor in the amount of heat generated when a fish is spinning the drag quickly, as well as the torque applied during a hard run. They can cost a pretty penny depending on the materials, but if you're chasing salmon, steelhead, striped bass, or tuna that are going to take a lot of line, you'll definitely want reliability. Many are also sealed within the reel frame by a metal housing (particularly important if you're exposed to saltwater) to thwart corrosion and ensure moisture doesn't damage the system.

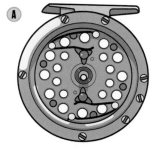

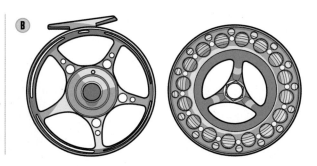

58 FIX YOUR HOLY CORK

A rod's cork handles deteriorate with use. After repeated soakings and dryings, the cork will weaken and chip, creating holes. If these holes are left untreated, then the surrounding cork grows even weaker and may break. This quick patch job will extend the life of your grip.

SAND Take a clean, dry wine cork and sand it with 220- to 240-grit sandpaper to make a fine cork dust. You will need to collect about $^1/_2$ teaspoon to fill a 1-centimeter hole.

GLUE Mix the powder with wood glue. Add sufficient adhesive to create a smooth and dry consistency, like that of cookie dough. Your patching material should not be fluid, or it'll run out of the holes and gaps.

PATCH Use a sharp, pointed tool to clean out pitted areas. Fill them with your patch material. The filler will shrink when it dries, so you must repeat the process to get the holes flush with the good parts of your grip.

SEAL When the filler has dried, buff with 220-grit sandpaper, wash with water and mild soap, and dry. Seal the cork with gunstock finish or a splash of cork seal.

59 CRAFT A MAKESHIFT MINI CASTER

If you've ever wandered from a main river into a small feeder stream, you've probably wished for a shorter rod. A couple of predrilled wine corks stowed in your vest will help you build your own short stick on the spot. Simply separate the tip from the rest of your rod; usually about 2 to 4 feet of length is all you need. Place the butt section that holds the reel in your wading belt, and pull out about 20 feet of line. Slide the corks onto the butt of the tip section to create a new handle.

STEP 1 Measure the diameter of the female ferrule and select an appropriate drill bit. A $^1/_4$-inch bit should cover most tip sections.

STEP 2 Put one end of the cork in a vise and position the drill bit at its center on the opposite end.

STEP 3 Use the fastest speed possible to avoid tearing the cork wall.

STEP 4 As the drill nears the end of the cork, stop and remove the cork from the vise. Hold it in your hand and carefully finish drilling. (Otherwise the vise's pressure would break the cork.)

STEP 5 Before use, soak the corks in river water. This softens them enough to fit over the ferrule.

60 PERFORM EMERGENCY GUIDE REPAIRS

A broken guide shouldn't be the end of a perfectly fine rod or a great fishing trip. For strength, speed, and durability, nothing beats a strip of shrink-wrap to attach a new guide. In the fall, local marinas or boatyards have scraps from winterizing that you can pick up for free, and you can buy an assortment of guides at local fly shops. Make a repair kit and keep it in your truck. You won't win a beauty competition with this fix, but you'll still catch fish when the bite is on.

STEP 1 Cut a triangular piece of shrink-wrap long enough to wrap three times around your rod. The width of the triangle's base should extend beyond the foot of the guide.

STEP 2 Cut off the threads and foot of the broken guide with a razor.

STEP 3 Select an appropriately sized replacement.

STEP 4 Tape the new guide to the rod blank.

STEP 5 Wrap one foot with shrink-wrap.

STEP 6 Heat with a hair dryer. For this step, you'll need electricity, so swing by a gas station or 24-hour mart. They'll usually let you plug into an outlet.

STEP 7 Repeat on the second guide foot.

61 GET GREASY WHEN IT'S COLD

The one thing I can't stand about winter is ice forming in the guides of my rod. Luckily, there's a cheap, simple fix: Just spray some nonstick cooking spray on those guides before you head out. Don't gunk it on, and wipe away the excess. You can give the smaller guides at the end of the rod an extra shot right before you string up. I know other anglers who like to use things like WD-40, but I prefer a slightly less "industrial" solution, and PAM seems to work pretty well. It will last a good couple hours or so, depending on how cold the air is. Besides, if the fishing is really slow and you use olive oil cooking spray, you can always chew on your line and pretend it's spaghetti.

ESSENTIAL FLIES: BLUE WINGED OLIVE

TYPE: Dry Fly
PRIMARY SPECIES: Trout

Often labeled "BWOs" in fly shops, this pattern represents one of the most prolific and long-running hatches from coast to coast. Olives are mayflies that can start hatching as early as February in some parts of the country, and can last well into late fall. With that in mind, BWOs are often the first dry flies anglers tie on in the beginning of the season, and the last before winter sets it. When nothing else is hatching, you can count on seeing a few olives drifting down stream. When there is a major hatch of bigger bugs, you can bank some olives still in the mix. The trout's willingness to eat these flies depends on what other food is available, but hitting any given river without some BWOs in your box will bite you sooner or later.

62 GO FIBERGLASS FIRST

Many trout anglers start out with 9-foot 5-weight graphite rod, which is a great choice. However, if you're considering a beginning lighter rod, say 3-weight or less, you should seriously consider fiberglass over graphite. Here's why.

SENSATION That classic slow action of a fiberglass rod really helps you feel your casts. You sense the rod loading and unloading the line, which will help you develop a good stroke. And that's exactly what all anglers should work on, especially beginners.

ACTION When are you really going to boom out big casts in the small-stream environment? Better to have a rod with which you can roll cast, mend, and pop short casts at small target zones, rather than a super fast action rod that you won't really use to full capacity. Sometimes the super-fast modern graphites are about as functional in light rods as a V-8 engine would be on a riding mower. Fiberglass gives you feel and all the casting oomph you practically need for most in-close fishing environments.

COST Lastly, fiberglass can be much more affordable. You don't have to spend several hundred dollars to find a perfectly fun and functional fly rod.

Here are some solid options.

	RODS	NOTES
LOW COST	Cabela's CGT rods	Probably the best value-priced option out there.
MODERATE COST	Redington Butter Stick	One of the darlings of the fiberglass world right now, with good reason.
HIGHER COST	Orvis Superfine	Some nicer "made in America" components and construction, and very consistent action.
HIGH COST	Scott F2	These rods still offer a full flex, but a faster recovery than many others. And they're heirloom quality.

63 TAKE CARE OF YOUR GUIDES

With the exception of the thick, wide first guide—known as the stripping guide—fly rods are built with light, thin-wire guides, often called "snake guides." Since the reel never comes into play in terms of cast distance or accuracy, snake guides are designed to simply let the fly line pass through freely and without obstruction while adding as little weight to the rod as possible. To that end, it's important to always make sure snake guides are aligned properly and don't have any grit or residue buildup on the inside. You want the guides to remain as smooth as possible to maximize your casting distance and accuracy. The stripping guide is wider and beefier because it takes the most strain when stripping streamer flies. You'll often find two stripping guides on heavier fly rods used for saltwater fishing.

64 TRY A CANE ROD

Even today, in the age of graphite, many fishermen yearn to cast finely crafted rods handmade of superior cane blanks, silken wraps, and high-grade cork. The rods have a romantic history, but they're also practical; many feel they deliver a small dry or emerger better at 10 to 40 feet than the best graphite rod.

Quality new rods run $1,000 to $4,000, while used ones range from a few hundred dollars to many thousands. Beware of the deal that sounds too good to be true. Some rods listed in the $500 range are made from blanks built in China and may have flaws. Others might come off an assembly line. If it isn't built by hand, the quality will not be there.

Perhaps the most important criterion when you're choosing a new or used bamboo fly rod is feel. Bamboo rods are made in a variety of tapers, and they all load more slowly than their graphite counterparts. Some anglers like this action; others don't. Always cast it before committing.

Really check the rod out before you buy. Make sure it's straight, not bent. Look for shoddy glue seams where water may get into the bamboo. Examine the ferrules to make sure they aren't oxidized, pitted, or warped. If you pick up a rod that looks good and casts well and you like it, buy it.

ESSENTIAL FLIES: PRINCE NYMPH

TYPE: Nymph
PRIMARY SPECIES: Trout

Developed in California in the 1930s by Doug Prince, there's no question that this nymph is a true classic fish-catching machine. While the Prince is technically a stonefly imitation designed for fishing in fast water, anglers have learned in all the decades since the pattern's inception that it will catch trout anywhere, any season, in any kind of water. The combination of shimmering peacock herl body, gold tinsel ribbing, and sharp white wings give the fly a distinct profile and contrast underwater. Regardless of clarity and water speed, trout just seem to be able to pick it out. No matter where I'm trout fishing, if the situation calls for me to use nymphs, I usually tie on a Prince first.

65 TURN JAPANESE WITH TENKARA

Developed in Japan about 200 years ago, tenkara fishing was introduced to American anglers in 2009. This method uses a very long fly rod with no reel; the line is tied directly to the tip. By using a truncated style of short-distance casting, anglers can use these rods to reach across any conflicting currents and prevent a faster (or slower) current from pulling the fly and causing drag. Adherents nearly worship tenkara, which they say emphasizes skill more than gear.

RODS Tenkara rods telescope, and some can extend to nearly 15 feet. With a base length of less than 2 feet, they're great for packing into tight headwaters. "Use the longest rod you can," says Daniel Galhardo, owner of Tenkara USA. The limiting factor is how much canopy might impede the cast, not overall length. "You'll quickly get used to the length, and you'll want the line control."

LINES These are about the length of the rod and attach to the rod's tip. There are two broad types: More traditional tapered lines which afford a super-delicate presentation, and newer level lines which are more easily altered on the stream but are harder to cast. Lines are tipped with a short 3- to 4-foot tippet.

FLIES Most tenkara flies feature a reverse hackle in which the feather is brushed forward toward the hook eye. This gives the fly a pulsing profile.

66 MAKE A POOR MAN'S CASE

You don't need an expensive rod case for travel. In fact, that might entice thieves with its promise of a pricey rod within. This simple trick allows you to stash your rod safely in your checked luggage. Cut a piece of 4-inch-diameter PVC pipe long enough to fit the broken-down rod and still fit inside your suitcase. Break the rod down, wrap it in newspaper, and stash it in the pipe. Nestle it into your suitcase, and travel safely and discreetly.

67 CAST, DON'T WIGGLE

Wiggling a rod won't tell you much about its action and feel, so walk into the store with a reel loaded with your favorite line, with leader attached, and a few flies with the hook points snipped off. Ask if you can try a few casts in the parking lot, on a nearby lawn, or off the loading dock out back. If you ask really nicely, they'll let you.

68 STORE GEAR FOR A WINTER'S NAP

Too many of us make the mistake of stowing dirty fly gear in winter. Don't be lazy. Take an hour or so when the season ends to properly winterize your tackle. Those rods, reels, lines, waders, and flies you spent good money on will last longer if you store them clean and dry. And you'll be better prepared to hit the water when the spring hatches turn on.

FLY LINE If you leave a gritty, gunky fly line wrapped tight on a reel for months, it's almost certain not to float properly next time on the water. Clean it with warm water and mild dish soap. Pull the line through a wet paper towel or cloth, feeling for major nicks and abrasions. If you do find some, it's time to toss that line and buy a new spool. Otherwise, store it on a wire coat hanger by bending the "elbows" of the hanger to create two notches. Loosely tie the end of the line to one notch, and then wrap it lengthwise around the hanger. This minimizes memory and will ensure that the line fully dries. Label each hanger with the line type. In spring, as you respool the line, pull it back through a pad or towel treated with fly-line conditioner.

GORE-TEX WADERS Hose down the outside of your Gore-Tex waders, and hang them overnight to air-dry. Once they are dry, turn them inside out. Dab rubbing alcohol, which shows up leaks better than water, on any suspicious areas to examine them for pinholes and abrasions. Smear some Aquaseal on the holes, and let it set. Store waders on a rack or a coat hanger, in a dry, cool place. Don't wad them up. Don't put them back in the box they came in. And don't store them in the garage if your

temperatures drop well below freezing or fluctuate significantly in winter months.

REELS Use a mixture of water and mild soap, and an old soft-bristle toothbrush, to clean away grime. Pop the spool and remove any grit. (I suggest removing the backing; wrap it around an old coffee can for the winter.) Rinse the reel and towel-dry it. Leave the spool and case apart overnight to air-dry. Sparingly lube the reel, and then reassemble and stow the reel in its case.

RODS Wipe the surface grit off of your rod, let it air-dry, and then pack it in its sleeve and tube for the winter. For rods that don't break down, clean the cork handles with mild soap and

water, and stand them upright (handles down) against a wall in a place that won't get too hot or too cold. If that means your basement, stand them on a plastic bucket as a base to guard against any damage from moisture.

FLIES Organize your flies in a large plastic compartment box or bin. Put three dry paper towels inside the box's lid to wick moisture from the flies. You can also get silica gel packs at a camera store to place in the box for added moisture protection.

VEST OR CHEST PACK Leave it unzipped, and drop a silica gel pack in a couple of the compartments to dry it out over the winter. Hang in a cool, dry closet.

69 PACK FOR YOUR FLIGHT

I get many questions about how best to pack fishing gear for a flight. After thousands of miles and having gear broken and/or lost, I've come up with these five tips.

CHECK YOUR RODS Airlines are so inconsistent about how they handle rods as carry-on (no matter what they tell you up front) that I recommend always checking them—inside tubes, inside your luggage (see item 66).

KEEP IT TIDY Assume that the TSA is going to go through your stuff. Don't leave items such as pliers or fly boxes laying loose; keep them in your pack, or in your vest in your luggage, or put them in plastic bags and pack them.

GO LIGHT Assume you will be 5 pounds heavier coming back than when you leave. If you want to avoid excess baggage fees, don't pack your outbound bag right at the 49-pound limit. When your stuff gets wet, it gets heavier. I always pack at 45 pounds or less on my way to go fish.

DRESS LIGHT For the same reason, I usually travel with light, crushable rain jackets, and sometimes even lighter waders or boots. I'll trade an extra layer of Gore-Tex for a few pounds, unless I'm going to a place where I know it'll be raining the whole time. Check the weight of boots before you buy—an extra pound or two won't matter as much in the river as it will at the airline counter.

DON'T TEMPT THE TSA Check your flies, pliers, and knives with your luggage. Don't even try to carry on flies. You're asking for extra inspection, and if the hooks are large enough, TSA agents will confiscate them.

FLY TYING CAN BE EVERY BIT

as addicting, challenging, and rewarding as flyfishing. You can purchase a thousand bugs and catch a thousand fish with them, but hooking just one on a fly you tied is always a little bit sweeter. While you can sit at the vise and spin up the same patterns you'd purchase at a fly shop, the real fun lies in the creative freedom you have to add your own touches to proven flies, or even experiment and create ties that are uniquely yours. No matter what you take from tying, or what it gives to you, having a working knowledge of how flies are made, even on a basic level, will only make you a better angler. To cover every aspect of fly tying in one chapter isn't possible. The subject accounts for hundreds of books already out there on the shelves. What this chapter will do, however, is make it easier to inspire beginners by taking away some of the mystery, and even help seasoned vets learn a trick or three that will make them faster, more creative, or more efficient at the vise. From breakdowns of common tools, to new ways to tie old bugs, to tips on using household materials to make magic, there's something for every skill level.

70 BUILD THE BASIC TYING KIT

For a beginner, choosing the right tools for tying flies can be intimidating. Look on the pegboard at the fly shop, and you'll see everything from dubbing rakes to tapering scissors. While all of these tools have a use, most of them are not necessary for tying the basic patterns you'll use most often. As you advance as a tyer, you can always add precision instruments down the line, but the tools detailed here are all you need to start spinning the bugs that will get you hooked up on the water.

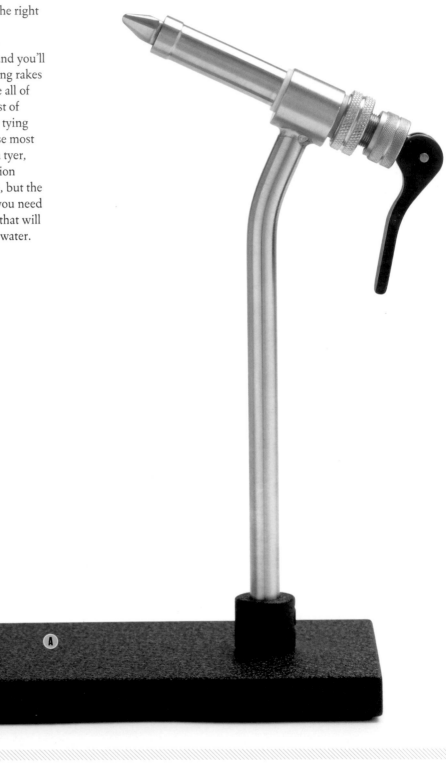

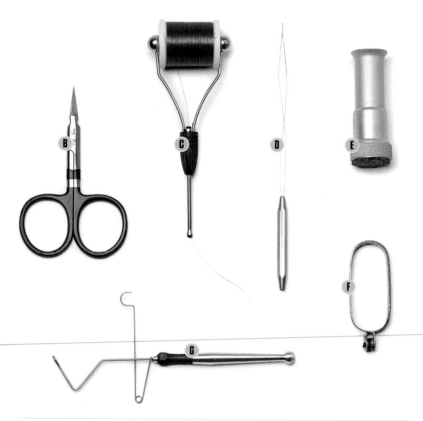

bobbin, use the threader to pull the tag end of the thread through the feeding tube. You'll never get it through by hand, and trying to suck it through with your mouth gets old.

E HAIR STACKER When you snip a clump of deer or elk or fox hair from the skin the cut ends will be even, but the tapered ends will not. If you tie it onto the hook like that, your fly will look like it's having a bad hair day. After cutting a clump of hair, drop it into the stacker points first. Tap the stacker on the table, and it will evenly align all the pointed ends. Stackers are available in multiple sizes to accommodate big and small clumps of hair.

F HACKLE PLIERS Wrapping hackle feathers around a hook comes into play while tying a wide variety of fly styles. To give the proper appearance, you want to wind hackles tightly. The problem is, if you're holding the feather in your fingers, it'll often slip out right at the end of the wrapping and unravel. Hackle pliers with rubber on the grippers hold feathers securely without breaking them, allowing you to nail a tight wrap on the first pass and secure the feather at the end without it slipping.

G WHIP-FINISH TOOL Whip finishing—making a series of wraps that tuck the thread under itself to secure it at the head when finishing a fly—is the bane of many tyers. Getting it right takes some practice (I recommend watching instructional videos on YouTube). Some tyers like to do it with their fingers, but once you master the whip-finish tool, you'll find that it's the easy way to complete the task.

A VISE A vise holds the hook so you can tie the fly. These can be found in countless varieties; some look like NASA instruments, but you don't need a high-tech vise to tie effectively. A cheaper model that clamps on the edge of a table gets the job done, though I'd recommend a vise mounted on a pedestal base as you can move it far more easily than a table clamp model. Being able to move the vise allows you to position it where it's most comfortable for you to work on the table or where the best light is cast.

B SCISSORS It might be tempting to use a cheap pair of nail scissors, but I don't recommend it. What makes fly scissors unique is that

they taper to an incredibly thin point, and a good pair is razor-sharp right down to the tip. This is important for getting in close and trimming those minuscule feathers and threads. Nail scissors won't be nearly as sharp or as precise.

C BOBBIN A bobbin holds the thread and keeps tension on the spool as you wind it onto the hook. There is some variation in bobbin types—different tube diameters and tension-applying devices—but a standard $5 or $8 model will do the trick.

D BOBBIN THREADER Although it's a simple tool, a bobbin threader will save you much frustration. After attaching a thread spool to the

71 GET HOOKED (IN THE DETAILS)

Just as there is a near-endless variety of hooks for bait fishing, the amount of specialty fly hooks that you can purchase is likewise staggering. Many of them are intended for very specific fly styles, but these three will get you by when tying the basics. All you have to do is select the right size based on the pattern you're creating or forage you're trying to imitate.

DRY-FLY HOOKS Standard dry-fly hooks are typically very thin in diameter (a style known as "light wire") and have a downturned eye. A thin hook will weigh less than one with a heavier gauge, and the lighter the hook, the better it floats. The downside to dry-fly hooks is that they bend easily, which is part of the reason that you need to play lightly with a big trout hooked on a dry-fly. If you are tying patterns with extra-buoyant materials such as foam or elk hair, you can get away with a dry-fly hook that has a slightly thicker diameter.

NYMPH/SCUD HOOKS Sometimes packaged as scud hooks, sometimes as nymph/scud hooks, these hooks feature a curved shank and are thicker in diameter than a dry-fly hook. Their main purpose is for tying nymphs, which imitate aquatic insects in their larval stage. While nymphs are frequently tied on straight-shank hooks, I tend to tie mine on curved shanks. Not only do I feel these hooks stick in a trout's mouth more effectively, I believe the curve makes the flies look more natural, as a live aquatic larva flutters its body when swimming.

STREAMER HOOKS As streamers represent larger forage such as baitfish and leeches, streamer hooks are naturally longer. They are also heavier gauge, as streamers are not presented as delicately as dry flies and need to withstand fights with bigger fish. Some streamer hooks feature a downturned eye, though I prefer to tie my streamers on hooks with a straight eye. When a streamer is stripped, a straight eye will help it move directly forward, which makes a pattern look more natural.

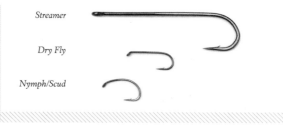

Streamer

Dry Fly

Nymph/Scud

72 TAKE A DRY-FLY ANATOMY LESSON

Before you can perfect your dry-fly tying, it's important to understand the different parts of your bugs, and what roles those various parts play in making them float or look more natural.

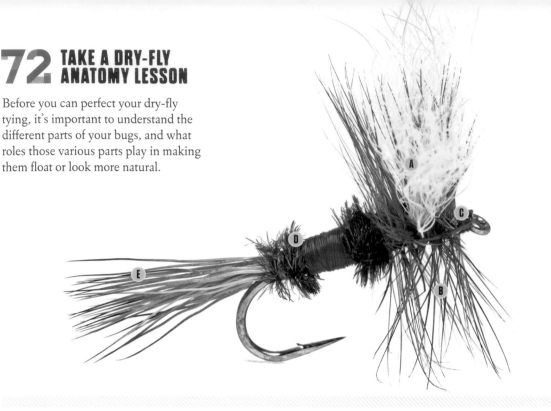

A WING When carefully cut from delicate feathers, a wing serves mainly to make a fly anatomically correct. However, a fly's wing also serves as your point of focus during the drift. It's often the only thing you'll see as the fly floats through a fast riffle. With that in mind, parachute-style wings, which are usually made of hair and tied in an upright post, are less about making a fly look natural and more about giving the angler something easy to visually track. Parachute hair wings are also more buoyant than feather wings, so they won't sink as easily. From underneath, a trout doesn't really see the wings in most cases, so don't be afraid to opt for white or another bright color that is easier for you to see, even if it's not the true wing color of the bug you're trying to match. Keep in mind that if you opt to tie or split hair wings, they need to be even, as unbalanced wings can cause a fly to float on its side.

B HACKLE The hackle is arguably the most important part of a dry fly's anatomy, as it is more responsible for keeping the fly floating than any other part of the bug. Hackle feathers are stiff and bristly, which, if splayed around the hook shank, allows them to rest on the surface film without breaking its tension. You can spin hackles vertically behind and around the wing, or horizontally around just the base of the wing. In either case, the hackle will touch more water than any other

part of the fly, so keep dressing it to make sure it stays as waterproof as possible when fishing. Whereas you can get away with an unnatural wing color, hackles should match the live bug's coloring as closely as possible.

C HEAD To reduce fly weight, tie your dries with fine-diameter thread, and keep the amount of wraps you use to secure each section minimal. When building the head, use just enough wraps to achieve a slight taper, and finish with a pin-size drop of thin head cement. Thick gel glues or epoxies can add extra weight to the front of the fly.

D BODY A fly's body doesn't add much to its floatability. It's really just there to make a tie look more natural. But bear in mind that the material you choose to craft that body can detract from the fly's ability to stay afloat. Opt for synthetic dubbings, wraps, and thread that won't absorb a lot of water. Likewise, regardless of the material, keep a dry's body sparse to minimize overall weight.

E TAIL A fly's tail might not seem very important, but it plays a huge role in floatation. Its job is to stop the rear of the fly from breaking water's surface tension and sinking. Without a tail, the weight of the hook could cause the fly to dip below the surface. You can create tails with a wide variety of materials, but stiff hair or feather strands are most common.

73 PICK YOUR EYE CANDY

Need to add some weight to your streamer? There is no better way than with a pair of dumbbell eyes. All it takes is a few figure-eight wraps around the eyes and the shank, and your pattern will sink away. But how fast it drops all depends on the eyes you choose. Here are the most common styles.

LEAD EYES If you need a streamer to drop in a hurry, opt for lead dumbbell eyes. No other material sinks as quickly. However, you should also consider splash when choosing lead eyes. As lead is heavy, it's going to plop hard when you cast, so don't automatically spin in the heaviest lead eyes you can find. Even if fish are holding fairly deep, if the water's clear, drop back a few eye sizes to reduce the chance of spooking your target.

ALUMINUM EYES Aluminum eyes are an excellent choice for targeting fish holding in shallow water or hovering in the middle of the water column. They'll help a fly fall steadily, but as they're lighter than lead, they won't splash hard or cause your bug to sink like a stone.

BEAD-CHAIN EYES These eyes are lighter than lead or aluminum eyes. As they're also smaller than the other eye options, they are a great choice for adding a touch of weight to smaller patterns. Bead-chain eyes are a staple in bonefish flies used on saltwater flats to imitate shrimp. They splash gently, fall quietly, and cause flies to hop when stripped across the bottom.

Aluminum Eyes *Lead Eyes* *Bead-chain Eyes*

74 FLUFF THEM ON THE CHEAP

Dubbing needles are used to pick body dubbing out after wrapping it on the shank to make it look more leggy and "buggy." A dubbing brush fluffs out materials on your larger streamers. You can shell out for these specialized tools at the fly shop, or you can hit the dollar store and buy some large sewing needles and a toothbrush. They'll do the same jobs just as effectively.

75 TIE ONE ON THE FLY

Here is one of the most frustrating experiences in flyfishing: You just lost your last size 16 Pale Morning Dun and don't have the right fly to match the massive hatch erupting all around you. Trout slurp up naturals with abandon but snub your next-closest imitations. What do you do?

Try tying flies right on the stream bank. It's easier than you think. This simple kit fits easily in a vest pocket, and can help you create variations on caddis, mayfly, midge, and small stonefly patterns that will match nearly any hatch you may encounter.

TOOL UP Leatherman's Crunch multitool has a pair of locking pliers rather than the usual needle-nose, which makes for a great travel vise. Just open and lock the knife blade, jam it into a dead tree trunk, and clamp a hook in the jaws. Other tools you'll need: a small pair of scissors (A), hooks (B), bobbin (C), thread (cream, yellow, olive, black, and brown), and head cement (D).

GET SOME TAIL Use some chicken neck feathers (hackles) (E) to make tails for mayfly patterns. You need them in a variety of colors, from white to dun to brown. Choose those with the longest and stiffest fibers. Sandwich the butt sections of individual feathers between two pieces of tape to keep them from blowing away.

FIND A BODY Dyed beaver fur (F) makes great dry-fly bodies; so do various waterproof synthetic dubbing materials. Most fly shops or fly-tying suppliers carry variety packs.

WING IT The tufts of hairs on the bottoms of snowshoe hares' feet (G) have evolved into a waterproof fluff that makes perfect dry-fly wing material. Include one foot each in cream and light, medium, and dark dun colors, as well as a short length of white polypropylene yarn with which to imitate the clear wings of spent adult mayflies.

A small tackle binder's clear vinyl sleeves will keep loose materials organized even on windy days. Put your hooks in a small utility box with curved compartment bottoms. Fasten the box and sleeve together with a rubber band and slip them into your vest pocket or glove compartment.

76 ORGANIZE YOUR FIBERS

It seems the digital camera has replaced the 35mm SLR, but the plastic film container has had a rebirth: I store my chenille, Antron, and yarn in individual bottles, by color and size. Drill a 3⁄16-inch hole in the center of the removable cap. Then just thread the material through, and snip off what you need for the particular pattern you're working on.

77 GET SATURATED

That fly you just tied might look great in the vise, but how it looks when wet really matters. Don't be afraid to fill the sink with water in order to find out if your dry flies are balanced when they float, or if your streamers have a nice shape when saturated.

78 WRAP IT WITH ICE DUB

Flies fall into two categories: They can either imitate natural bugs or they attract the attention of fish. A relatively new synthetic called Ice Dub, when wrapped into the body of a fly, does both. Classic nymph patterns such as the Hare's Ear and Prince Nymph look just as realistic when they are tied with Ice Dub, yet they also flash and draw eyeballs—especially in low-light conditions—better than the same patterns tied with only natural fur and feathers. In flyfishing, seeing is half of the believing equation for trout, and Ice Dub commands notice better than anything else.

79 MAKE YOUR OWN DUBBING

If you're like me, on more than just one occasion you've left your local fly shop frustrated because they didn't sell that just-right, match-the-hatch-perfect shade of fly-tying dubbing that you wanted. Fear not. Chances are, the craft store will have it—and at a fraction of the cost. There, you can purchase a skein of acrylic knitting yarn. A few bucks buys you 100 yards—practically enough for a lifetime supply of nymphs and dry flies. At home, cut a 3- to 4-foot length of yarn, wrap it around your hand, and snip the coil into 1-inch pieces. Place the cut yarn in a coffee grinder and pulse for about one minute. The result is enough dubbing for dozens of flies.

To store the dubbing, drill a ¾-inch hole in the cap of an empty prescription bottle, stuff the dubbing inside, and replace the cap. Pull the dubbing out just as you would with any other dispenser. Later, if your fishing buddies inquire about your deadly custom-colored flies, you should share the wealth—at two bucks apiece, of course.

ESSENTIAL FLIES: ZONKER

TYPE: Streamer
PRIMARY SPECIES: Trout, Bass, Steelhead, Pike/Muskie, Saltwater

Most streamer enthusiasts will agree that nothing looks sexier than a long, fluttery piece of rabbit fur getting stripped through the water. These days, thousands of streamer patterns incorporate this material, but no matter how complex they may be, they are all cousins of the Zonker. In its most simplistic form, this baitfish imitator is nothing but a single strip of rabbit fur and a flashy body made of Mylar or tinsel tubing. And in truth, you don't need anything more sophisticated than the original recipe to catch almost any fish that swims. Strip a Zonker quickly across fast water and hang on. Work it erratically with long pauses in still water and it'll get blasted. Versions tied with a heavy-gauge hook will also fool species like false albacore, striped bass, and redfish in the salt.

80 MAKE GLOW-IN-THE-DARK FLIES

Many of the best mayfly hatches happen after dusk, when it can be more than a little difficult for mere mortals to actually see the trout eating those flies you're offering them. To avoid missed strikes, you're going to want to organize a dedicated late-night fly box. Set aside some of your key patterns, and use a fine-point paintbrush to dab the tips of fly wings (or the posts of parachute patterns) with glow-in-the-dark paint. Be conservative, so as not to add extra weight to the flies, and only treat the top sections (where you'll see it, but the trout won't).

Paint your flies at least 24 hours before fishing them. Before you hit the river, spend a good five minutes or so shining a bright flashlight beam into the box, so the paint absorbs the energy. If the glow-in-the-dark spot on the water disappears when you hear a slurp, set the hook.

81 EMBRACE MODERN MATERIALS

Synthetic materials have not only superseded natural fur and feathers, they've also led to the creation of new patterns. Synthetics often are easier for tyers to shape and fit, add more flash and movement than natural components, float higher or sink faster, and last longer. Here are six popular types.

	WHY IT'S COOL	USED FOR
ICE DUB	This synthetic dubbing material is easier to wrap and more durable than fur dubbing. The ultraviolet hues pop and flash.	**PSYCHO PRINCE**
LOCO FOAM	It's high floating and durable like sheet foam, but with an iridescent skin layer—which helps trout find it in dim light.	**LOCO HEXAGENIA**
SHEET FOAM	This flat, rectangular rubber is akin to conventional skirting material on bass lures.	**AMY'S ANT** **CHARLIE BOY HOPPER**
SILI LEGS	You can cut this material to body size, and it floats higher and longer than fur or yarn.	**SUPREME HAIR SHRIMP** **CATHY'S FLEEING CRAB**
THIN SKIN	You can cut this very thin clear or mottled plastic exactly to shape to create wing cases, and the backs of nymphs.	**DEAD DRIFT CRAYFISH**
Z-LON	The crinkly, sparkly synthetic can form wings and tails, and serves as a very coarse dubbing.	**MISSING LINK CADDIS**

82 STOP THE BLOODBATH

Having sharp hooks on your flies is always a good idea, but when it comes to large trout, saltwater, or muskie streamers, it's crucial. If you buy quality streamer hooks, they should already be razor sharp, and the easiest way to figure out just how pointy they are is to tie on them. When tying streamers you are constantly pulling the materials backward after you lash each new segment to the shank, and if you tie a lot, you're going to end up turning your finger into a pincushion. To avoid getting jabbed, pick up a few thin plastic coffee stirrers in the convenience store next time you grab a cup of joe. Cut them down to small lengths, stick a piece over the hook point after you put it in the vise, and you'll be saved from spilling blood.

ESSENTIAL FLIES: SAN JUAN WORM

TYPE: Wet Fly
PRIMARY SPECIES: Trout, Steelhead, Bass, Panfish, Carp

Some flyfishing purists call the San Juan worm cheating. I call it the ace in the hole when you're struggling with more traditional patterns. No matter how keyed in a trout may be to a particular bug, it's hard to get one to pass on the old squirmy worm. But there are many cases where this simple piece of chenille lashed to a hook is no backup, but rather the go-to. In winter, when bugs are scarce and trout need protein, the worm reigns. When the water is murky, a bright pink worm stands out.

83 BE A COLOR GUARD

The amount and variety of materials available in a good fly shop can be pretty overwhelming. Facing thousands of feathers, furs, and synthetics in thousands of colors, you can easily end up buying too much. Of course, that makes the shop owner happy, but if you remember these simple color rules, they'll help you focus on the hues that you'll use most often to tie subsurface streamer patterns.

DARKS Colors such as black, deep green, and dark brown create better silhouettes than light colors. Because of this, these tones shine in low light and stained water. However, they are not as easily seen from a distance. This makes dark colors great choices when you are casting to ambush points (behind boulders, below undercut banks) and less effective while working large open pools or lakes where fish are more spread out.

LIGHTS Brighter, more reflective colors, such as white, tan, light pink, and yellow, will catch fish for you in just about any water clarity, though they will lose some potency during extremely low light and after dark. It's hard to go wrong with white in any situation where you're trying to mimic baitfish, as the vast majority of bait species in both salt and freshwater have white bellies.

BRIGHTS Fluorescent orange, red, pink, and chartreuse are the tones you want to bring into play when the water is very dirty. In situations where silt or mud has dropped clarity to almost nil, these colors may be your saving grace. Bright colors are also key in fishing the salmon and steelhead worlds, regardless of water clarity, as these fish are largely reaction strikers that have a habit of keying in on "hot" colored streamers.

84 STICK TO IT

Just as you'll find loads of tying materials in stores, you'll also find a big selection of glues, cures, cements, and epoxies. Here are the three you should be most familiar with, and when each comes into use.

	SUPER GLUE	HEAD CEMENT	CLEAR CURE GOO
PROFILE	Fly tyers have a bad habit of using fast-drying glues like Zap-A-Gap for all their tying needs. That's a mistake, because they are thin and difficult to control, and often end up making a mess or ruining flies, especially when they are used to finish creating the head of a fly.	Head cement is thicker than super glue, but thinner than clear nail polish. You can apply it with a tiny squeeze bottle, a brush, or the tip of a toothpick. Head cement takes a little time to cure, but it leaves no foul odor and adds very little weight to a fly.	A relative newcomer to the fly-tying market, Clear Cure Goo (CCG) is a thick epoxy that cures instantly when hit with a UV light. Before its invention, using epoxy meant mixing a resin and a hardener, and then turning the fly on a motorized wheel to ensure even drying.
PRIMARY USE	Use a tiny dot of super glue on your wraps between steps when tying larger streamers and bass bugs. This will help secure thicker bunches of material so they don't come loose later. Never use super glue on dry flies or nymphs, as it has an unnatural odor that sticks around long after it dries.	Use head cement to coat the finishing wraps of your dry flies, nymphs, and smaller streamers. With larger flies, you might want to apply two coats. You can also spread some on nymph backs to make them glisten just like a live nymph.	CCG is my go-to for finishing any flies that require a thick, clear head, such as a saltwater Deceiver. As you can layer this material, it's also ideal for building epoxy-body flies such as the Surf Candy, which imitates a sand eel.
SECONDARY USE	Super glues—particularly the thicker gel varieties—are ideal for sticking eyes on a fly after tying, or keeping a foam popper head secured to the hook shank.	Since head cement is thin but dries slowly, I like to brush a bit on my thread before I spin on dubbing. This helps keep the dubbing in place once it's wrapped on the hook shank.	Add one drop of CCG to the backs of your nymphs to create an extra reflective surface and give them a little more flash.

85 HACK A HELLGRAMMITE

It's difficult to find a big smallmouth or trout in a rocky river that will pass up a live hellgrammite. It's also difficult to find live 'mites in the bait shop—and time-consuming to catch your own. For fly anglers, large black stonefly nymphs are the standard hellgrammite imitators, but they're not the only option. If you make a few modifications to some common trout and smallie patterns, you can turn them into bugs that are almost as lethal as livies. Here are some top hacks.

Girdle Bug   *Woolly Bugger*   *Clouser Minnow*

GIRDLE BUG This fly, in all black, does a fine job of imitating a hellgrammite, but it's even better if you replace the rear legs with a long piece of flat rubber band. After you finish the tie, blacken the rubber band with a marker and trim the end to a point. This lengthens the fly's profile, and the modified tail flaps and waves just like a real hellgrammite abdomen as it drifts through the riffles.

WOOLLY BUGGER To spice up a plain dark Bugger, opt for a longer marabou tail for extra wiggle, skip the beadhead, and tie in black bead-chain eyes. These make the head appear wider, like a

hellgrammite's. Wrap the body chenille over the head, whip-finish, and coat the entire head in epoxy to give it a glossy glisten. Fish it like a nymph, or strip it close to the bottom.

CLOUSER MINNOW Make a tail with a length of black bunny strip. Wind in some black chenille to create a body, stopping behind the dumbbell eyes. Instead of tying in a long length of bucktail, spin in a sparse clump of short, black, deer belly hair in front of the head. Finish with a puff of black flash material. Slow-hop this across the bottom in deep holes.

86 BOB FOR GLORY

A few years ago, Thingamabobbers took the fly world by storm. These light strike-indicator bubbles cast well, you can add or remove them easily, and they'll never, ever sink (unless a fish pulls one under). The makers of Thingamabobbers also recently introduced the Unibobber. A shrunken version of the popular

strike indicators, these mini bubbles are designed to tie into a dry fly in place of traditional hair or feather wings. They're much easier to spot in low-light conditions, and the tiny globe of trapped air assures that your dry fly won't sink.

87 TIE A HOPPER NYMPH FOR NON-HOPPER SEASON

You've seen or heard them buzzing about in fields on hot summer days, in crude flight with their diminutive wings and clumsy bodies. If they accidentally land with a splat in a stream, hungry trout gobble them up. This is why so many fly patterns such as the Dave's Hopper and Letort Hopper imitate adult grasshoppers.

But these flies imitate the final life stage of the insect. The first half-dozen life cycle stages are all wingless as the hopper develops, sheds its exoskeleton, and then grows some more. It takes 40 to 80 days before a hopper becomes an adult and sprouts wings. That means, for much of the fishing season, typically from April or May into early July, winged adult patterns are inappropriate.

To fill this gap, I invented the Nymph Hopper. It imitates the immature, wingless stage of the grasshopper, which often jumps into the water and is feasted upon by trout. It's a simple pattern, with legs and a body that floats low in the surface film. It's easy to make and easy to fish.

My original pattern has a thickly dubbed rabbit-fur body and two short deer-hair legs flared out on the sides, which also act as outriggers. Alternately, you can use polypropylene or other synthetics for the body. I've even tied some patterns with a cork or balsa body and two trimmed-down hackle quills on the sides for legs. The point is to attain the clean, torpedo-like silhouette of a hopper body and two distinct legs on the sides.

Fish the fly so it lands with a slight plop, instead of trying to present it delicately. This mimics the naturals and seems to attract attention from trout, usually resulting in a lunging, boiling take.

To tie the Nymph Hopper, dub rabbit fur halfway up the shank of a size 12 to 18 dry-fly hook, adding more as you work toward the hook eye. Add a clump of deer hair so the tips extend just beyond the hook. Take several turns of thread over the hair and tighten, flaring it. Trim excess hair butts. Use that thread to split the hair into two bunches protruding at an angle toward the rear. Secure with a figure-eight. Dub more fur on the thread and wind forward to form a thick thorax and head. Whip-finish and apply a drop of cement to complete the fly.

88 CRAFT A CLOUSER MINNOW

Fly fishers frequently mention the Clouser Minnow as one of the best all-around flies ever tied. It catches trout, smallmouths and largemouths, and saltwater fish. And, best of all, it's a cinch to tie.

STEP 1 Lock a hook—such as a size 4 Mustad 34007—into the vise. Create a base with white 3/0 thread, starting near the hook eye; attach a dumbbell-weighted eye with figure-eight wraps. You want the eyes to be on top of the hook one-quarter of the way down the shank. Dab head cement at the base of the dumbbell wraps.

STEP 2 Attach a sparse strand of white bucktail in front of the dumbbell. Secure it with thread wraps behind the dumbbell. The length of the bucktail depends on the size of the fly; you want 2 inches trailing behind the bend.

Wrap the thread in front of the dumbbell, and turn the fly upside down in the vise.

STEP 3 Put a few strands of Flashabou in front of the dumbbell and wrap back, with the Flashabou lined up on the bottom of the hook shank. Repeat with another strand of colored bucktail (chartreuse is great), fastening in front of the dumbbell, and wrapping the material along the bottom of the hook shank.

STEP 4 Taper the thread from the dumbbell forward toward the eye, make a double whip finish, and add a dab of head cement. This fly works well because it will sink quickly into the feeding zone and undulates as you strip it through the water, enticing reaction strikes in various water conditions.

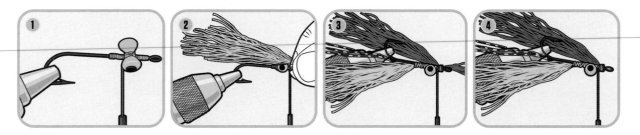

89 GO NUDE

Al Troth created the elk hair caddis, one of the greatest flies ever, to fish the caddis hatches on Western streams. But back on heavily pressured Eastern waters, like New York's Beaverkill and the spring creeks of Pennsylvania, I've found that a revision of this classic pattern works better. I call it the Nude Caddis. This is Troth's fly, but with no hackle wound around the body. This allows the fly to float low on the surface, imitating a caddis pupa rising from the bottom and struggling to emerge. In slick glassy currents, this simpler fly can outscore the original 2 to 1.

The weight of the hook is sufficient to make the body float in or actually penetrate through the surface film, while the hollow elk-hair wing stays on top, making it easy to see the fly.

If you don't tie flies or are short on time, simply buy some of the original patterns, then take a pair of scissors and trim away the hackle. This will give you a deadly caddis pattern for difficult slow water and wary spring-creek trout.

To tie the fly, dub a thin rabbit-fur body on a size 12 to 18 hook. Wind on very fine copper or brass wire ribbing if you want the fly to sit a bit lower in the surface film. Then tie in a down wing on top using elk or deer hair that extends just beyond the bend of the hook. Clip the hair at the head. If you want to be neat about it, wrap thread over the ends.

90 FOLLOW THE RULE OF 3

Some tyers can sit down and keep spinning the same bug over and over until they knock out a few dozen. I'm not one of them. Though I love to tie, I hate all the repetition. If you're like me and you find it difficult to stockpile one pattern, try the rule of three. If I know I need certain bugs for a trip in a week or two, I'll focus on the three patterns I'll use the most, and tie just three of each per night leading up to the outing. It breaks the repetition, stops you from spending hours on end at the vise, and by the time you're ready to fish, you'll have plenty of fresh bugs in your box.

91 TURN PURPLE

The hot patterns in my fly box aren't new patterns, but purple variations of the old standards—purple Prince nymphs, purple San Juan Worms, purple Woolly Buggers, even a purple Parachute Adams.

No matter how many river rocks you turn over, you won't find an insect that looks even remotely like a purple Prince nymph. But it's widely considered a "money bug" by fly guides when the fishing is tough, maybe because purple is easy to see.

According to Dr. Robert Behnke, author of *Trout and Salmon in North America*, trouts' eyes are more perceptive to shades on the blue side of the color spectrum. He adds, however, that trout "exhibit different feeding patterns at different times; during some periods imitation of the food item of the moment is required." The takeaway? When fish are on a specific bite, match fly size and color to the hatch. But next time you're tying, spin up some purple variations for those slow days when you just need to get their attention.

ESSENTIAL FLIES: GIRDLE BUG

TYPE: Nymph
PRIMARY SPECIES: Trout, Bass, Carp

Technically a stonefly nymph mimic, girdle bugs are sold in hundreds of colors, but all share a heavily weighted core and rubber legs that wave seductively in the water. You can dead drift them solo, or in a double nymph rig as an edible weight—if you will—to help get a smaller nymph down deep. They just look "buggy;" even in waters void of stoneflies, they'll get eaten. They're a favorite for pressured stocked trout, an excellent crayfish imitation for smallmouth bass, and carp snap them up when you slow-hop them over a soft bottom. The legs are full of action; try stripping a girdle bug back like a streamer after each drift.

92 RAID YOUR EASTER BASKET

Carol Anne Corely is a nun, a teacher—and a long-time fly tyer and trout fisherman. She also teaches the kids at St. John's School in Arkansas how to spin up bugs; one of her signature patterns is the Resurrection Fly, which incorporates Easter grass. A few Easters ago, I was at the drugstore, and was suddenly drawn to the entire aisle devoted to this colorful shredded plastic. I took a cue from Sister Carol Anne and decided to see what I could come up with at the vise. I figured for 89 cents a bag, it was worth a shot, and if it was any good, I'd have a big enough supply with just two bags to last until the Rapture. Here are the five patterns born of this madness.

A **OL' DIRTY GRASSTARD** Easter grass, I found, is much more durable than Mylar or Flashabou. That means this fly can handle several pike chomps before retiring. The grass is pretty kinky out of the bag, but give the strands a stretch; they straighten easily and breathe nicely.

B **BRUNCH WORM** Easter grass makes stellar body wrap that creates the look of real thorax segments. Though I'm sure it would work nicely on just about any nymph or stonefly, I went wormy. I drift this grassy green weenie for everything from spring stockers to fall steelhead.

C **SILLY RABBIT** You bonefishermen have heard of a Crazy Charlie. This is the Silly Rabbit (work with me, here). The stiff grass tail scratches away at sand and mud a little better on the strip, perhaps creating a stronger visual cue for bones. The material also mimics the mouth feel of shrimp shell pretty well. This may not become your go-to bone fly, but if the fish are being finicky, throw the grass at them.

D **CADBURY CARP EGG** Green Easter grass makes an excellent berry stem. Then again, we're talking about carp, which could likely care less about anatomically correct morsels. Bottom line: they'll eat this egg.

E **PEEP TOAD** I've tied similar diving frog patterns for largemouths, but Easter grass arms and legs add a new twist. I didn't stretch the strands for this pattern; I just left them stiff and kinky, so that the extra rigidity will help them stay flared when the frog dives and hovers back up.

93 TINT YOUR OWN TAILS

The long, flexible hair from a deer's tail is widely used in making streamer flies such as the Clouser Minnow. Deer body hair, meanwhile, is shorter, stiffer, and hollow. You can spin it around a hook shank with thread, or trim it to make floating bass bugs. In either case, you have the satisfaction of catching fish with flies made from your own trophy, if you happen to hunt. Here's a quick cut to get you there.

CUT AND CURE Start with a fresh deer tail cut at its base from the hide. Slice open the hide to expose and remove the tailbone, starting at the base and working on the underside. Scrape away as much fat and tissue as possible. For deer body hair, cut a few hide pieces about 4x4 inches in both white (belly) and brown (back or side) shades, and scrape. Coat the scraped hide with salt and allow it to cure, which will take a few days.

CLEAN AND DYE After the hide dries, gently wash your bucktail or body-hair patches in lukewarm water with household detergent. Rinse thoroughly to get rid of grease and grit. Air-dry the natural-colored hair, unless you plan to dye it, in which case keep it wet while you ready a dye bath. You can easily color deer hair with common fabric dyes such as Rit or Tintex. Believe it or not, one of the best dyes to use for colors such as orange or purple is unsweetened Kool-Aid.

The most useful color for both flies and jigs is natural white; save at least one tail without dyeing it. For, say, smallmouth bass flies, you'll probably want to dye some tails in green, brown, and orange shades so your bugs will imitate crayfish.

94 SPIN THE FLY WHEEL

Fly innovator Jack Gartside created some of his best patterns (such as the Gurgler) while sitting in his Boston taxi, tying them on a vise clamped to his steering wheel. With a standard clamp vise and a 2-inch piece of flexible foam pipe insulation to protect your wheel (if that matters to you), you can apply that concept to make sure you always have the fly you need. Here's what to pack.

THE MATERIALS Keep your inventory to a minimum: several spools of different colored 6/o and 8/o thread, some basic dubbing colors (including olive, brown, and PMD yellow), foam, calf tail, deer or elk hair, beadheads for tying nymphs, marabou, Z-lon, copper wire, a few hackles or capes (in brown, grizzly, and cream), an assortment of hooks, and head cement. Also bring any fly-tying tools essential for creating the basics.

THE FLIES If you're tying on the fly, you've got to tie quickly. The 30-step intricate patterns are out; instead, memorize seven down-and-dirty staples you can spin up in a few minutes: parachute mayflies, emergers, mayfly nymphs (like Pheasant Tails), Elk Hair Caddis, caddis nymphs, Woolly Buggers, and foam terrestrials are all great road patterns.

95 DO YOUR PREP WORK

The mark of a good fly tyer is consistency; if he or she turns out a dozen patterns, they should look almost identical. Commercial tyers who earn their paychecks by whipping up bugs have to be especially consistent, and one way they pull it off is by prepping their materials before making that first thread wrap. It's a trick that can help even beginners tie cleaner flies. If, for example, you're going to tie four Woolly Buggers, select four hackle feathers of similar length, clip four marabou tails of the same length, and clip four strands of flash material of the same length first. Lay them out

next to your vise before you start tying, creating an assembly line. Provided you matched feather sizes and tail material lengths, your four flies should look very similar when completed.

96 FISH WITH PROTECTION

Leave it to fly tyers to invent new uses for household (or should I say bedroom) items. Believe it or not, condoms are quickly becoming a staple material at the benches of some well-known and creative tyers. When cut into strips, the thin latex makes an excellent wrap for worm flies or nymph bodies. What makes it so useful is that when stretched very tight, it becomes almost clear, allowing any underbody colors you've already added to the fly to show through. Condom strips also create a rubbery texture, making your bugs look, well, "buggier." Non-lubricated condoms work best, but if you've still got an old lubed one in your wallet, split it open with scissors, rinse it thoroughly with water and a little dish soap, and let it dry before cutting it up and tying it in.

97 SLAP SOME ELK SKIN

The hide of one bull elk will produce enough hair for 984,376 flies—give or take. So if you're a hunter (or if you get a hide some other way) don't let it go to waste. Here's how to make a range of cool flies with all that hair.

STEP 1 Cut 6-inch squares of hide. Flesh them with a knife blade by removing as much fat and meat as possible without slicing through the roots of the hair.

STEP 2 Salt each square with ¼ cup of salt, rubbing it into the flesh side of the hide with your fingers. Let it sit for eight hours, shake off the wet salt, and repeat.

STEP 3 Hang the squares from the game pole and air-dry them until it's time to break camp.

STEP 4 To get them home, store the squares in an air-permeable bag, such as a pillowcase.

Think outside the caddis box. Sure, elk hair is perfect for caddis imitations. But use your hide for other dry flies such as Humpys and Stimulators; for nymphs such as little yellow stoneflies; and for terrestrials like the Henry's Fork Hopper. Elk hair is a little coarser than deer hair. It also floats better, so you can use it for poppers and bass bugs.

98 TIE DRAB COLORS TO HOOK BONEFISH

Headed to some place tropical with miles of bonefish flats? Here's some advice. While getting creative with fly colors can pay off for species such as trout, bass, and pike, when it comes to bonefish, stick to white, tan, and light pink. These colors may not be eye-catching to you, but they are perfect matches for the tiny shrimp and crabs these fish eat. Unlike predator species that you can find in various water clarities and conditions where wild colors can score an eat, bone flats need to be crystal clear (or else you can't fish them properly), and whether you find them in Florida or Mexico, these fish are wary. A hot pink or screaming red fly is no advantage; it would be more likely to spook than attract them. If you keep your fly colors muted, you'll hear your drag scream more often.

ESSENTIAL FLIES: MARCH BROWN

TYPE: Dry Fly
PRIMARY SPECIES: Trout

The first March Brown dries were reputedly tied in England in the 1600s, as the mayflies they represent were then and are now one of the most significant hatches in the United Kingdom. Those hatches are pretty spectacular in the States, too, and most often occur in spring and early summer. You can bump into March Browns on almost any trout river in the United States, and as these bugs are larger than many other mayflies, they have a tendency to coax big, bottom-dwelling trout to the surface. You can use several other dry fly patterns to mimic March Browns, but none are as spot-on and deadly as this classic pattern of the same name.

99 CRAFT A MONEY BUNNY

At the tying vise, you can make streamers as complex as you want—creating jointed bodies and adding rubber legs or plenty of other enticing materials. But any streamer junkie knows it doesn't take much more than a fluttering strip of rabbit fur to entice an aggressive gamefish. This pattern, which I call the One-Trick Bunny, is great for novice tyers or seasoned vets looking for a quick streamer that'll catch lots of fish. It may not be the sexiest pattern in your box, but it often outfishes those fancy ones that'll cost $5 a pop at the fly shop.

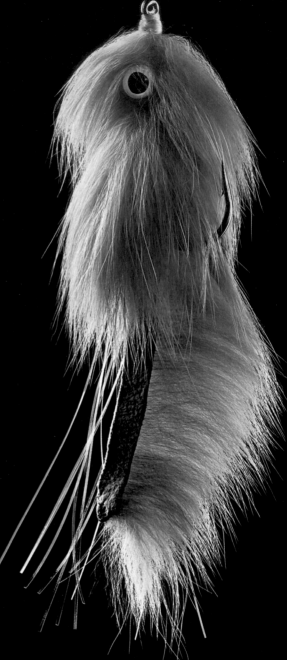

MATERIALS

Tying thread • Size 1 popper hook • Dumbbell eyes • One long cross-cut bunny strip (color of your choice) • Flashabou (optional)

STEP 1 Lock the dumbbell eyes into the notch on the popper hook. I use these hooks because the groove prevents the eyes from rotating and keeps them closer to the shank, reducing the fly's overall profile.

STEP 2 Tie in the bunny strip just forward of the hook bend, leaving a 2- or 3-inch tag for the tail. If you'd like to add some flash, tie in a few strands of Flashabou on top of the wraps that anchor the strip.

STEP 3 Wind the bunny strip forward over the shank, making sure to pull fairly hard to create tight wraps. Lock the strip in place with thread just behind the eyes. Crisscross the strip once around the eyes, make a few more spiral wraps with it around the shank in front of the eyes, and then lock the strip down with the thread. Trim the excess rabbit strip. Add some final thread wraps, whip-finish, cement, and go fishing.

100 LET NATURE BE YOUR TYING MUSE

Anyone can learn to tie by copying the patterns that they find in the fly shop, or by watching videos online, but some of the best tyers in the world use nature as their inspiration. When you're out on the water, pay close attention to how different species of live caddis and mayflies look while floating on the surface. Do they flop on their sides? Do they drift with their wings perfectly erect, not moving at all? These observations can help when you want to experiment with new materials, or tweak patterns to make them look more natural. Flip rocks to find live stoneflies, and note subtle variations in their coloring that can help you to create a more realistic imitator. Take note of the way baitfish move in flowing versus still water. Their action might prompt you to add a joint or some extra flash material to your next streamer.

101 STAY CLASSY

You can watch hours of online video, but one of the best ways to get started in tying, or keep sharp if you're already seasoned, is to take a class. Many local fly shops offer courses on tying specific kinds of bugs ("classic" dry flies, bass bugs, and so on), and they also have "open tying" nights where anglers hang out together, swap tying materials, and make bugs. There is no replacement for having an expert sitting next to you while trying to learn a new technique, and tying with a group is an excellent way to pick up new tricks.

ESSENTIAL FLIES: MUDDLER MINNOW

TYPE: Streamer
PRIMARY SPECIES: Trout, Bass, Steelhead

The Muddler is a true classic, developed in the 1930s to imitate a slimy sculpin, a bottom-dwelling baitfish preyed upon by large trout. Though its design was specific to this particular forage, it blossomed into an all-around baitfish imitator, thanks in part to its wide, full profile, which many streamers of that era lacked. These days, the Muddler has largely taken a back seat to streamers that lean on modern materials with more action, but don't rule this old fly out. On a clear stream full of wary fish, an unweighted Muddler stripped through pools and eddies can be a trout magnet.

102 THROW THIS JOINT

Over the last few years, multihook, multijointed streamers have become very trendy, and with good reason. Many anglers subscribe to the theory that the bigger the fly, the bigger the fish it will entice. I can tell you from personal experience: It's true. Not only will these monster ties hook the biggest trout of your life, their extra-sexy wiggly action does a number on giant pike and muskies, too. Creating the flies is easy, and requires nothing more than a spool of coated beading wire from the craft store, a bag of cheap plastic beads, and some crazy glue.

STEP 1 After locking the fly's front hook in the vise, tie in 3 inches of beading wire near the bend with the tag end extending off the back of the hook.

STEP 2 Slip 2 to 4 beads on the wire. These act as spacers, and the more beads you add, the wider the gap between the front and rear sections of the fly.

STEP 3 Thread the wire through the eye of the pre-tied tail section. Now run the wire back through the spacer beads, and lash it down tightly to the shank of the front hook again. Clip off the excess wire and give the thread wraps a few coats of super glue before tying the front half of the fly.

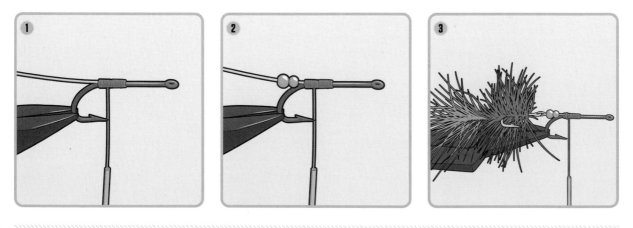

103 TIE AN EASY, DEADLY MOUSE

When most people think of mouse flies, they imagine complicated patterns with spun deer hair, leather ears, and intricate whiskers. But a big brown trout doesn't care how much *you* think a fly looks like a mouse. All an effective fly has to do is create a "mousy" silhouette when it is seen from below. The Master Splinter—named after the Teenage Mutant Ninja Turtles character— is so easy to tie, a beginner can bust out an dozen in a flash, and this fly has already proven itself a killer on several noted East Coast brown trout rivers.

MATERIALS

210 denier black thread • 5" length of black cross-cut bunny strip • 1"x3" piece of thin black foam • 3" thin sliver of black bunny strip, hair removed except for a puff on the end • Size 2 stinger hook

STEP 1 Tie in the thin bunny strip tail near the bend in the hook skin side (the side that was always hairless) facing up.

STEP 2 Wrap in the first half-inch of foam backwards so the remainder extends over the tail.

STEP 3 Tie in the cross-cut bunny strip and wind it forward towards the eye of the hook and secure it at the head.

STEP 4 Part the cross-cut hair so there is equal length on either side of the hook shank. Now bring the foam forward over the shank, and cinch it down near the eye with three tight wraps. Fold the foam back on itself and lock it with three more tight wraps to create the mouse's head.

STEP 5 Trim the excess foam to create a collar behind the finishing wraps. From underwater, the collar helps to create the illusion of ears.

104 TIE A FIVE-MINUTE FLY

The Woolly Bugger is the perfect pattern for a learning fly-tyer. It's big, so you can see what you're doing, and it involves only a few inexpensive materials. Even more importantly, it's a proven producer for trout, bass, and almost anything in between.

STEP 1 Wrap black 6/0 thread along the length of a size 10 streamer hook. Always wrap away from yourself, over the top of the hook. If you want a beadhead bugger, slide the bead on the hook before starting your wraps.

STEP 2 Secure one large black marabou feather at the front of the hook, and wrap all the way back to the bend. You want to leave enough feather exposed to create a tail.

STEP 3 Connect a 2-inch piece of fine copper wire by the tail, and also a strand of black chenille. Wrap the thread forward, then the chenille, but leave the wire behind. Tie off the chenille with a half hitch.

STEP 4 Now tie on a saddle hackle feather (black or grizzly), palmer it back (wrap with spacing), and secure this with a couple of wraps of the wire. Trim the leftover hackle. Wrap the wire forward, and tie it off with the thread. Trim the excess wire.

STEP 5 Finish the fly with a tapered thread head. Whip-finish, apply a dab of head cement, and you're done.

105 FLASH YOUR STACK

When stacking deer hair for bass flies, mix in small bunches of Krystal Flash or Flashabou. This will give you some nice flash accents when you spin the hair onto the hook. The extra flare can go a long way, especially with diving hair bugs.

106 KEEP YOUR EYES ON THE PRIZE

Large predator species, such as pike, muskies, striped bass, and brown trout, tend to attack a streamer head first. With this habit in mind, it's never a bad idea to add bigger eyes to your streamers than you think you need. These gamefish recognize the eyes of their prey, and you'd be surprised how a streamer lacking eyes often draws fewer strikes than one with them. Clear Cure Eyes are relatively new to the market, and are very lifelike. They're made of plastic and tie in just like weighted dumbbell eyes. However, if you want to keep it simple, head to the craft store and buy a cheap bag of large googly eyes. After you finish a streamer, stick the eyes either side of the head with a dab of thick super glue.

107 LOOP THAT BUNNY

Soak a bunny strip in water, and it shimmies and wags more seductively than any other material when you strip it. Some of the most effective streamers for big trout, pike, and saltwater species rely on bunny strip tails. The problem with them is that they have a habit of fouling around the hook when you cast, leaving you with a knotted pile of fur that won't seduce anything. The easiest way to thwart fouling is to tie a loop of stiff monofilament behind the hook bend before lashing on that bunny tail. The loop acts as a kind of flop guard, making it more difficult for the bunny strip to spin around the hook point.

ESSENTIAL FLIES: CLOUSER MINNOW

TYPE: Streamer
PRIMARY SPECIES: Saltwater, Bass, Pike/Muskie, Trout

First tied by the renowned flycaster Bob Clouser, this historic streamer is perhaps the most versatile baitfish imitator ever created. Though sizes range from an inch or less to six inches or more, the materials are universal; bucktail, dumbbell eyes, and a little bit of flash. Not only do these flies get down faster than any unweighted streamers, but the design causes them to rise and fall in an enticing jigging action. If what you're chasing eats baitfish, it'll eat a Clouser.

TECHNIQUES

DURING MY FIRST VISIT TO ELK CREEK

in Pennsylvania, the water was horribly low and gin clear. My guide, Chris Kazulen, explained that if I dropped even one little split shot in the hole in front of us, I'd scare the fish. The trick, he said, was to use a tiny nymph, a light tippet, and no weight. Given how hard steelhead fight, I was a wreck when I tied into the first fish on this rig. But Kazulen calmly walked me through how to bend the rod to keep the micro hook planted, when to let the fish run so I didn't break the meager tippet, and where to position myself so he could nail the net shot on the first attempt. Everything came together, and I ended up landing a near 20-pounder. I credit Kazulen's technique entirely.

The best way to learn to fly cast is at a lake on a calm day where there is nothing behind you to snag. Of course, most of the time, you won't have such perfect conditions. Wind, trees, currents, bushes, and rocks are just a few of the obstacles that will get in your way. The techniques you'll find in this chapter will help you overcome these obstacles, whether in a case where you need to cast under a low-hanging limb, spot fish on a cloudy day, or land a huge steelhead on hair-thin tippet.

108 CONQUER TROUT CAMOUFLAGE

You might assume that trout in a clear stream would stick out like sore thumbs. Unfortunately, spotting the masters of camouflage takes a little practice. First, find glare-free viewing lanes that give you the clearest possible picture of the bottom. Next, take some focus on the contrasts in rock colors. Familiarize yourself with the piece of water, and then focus on spotting fish.

Imagine a sketch of a fish, a heavy outline filled with color. Now remove the outline. That's the target: a ghostly underwater smear (A). Now, look for a fish that moves slightly, and then returns to the same location in the stream (B). That's a feeding fish. Analyze every speck of white on the bottom. An on-off glint of white is the inside of a trout's mouth. A broken pattern of glints is your target: a feeding trout (C). Here's how to catch it.

STEP 1 Force your eyes to adjust to the stream bottom. Fix your eyes on the bottom without blinking. Going into this "soft-focus mode" opens your peripheral vision to take in a big swath of the viewing lane.

STEP 2 Now, sharpen your focus to pinpoint any object that resembles a trout—a silhouette, a movement, a glint of white. At this point, most anglers wind up for the cast. Hold off.

STEP 3 Let your eyes adjust back to peripheral vision while keeping your target centered. Now you can pick out the contextual clues (water current and casting and drift obstacles) that you need to plot a perfect cast.

STEP 4 Focus back on the target to watch for a feeding pattern and dial down the precise timing of the cast.

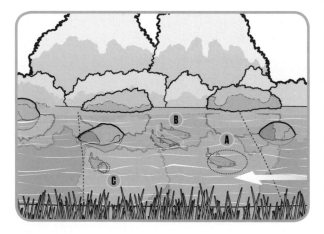

109 LET BAD CASTS GO

A trout rises in a riffle, gulping steadily. You wade into position, make your false cast, let fly, and—pow!—a gust of wind tosses that cast 2 feet to the left of what you thought would be a perfect shot, just outside the fish's feeding lane. Like most people, you quickly reload and try again. Bad call.

"Live with it," says Missouri River guide Pete Cardinal. "If you make a bad cast, let your fly float out of that trout's range of vision, then go again, but not before." If you miss, let the fly slide behind a trout, and then recast. Ripping the line off the water while it's still in front of the fish may cause it to spook.

110 CONTROL YOUR WRIST

The No. 1 mistake novice fly casters make is going back too far on the back cast. The tip-offs are noises of line slapping the water or the rod tip scraping the ground. This usually happens because the caster is allowing his wrist to cock too far back.

Remember: The arm is the engine; the wrist is the steering wheel. Sometimes it may be "all in the wrist," but that's for aiming the cast, not powering it. Let your wrist power your cast and you'll crash.

To correct this tendency, get a large, thick rubber band, wrap it around your casting wrist, and then insert the rod butt inside the band when you cast. If the band flexes too much, odds are you're breaking your wrist too far.

If you're wearing a long-sleeved shirt, tuck the butt inside your cuff to get the same effect.

111 POINT YOUR SHOTS

It's axiomatic: The fly line, and thus the fly, follows the rod tip. Taking that one step further, the rod tip follows the thumb—the strongest digit and the one most anglers place atop the grip for power and direction. Lee Wulff used to cast with his index finger on top, because he felt it gave him better control. He was an exception to the rule. But as long as you keep your thumb—or index finger—pointed at the target, your cast will go where you want it to.

112 FISH THE CYCLE

In 1496, dame Juliana Berners described fly imitations for about a dozen mayflies in her *A Treatyse of Fysshynge wyth an Angle*. And so it began. There are more than 500 species of mayflies known to North America, and no telling how many mayfly patterns. Here's how to match the fly to the mayfly life stage.

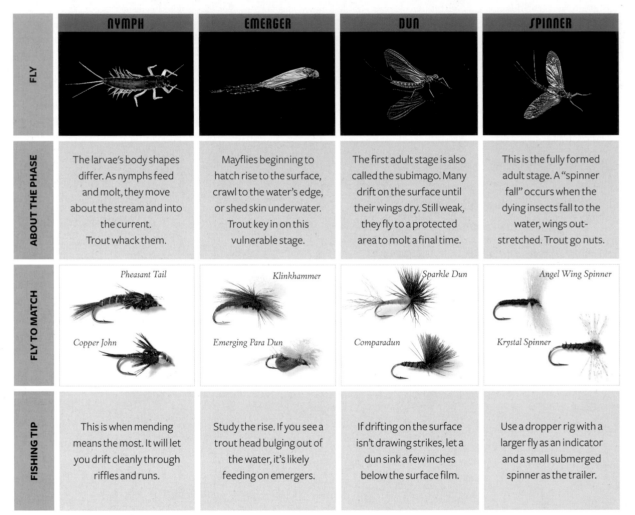

	NYMPH	EMERGER	DUN	SPINNER
ABOUT THE PHASE	The larvae's body shapes differ. As nymphs feed and molt, they move about the stream and into the current. Trout whack them.	Mayflies beginning to hatch rise to the surface, crawl to the water's edge, or shed skin underwater. Trout key in on this vulnerable stage.	The first adult stage is also called the subimago. Many drift on the surface until their wings dry. Still weak, they fly to a protected area to molt a final time.	This is the fully formed adult stage. A "spinner fall" occurs when the dying insects fall to the water, wings out-stretched. Trout go nuts.
FLY TO MATCH	*Pheasant Tail* / *Copper John*	*Klinkhammer* / *Emerging Para Dun*	*Sparkle Dun* / *Comparadun*	*Angel Wing Spinner* / *Krystal Spinner*
FISHING TIP	This is when mending means the most. It will let you drift cleanly through riffles and runs.	Study the rise. If you see a trout head bulging out of the water, it's likely feeding on emergers.	If drifting on the surface isn't drawing strikes, let a dun sink a few inches below the surface film.	Use a dropper rig with a larger fly as an indicator and a small submerged spinner as the trailer.

113 DRESS A DRY FLY RIGHT

Guides often see anglers fatally alter a fly's profile by smashing and grinding floatant into the material, but here's how to make your fly float. Grasp the hook point between your thumb and index finger, and place one drop of floatant directly on the top of the hackle fibers.

Don't put it on your fingers and then work it into the fly; you'll destroy the silhouette that you're hoping will attract a fish. Instead, with your other hand, use a fingernail to flick the floatant into the fly materials.

114 HUNT FOR SHADOWS

In a trout stream, currents and rocks on the bottom will make it much trickier for you to spot shadows created by hovering fish. But on sandy saltwater flats, shadows might be all you have to go by. Flats bonefish blend incredibly well with the light sandy bottom, which is why they're nicknamed "gray ghosts." Looking down into the water, you may never see an actual fish, but they can't hide the shadow that lies between their bellies and the bottom on sunny days. If you see dark shadows moving, remember that they'll be positioned slightly behind the actual fish. You want to lead a bonefish by 3 to 5 feet when you cast, so you should lead a shadow by 4 to 6 feet.

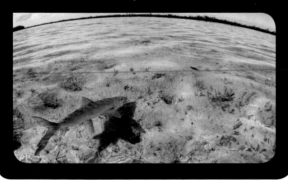

ESSENTIAL FLIES: DAVE'S HOPPER

TYPE: Terrestrial
PRIMARY SPECIES: Trout, Bass, Panfish

In late summer when the grass is high, the air is muggy, and major hatches wane prior to fall's cooldown, trout go after grasshoppers. There are nearly endless styles of hoppers on the market today, but Dave Whitlock's original variation is tough to beat. Perfected back in the 1950s, Dave's Hopper is super-buoyant, riding high on the surface and making a nice splat when it lands. This is important; trout actually recognize the sound of a live hopper falling into the water, and it's the splash that draws them to these big, juicy, targets. Drift this fly tight to the bank, and dangle a Pheasant Tail Nymph under it for a "hopper-dropper" combo.

115 MATCH THE MOTION TO THE MEAL

It's one of the most basic things you need to know: What are the trout eating, right here, right now? Here's a way to read behavior, from expert guide Craig Mathews.

A trout whose fin cuts the water surface (A) is almost always taking nymphs.

If you see noses, heads, or backs breaking the water surface (B), those fish are taking duns.

Bulging, splashy rises in fast currents (C) are often made by fish hammering caddis flies skipping on the water's surface.

If you see a casual, almost slow-motion rise (D) and hear a soft kissing sound, that's a fish taking mayfly spinners in the surface film.

Trout that dart like knives (E) are taking damselfly nymphs, which move very quickly from the water column toward the stream bank.

116 PLAY THE ANGLES

When sight-fishing for anything from carp to bass, your inclination is to always look for fish ahead of you. That's fine when you're fishing wide-open spaces, but as soon as trees come into the picture, especially on tight waters, you need to alter your approach. Trees create shadows, and while you may have a clear picture of what's swimming in the sunny spots, seeing into the dark water will require changing your viewing angle. Walk extra slowly, and periodically look back over your shoulder as well as ahead. A mudding carp you couldn't see in the shadows ten steps ago can suddenly stick out like a sore thumb when you slightly shift your position.

117 DON'T BARGE IN

A number of years ago, I interviewed 10 trout fishing guides for a *Field and Stream* story on their favorite tactics and techniques. Their input was diverse, and everyone seemed to have a different point of view (perfect for the story.) But when I asked them all about their pet peeves, they gave nearly uniform answers. "People don't look where they walk." "People forget to look at the water right in front of them." "Most folks forget to notice that some of the best trout are right near the bank." In other words, you're standing on your fish, stupid.

Don't take anything for granted. By dashing into the middle of a run, the only thing you guarantee is that any fish that were there will be gone.

118 MOW THE LAWN

Casting to a tailing redfish 40 feet away when a mass of protruding grass separates you and your target is not easy. First, figure out which way the fish is moving and aim 2 feet ahead of its course. Your line may land across the grass tops, and your fly will get stuck on the grass above the surface. Instead of trying to strip the fly, wiggle the line with your wrist when the fish is close. The fly may plop into the water and get hit, or the wiggling grass may draw the red's attention, and it'll strike the crab.

119 TIE AN ARBOR KNOT

The best way to connect line to a reel is also the simplest. The arbor knot works with any type of reel and line, including the gel-spun or Dacron backing you need to put on your fly reel before winding on the actual floating fly line.

STEP 1 Pass the backing around the reel spool and back out again the same way that the line entered.

STEP 2 Tie a simple overhand knot with the tag end around the standing backing. Tighten the knot.

STEP 3 Tie an overhand knot in the tag end, and then tighten and trim the tag end. This will keep the first knot from slipping free.

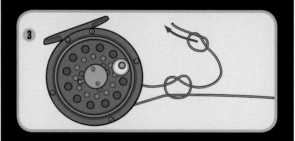

STEP 4 Pull the standing backing to tighten on the spool, binding the knots together securely. Spool the reel.

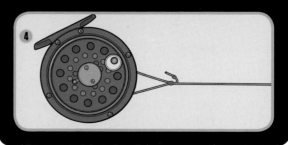

120 DON'T BE THAT GUY

Fly fishing has the reputation of being a refined sport, and yet I am often amazed by the behavior of anglers who should know better. The onus is on seasoned anglers to make the experience positive for everyone, and not just for themselves. Good etiquette is really just a matter of common sense—which, as the old saying goes, is not so common.

DON'T CROWD IN If you are second (or third, or 25th) to the river, that's your problem, not everyone else's. Find somewhere else you can fish, or wait. Watch the direction in which other anglers are fishing (are they going upstream or downstream, moving right or left along a shoreline?), and never block them. You should yield at least a couple runs in front of another angler, especially when that other angler is on the move.

SHARE AND BE FAIR Don't camp in one run all day. It might be the most productive spot in the river, but courtesy dictates that you share with others. And don't do things that will mess up the water someone else is fishing. For example, mind your shadows if you're walking next to a river. Don't splash around and stir up the water. And don't paddle your boat right through a run that someone else is casting into.

USE YOUR WORDS When in doubt, ask. "Do you mind if I wade in and fish that pool up there?" Tell others what your plans are. For example, leave a note on the windshield of your vehicle parked at a bridge. "I went upstream, 2 p.m." Unless the anglers who follow you are nuts, they'll head the other way. That said, your voice should only be heard by others when they want to hear it. It's great to get excited about fishing, but don't go whooping it up.

PLAY BY THE RULES Don't leave trash where it doesn't belong. Keep your dog on a leash (or leave your dog at home) if it's not the kind of dog that will heel right next to you as you fish. And if you're a catch-and-release angler, do your best to ensure that the fish you catch will live.

BE NICE Lastly, if you truly feel like somebody has done something wrong, don't yell at them, flip them off, or get into an argument. Odds are, they don't know what they did. If you can politely let them know, and then move on by saying "no worries," they'll be smarter, you'll feel better, and a future bad encounter will likely be avoided.

121 TEACH A KID TO FISH

Schooling your kids on flyfishing doesn't have to be as trying as helping them with their math homework. Just ask Scott Wood, a flyfishing instructor who has taught thousands of students. "You have to approach it like dog training," says Wood. "You're not going to take a puppy out for three hours of retrieving. Figure you have a half hour, and optimize it." Here's how.

KNOW YOUR STUDENTS Tailor your comments to the age level. A 14-year-old might understand what you mean by "feel the rod load," but an 8-year-old won't. Bring two rods so you don't have to take the rod from your kid while instructing, which feels like punishment. "Above all, don't let them get bored," says Wood. "Don't just sit and wait for perfection—introduce new concepts quickly."

TEACH TIMING Start off with sidearm casts so kids can watch the fly line and better understand the physics of casting. Emphasize that fly casting is about timing of the cast, not the strength.

MAKE A CASTING CALL Tell your kids to treat the rod like a ringing telephone: Bring the rod up close to their ear, say, "Hello, this is Drew Smith," and then set the "phone" down. That's the basic fly-casting movement: Sweep the

rod back, stop it, let the rod load, and then make a forward cast. If they struggle with the basics, switch to roll casting for the time being. It's easier to learn, and once they've had a bit of success, they'll be ready to tackle a standard cast.

FIND A LIKELY SPOT Choose a time and place where the fish are willing. Bream beds, Wood says, are perfect.

GO PRO Do your kids bristle at every suggestion you make? Sign up for a casting school, or hire a guide for a half day and outsource the tricky parts.

122 OUTFIT YOUR KID

The right gear can make all the difference between a fun trip that has Junior begging for more and a frustrating outing for all. Here are the basics.

Ⓐ ROD A soft action helps kids feel the rod flex and load. You might think that a short rod is the way to go for a short kid, but supershort rods can be difficult to cast. Go for an 8-foot, 6-weight, two-piece outfit.

Ⓑ LINE Overline the rod by one line weight, or use Rio's Rio Grand lines, which are one-half line weight heavier, for easier turnover.

Ⓒ FLIES Get a barbed fly stuck in your child's forehead and you can forget about having a future fishing buddy. Only use flies with barbless hooks. For practice, tie orange egg yarn next to the fly to make it more visible. On the water, cast big high-floating flies like Stimulators.

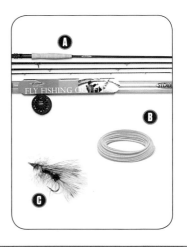

123 PLAY IN THE DIRT

The first few times I saw flyfishermen on local streams during spring runoff, I wrote it off to cabin fever. After all, I thought I knew that dirty water is not that good for flyfishing. I learned my error pretty much by accident, after driving two hours to a stream I was sure would be clear. When it wasn't, I figured I should at least give it a half-hearted try. Just by going through the motions, I began to pick up a few trout here and there—and I realized I'd been missing out on some great fishing.

The fact is, trout do well in runoff. In a normal spring flood, the water is comfortably cool and well oxygenated by the tumbling currents. This increased flow also dislodges aquatic nymphs and washes bankside terrestrials into the stream, so there's plenty to eat.

Visibility is your main issue. Stand in the middle of a bridge over a steam in runoff. The main channel will look like a brown, roiling mess, but check along the banks. If you can see even a few rocks in shallow water, string up your rod.

My standard rig is a brace of flies: a size 4 or 6 dark stonefly nymph, trailed by something like a size 12 or 14 mayfly or caddis larva. I'll use as much weight on the leader as it takes to get the nymphs to the fish. You don't want to snag bottom on every other cast, but if it doesn't hang up now and then, you're probably not fishing deep enough. And I'll probably use a strike indicator that's large and buoyant enough to use as a bobber, suspending the nymphs in the current.

I usually have a few great trips fishing the runoff every spring but, honestly, most are the kind where, after an hour or so, it's apparent that two or three trout is all I can hope for. Still, catching even a few small trout from a stream that few others will bother with until later in the season makes me feel pleasantly sneaky.

124 WADE FOR YOUR LIFE

Every year some 2,000 people drown in North American waters, most within 10 feet of shore. The majority are "flush drownings," in which an angler is swept off his feet. Besides common sense, the three most important tools for maintaining your balance are polarized sunglasses that let you see the streambed, soles that let you grip the streambed (felt, spiked, or sticky rubber soles for smooth rocks and moss, cleated rubber bottoms for sand and silt), and a wading staff.

Use the staff as a third leg. Establish it ahead and downstream of your position, place your weight on your upstream leg, then step to the staff with your downstream leg. Keep two points of contact with the streambed at all times. Wade with your body sideways to the current, and cross the water at a downstream angle. Avoid stepping over boulders. Take advantage of slower water and shuffle your feet near the bottom, where the current is the least powerful. Here are some specialized techniques.

TURN TOWARDS SHORE To safely turn around in heavy current, stick your rod into your belt (A), anchor your staff downstream, and grab it with both hands (B). Swivel your feet to face the staff, and then step around (C) toward the bank.

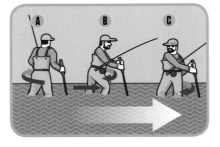

WADE WITH A BUDDY Two people are more stable than one. The stronger wader takes a downstream position and leads the way with his staff. The partner carries both rods. Each wader holds on to the upper wading belt of the other.

125 FOLLOW BUBBLES

One morning, while dry-fly fishing a Trico hatch on Montana's Missouri River, guide Pete Cardinal told me to stop casting and watch the water. We were working a seam where fast water, colliding with a slow pool, was creating a foamy bubble line. Sometimes, that bubble line would disperse and spread out in wide fronds of white, wispy water. At other times, the currents converged and collected hatching insects in a tight, white highway that ran straight through the run. Until Pete pointed it out, I hadn't noticed that the fish were keyed into this system. When the currents dispersed or collapsed, the fish didn't rise. When the foam line formed a hard seam and collected those mayflies, the trout began slurping away at the surface. The lesson? Follow the bubble line. When you see a foam or bubble line on the surface, there's a good chance that feeding trout will be underneath it.

126 FISH WITH YOUR EYES

"How in the world did you see that?" is a refrain fishing guides often hear. Spotting fish before you cast can dramatically increase your odds of hooking up. It doesn't require Superman vision or a carrot-rich diet to start sighting fish. Follow these rules and you'll see your way to instant gratification on the water.

A ZERO IN Instead of searching the entire waterscape, focus on one small zone at a time. Having tunnel vision is actually a good thing when you're contemplating where to place that next cast.

B WATCH THE SURFACE The motion of schooling fish reveals their locations. If a noticeable disturbance occurs as you stare at a smooth water surface, keep looking. Flashes of tails often follow in spots where you first see ripples.

C DISCARD DISTRACTIONS The sooner an angler can weed out distractions such as wind, ripples, and bird shadows, the sooner he can identify the position of feeding fish.

D LOOK UPSTREAM One key to seeing the things you want is to look upcurrent. This usually puts you outside of a fish's peripheral vision and gives you a more detailed point of view.

E SEARCH FOR THE SUBTLE Look for reflections, shapes, and shadows that might reveal a fish. A tail or a nose can be all you need to identify a target.

F SPOT INCONSISTENCIES Whether you're seeking out bedded bass or trout holding in a run, identify unusual marks in the water—color shades, shadows, and motion can tip you off to a lurking fish.

G LOOK THROUGH Practice looking through the water column instead of fixing your gaze on the surface or bottom. This makes you more adept

at seeing the motion and subtle color changes that pinpoint fish.

H GET THE EYES Polarized glasses are a must. You can't see fish without them. Different lenses suit different conditions. On bright days, you might want amber or copper lenses; when it's overcast, maybe yellow. Try to position yourself so the sun makes a spotlight on the water.

127 STEER BIG TROUT AWAY FROM TROUBLE

When a big trout runs, apply pressure above the fish by lifting the rod from the butt section—not the tip. The trout is forced into a head-shaking posture and blunts the surge.

Still going? Don't lift the rod tip. Sweep the rod in the same direction that the fish is moving so that the momentum of your rod and line movement guides the fish away from any obstruction.

If the bruiser does run into a logjam or root snarl, stick your rod tip into the water and free some slack line. You want the tip to carry the fly line, leader, and fly low enough to clear the sunken timber. The current will keep enough tension on the belly of the slack line. Once the fish clears the trees, bring the rod tip up and to the side to apply more side pressure and guide the fish out.

ESSENTIAL FLIES: ZUG BUG

TYPE: Wet Fly/Nymph
PRIMARY SPECIES: Trout

Created by Cliff Zug as an emerging caddis imitation, the Zug Bug has been roped into that category of "all-around producers." The natural reflectiveness of peacock herl—used in this fly's tail and body—gives it the shimmer of a live emerger, while its dark color stands out well in a wide range of water clarities. Zugs make terrific droppers under larger dry flies, or nymphs when dredging the bottom. My favorite way to fish them, however, is as a wet fly. Tied on a long leader, I'll let a Zug swing just below the surface at the tailouts of pools, and just wait for my line to come tight on a fish.

129 MAKE YOUR FIRST CAST COUNT

Fish the first cast with as much focus as the sixth or seventh. Don't just go to a pool and throw the line in; make the first cast count and treat all stops, ticks, or line tension as fish. Don't hesitate and think, "Oh, that's not a fish; maybe next time." That *was* next time.

128 USE THE (NET) BUDDY SYSTEM

Netting a big fish in current for your friend is a high-pressure job. To be the hero instead of the guy that flubbed the glory, always stay downstream of your buddy so he doesn't have to pull it upcurrent. Have the net partially submerged for the end game; wild stabs spook fish and break lines. Finally, net a fish headfirst whenever possible. Scooping at the tail gives the fish a chance to swim forward, which often ends badly.

130 TRY TENKARA

Tenkara is an old form of flyfishing developed on the small mountain streams of Japan, where the long, light rod and thin line made it possible for anglers to accurately and stealthily present flies in tight pockets and seams. Aside from the rod length and light weight, what makes Tenkara unique is there is no reel involved.

The 11- to 14-foot graphite rods taper quickly to a tip far thinner and more flexible than that of even the lightest traditional fly rod. At the end of the tip is a short length of string to which you loop-knot the fly line. Tenkara fly line is composed of multiple handwoven monofilament strands, making it light and springy. It unrolls, floats, and loops like regular fly line, but the design promotes less drag on the water and more stretch than with traditional line. It lands like a feather and won't absorb water. Lines, which range in length from 10 1/2 to 13 feet, feature an end loop that lets you add a 2- or 3-foot piece of 4X or 5X tippet.

Shorter Tenkara rods are for use on streams you could cross in about five bounds. Longer sticks were developed for U.S. anglers who fish larger streams. However, that doesn't mean a wide, roaring tailwater. Tenkara outfits shine in pocket water.

Japanese Tenkara anglers primarily chase trout under 10 inches, though the longer rod models can handle trout to 20 inches, says Daniel Galhardo of Tenkara USA. During my first outing with a tenkara rod, I hooked several trout in the 12- to 14-inch range. The rod kept pressure on well, allowing me to keep the fight within a 30-foot radius of where I stood. When the fish tired, I drew the rod back over my shoulder until the line was close enough to loosely grab with the fingers of my rod hand, so I could gently lead the fish to the net with my other hand. I can't say Tenkara caught more trout than my regular fly outfits, but it did get me fish in places where presenting a fly with my 5-weight would have been tough.

131 BUILD ACCURACY

Long casts, while impressive, are often overkill. Accuracy under pressure matters most in the real fishing world. Pro redfish angler Travis Holeman shared this practice drill that will help you lose the casting yips. Master shorter casts, and you'll hook more fish.

Set up five targets (like trash-can lids, hula hoops, or doormats) at 40 feet. A timekeeper calls a random target, one through five. Using a stopwatch, or shouting "one Mississippi, two Mississippi . . ." (like the pass rusher in a flag football game), he or she counts four seconds. The caster must hit the target before time is called. Mix it up, and then trade places. Want to improve your score? Here are some hints to do just that.

PAY IT FORWARD The drill makes judging distance a reflex; Focus on aiming the cast, not measuring line. Start by paying out 20 feet of line, draping 10 from the end of the rod, and coiling 10 near your feet (1). Then hold the fly in your off hand. With a 9-foot leader between line and fly, that is nearly three-quarters to 40 feet.

START RIGHT To get that slack line airborne, roll cast away from you, off-target, and release the fly (2). Don't yank backward and pull the fly out of your hand; you'll get yourself tangled. Next, fully load the rod on the back cast. Strip out the remaining line as you make one false cast.

STAY ON TARGET Once the line is in the air, focus on the target. Direct the cast with your thumb. When you shock the rod and make your final cast, if the target is lined up at the tip of your thumb (3), odds are your fly will land on the sweet spot.

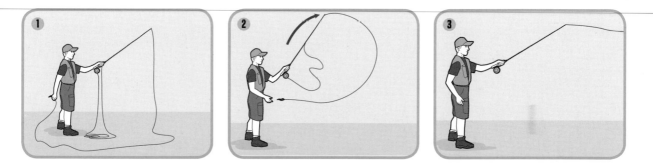

132 LIMIT YOUR FALSE CASTS

To really understand what a trout sees, I went scuba diving in Colorado's South Platte River. I slid right into a run without spooking the fish, as long as I moved slowly. But when my photographer moved the boom-operated underwater camera overhead, even subtly, the fish scattered in panic. Later, as the shadow of a blue heron passed above, I saw fish slink away to the rocks.

More significantly, I watched from below as a friend made several false casts over the fish. As the line flew back and forth, the fish went ballistic and hid against the bank. After allowing them to recover, he started limiting false casts, even using roll casts, and the trout

seemed undisturbed. The point: You get one, maybe two, false casts before the fish are onto you. Try to direct these at an angle behind the fish; only your final cast should target the run.

133 CAST THE WHOLE LINE

Is casting your whole line at once practical? No. (You probably wouldn't be able to set the hook.) Impressive? Oh yeah. Plus, it's a great training exercise. Let's assume you've made a couple of false casts to get 50 or more feet of line in the air straight out in front of you. Now, to toss the whole 90-foot enchilada, make an authoritative back cast. Add a haul (pull the line with your off hand) as you bring the line straight to the rear, running parallel to the ground or water. Shoot a little line backward. Then pause a second. Now haul again as you power the rod straight forward and snap it off with a solid stop. Too much oomph will cause a tailing loop. But if you harness the energy and stop the rod precisely, the line will carry. The more line you have out, the longer your stroke should be. No more than 70 feet should be dancing overhead before you shoot the remainder of the line. Keep in mind that a clean, straight fly line really helps. And remember—any more than three or four false casts, and you're bound to lose it.

ESSENTIAL FLIES: MARCH BROWN WET

TYPE: Wet Fly
PRIMARY SPECIES: Trout

Wet-fly fishing is now nearly a lost art, but has been effective since the dawn of flyfishing. Nymphing gets flies matching aquatic insect larvae down deep, but wet flies ride just below the surface, mimicking bugs rising from the bottom. Anglers tend to use nymphs with no extra weight for the presentation, but traditional wet flies are unweighted, resembling dry flies minus the spiky hackles. Keep a traditional wet fly or two on hand for fish feeding in shallow water just below the surface. The March Brown is a good choice; its neutral color allows it to match many species of emerging insects.

134 TIE AN ORVIS KNOT

The Orvis knot is a good connection for weak line; you can use it for tying small flies to light tippets. It is usually 20 to 30 percent stronger than the popular improved clinch.

STEP 1 Extend 6 to 8 inches of line through the hook eye. Form a large loop with the tag end on the far side of the standing line.

STEP 2 Form a second loop by bringing the tag end around the standing line and back, underneath and through the first loop.

STEP 3 Bend the tag end to the right and make two turns around the second loop. These turns must start from the far side of the second loop.

STEP 4 To tighten the knot, first pull in opposite directions on both the hook and the tag end. Then pull on the standing line to bring the knot firmly against the hook eye.

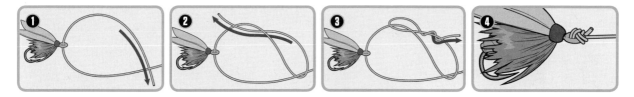

135 STRIP INTO A HAMPER

Anglers fishing from the bow of a boat commonly use waist-high, bottom-weighted, hard-plastic stripping buckets, designed to keep fly line from blowing overboard on windy days. Though functional, these things are pricey. They're also a pain to stow out of the way in a small open boat. An inexpensive polyester-mesh pop-up laundry hamper, however, does the job for a fraction of the cost. When fully open, the one I use is 25 inches high and 16 inches in diameter, providing a deep, wide reservoir to hold the line. When I don't need it, it collapses for convenient storage.

The hamper is light, so you must anchor it to the boat. You can weight it down with flat-sided water bottles, but I prefer to secure mine to the deck by stainless-steel hooks attached to a set of bungee cords, which hook into a pair of recessed flush-deck fittings already on my boat's deck. I also run a loop of braided nylon from the forward edge of the basket over the foredeck pop-up cleat. That way the hamper will never blow over.

136 RIG TWO FLIES

Drift-fishing western rivers is a two-fly proposition, with either a pair of dries, a dry with a beadhead dropper, or two wets—typically a beadhead with a San Juan Worm. This offers the trout a choice and also covers two feeding lanes in the river. To avoid tangles, the best rigging method is to tie a dropper strand directly to the hook bend of the point fly with a clinch knot. That puts the flies in line for tangle-free casting. Tie the smaller fly to the dropper strand.

137 AVOID DOUBLE-HAUL MISTAKES

Like most aspects of fly casting, the double haul is more about feel and timing than it is about power. Simply put, to double-haul you use your noncasting hand to pull the fly line away from the rod tip in an abrupt, well-timed burst—thus increasing the resistance and flex in the rod—first on the back cast and then on the forward cast. By increasing that flex, you boost line speed. And if you maintain a well-formed loop during your cast, that added energy translates to distance. The trick is to avoid these common mistakes:

TOO MUCH LINE You need to feel the effect to get your timing down, and that's hard to do with 60 feet of line flying overhead. Start short, with maybe 20 feet of line. Pull the line on your back cast (1), feel the resistance, let the line spring back through the guides, sliding through your fingers so you can pinch it again (2), and then give another tug on the forward cast (3), release, and shoot the cast (4). Don't try long casts until you get into the groove with short ones.

NOT GIVING THE LINE BACK TO THE ROD You're sunk if your cast ends up with your line hand down by your hip pocket, 3 feet away from your casting hand, with dead line flapping in between. All the energy is lost. You want your hands to spring apart and come together, like you're playing an accordion. If you're stuck on this problem, tie your wrists together with a 20-inch piece of string.

HOLDING ON TOO LONG When it's time to let fly with that cast, let go of the line! Haul on the back cast, haul on the forward cast, feel the flex, and, when your loop gets ahead of your rod tip, let go of the line as if you're shooting a slingshot through the guides on your rod. Hanging on kills the cast. You'll soon learn how to gently release and regather the line with your fingertips as you're double-hauling.

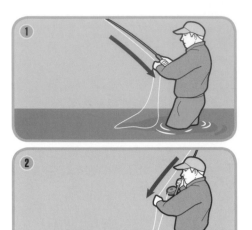

138 PERFECT THE SLACK-LINE CAST

There's a step-by-step process to mastering the short, accurate slack-line cast. First, choose the target, be it a rising fish or a rock. Account for current speed and drag, and guesstimate the exact spot where you want the fly to land. Second, as you cast, carry 2 to 3 feet of extra slack in your line hand. When you carry through that final forward stroke, aim precisely at your target spot. As the fly reaches the target, release the slack line, and, when the line straightens out, check the rod tip abruptly. That will cause the line to recoil and drop in a series of S-curves that will defeat drag.

139 FIRE THE CURVE CAST

The curve cast is a useful trick when you want to drop a dry fly in a specific spot, but a boulder or overhanging tree branch blocks the straight line between you and the rising trout. It also works where heavy currents or obstacles make a downstream presentation impractical. I've also heard this called a hinge cast, because the idea is to shoot the fly line forward with power, and then stop the line abruptly so the leader connection hinges and kicks the fly to the side.

STEP 1 Get within 20 to 50 feet of your target. As you start casting, move the plane of your rod from straight overhead to 45 degrees—or even sidearm—so the path of your line is nearly parallel to the water surface.

STEP 2 Accelerate the forward cast to generate line speed, but stop the rod abruptly as the line straightens. When the line is almost fully extended, flick your wrist so the reel curves (A) toward the direction in which you want your fly to land.

STEP 3 Stop the line by pinching it against the grip with the index finger of your casting hand, or by pulling taut with your line hand if you're double-hauling. As you see the leader cock sideways, drop the rod tip and let your fly fall gently to the surface.

ESSENTIAL FLIES: MICKEY FINN

TYPE: Streamer
PRIMARY SPECIES: Trout, Atlantic Salmon

Compared to exotic modern streamers, the Mickey Finn looks like a giant dry fly. Historians think it originated in the 19th century; it's still on sale, so you can bet it works despite its simple appearance. It may not be your go-to streamer for big trout, but it often outshines trendy new patterns on small streams full of wary native trout. The Mickey Finn barely makes a splash when it lands, so it doesn't spook the fish. Its bright colors stand out well in every water clarity, and it's light, so just a little movement of the rod or line gets it dancing through the riffles.

140 GO BLIND FOR CARP

When flyfishing for carp, the goal is to target fish you can clearly see. But in deep or stained water, this is a significant challenge, though still possible. In moving water, carp gather behind rocks, fallen trees, or logjams blocking the current. The soft water behind these structures is worth targeting, but look for bubble trails on the surface as signs of carp grubbing below. Cast a weighted nymph or berry fly above the bubbles to allow sink time. Once it hits bottom, try to keep the line taut; set on even the slightest stop or bump.

141 GO LONG

Spey casting—which requires long specialized rods and specially-weighted lines—has been around since the mid-1800s, but it's experiencing a major comeback, mainly because it allows you to put a fly in front of a distant fish without wearing your arm out. The easiest spey cast to learn, the double spey, is used (for a right-handed caster) when the river is flowing from left to right—called "river right"— although you can also use it on the other bank simply by reversing the hand positions.

Start with the fly line straight downstream. Drop your rod tip low to the water. Point your right foot and orient your body toward the target where you intend your fly to land. Lift the rod to head height, using the same motion you'd use to mount a shotgun, and then sweep the rod upstream in a flat plane (A).

Next, drop the tip toward the surface, positioning the tip of the fly line (not the leader or fly) about one rod length downstream from your position (B). Use too much force and you will bring the line tip upstream from you, which will result in the line fouling itself on the forward cast. If you position the fly-line tip farther downstream, it will create too much drag to lift the line out of the water.

Sweep the rod back downstream on a slightly inclined plane (C). The line should rip off of the water audibly, creating a slash of white water that spey casters call the "white mouse."

Then sweep the rod sideways and behind you, while keeping the path of the rod tip in a flat plane. In the same continuous motion, raise the rod at the back of the sweep to the one o'clock position, forming a D loop in the line behind you (D).

Finally, begin the forward stroke by sharply pulling your lower hand tight to your chest, just like a gorilla thumping his chest, while pushing forward with your upper hand. Use equal power for both motions. Stop the rod abruptly at 11 o'clock as the line unrolls forward in a tight loop. When you finish the cast, your bottom hand should be tucked under your opposite armpit.

Count the cast to waltz time: Lift-two-three, sweep-two-three, loop-two-three, cast.

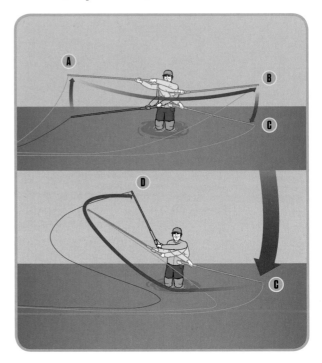

142 STRIP UNDERWATER

When you're flyfishing for muskies and pike, a strip-strike is a must, because these wide-jawed fish often spit out flies from a lift-up hookset. That's why many anglers who target these species keep their rod tips in the water during the retrieve. When a fish hits, the taut line helps set the hook into the fish's bony mouth and may thwart any instinctive lifting of the rod. The method also works well for any fish with a mouth positioned under the head, such as bonefish and redfish. Even if your target doesn't require a strip-strike, such as a trout or bass, keeping the tip in the water when working a streamer will help you maintain better contact with the fly and detect subtle takes more easily.

143 DUPE WARY TROUT AT CLOSE RANGE

Perfecting pro guide Landon Mayer's arm-roll cast will let you deliver a fly upstream of a feeding fishing without having to false cast over your target. Here's how it's done.

Begin with the rod tip at the surface and pointing downstream. Load the rod with the tension of the line dragging on the water (A). Keep your forearm and wrist straight and bring the arm up in a rolling motion (B).

To finish, roll your arm down to the water, pointing the rod tip upstream (C). Allow the line to unroll in front while reaching out (D) before the rod tip stops at the water's surface.

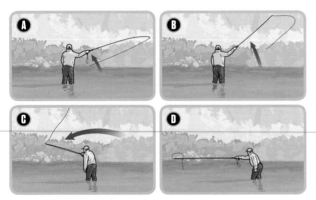

ESSENTIAL FLIES: DECEIVER

TYPE: Streamer
PRIMARY SPECIES: Saltwater, Bass, Pike/Muskie

Also called "Lefty's Deceiver" after creator and flyfishing legend Lefty Kreh, this is an essential baitfish imitation for targeting larger gamefish. Deceivers are tied in small sizes, but are most commonly found in sizes to match bigger baitfish. Tied in white and blue, they mimic the peanut bunker and mullet loved by saltwater species such as striped bass, tarpon, tuna, and snook. Spun in pink and green, they look like the juvenile trout that pike and big largemouths crave. There is virtually no limit to Deceiver color combos. Unlike Clouser Minnows, these patterns are not weighted, so they're most effective on fish that aren't feeding too deep. To get a Deceiver down more than a few feet, you'll have to fish it on a sinking line.

144 TAKE A SHOT AT SHAD

Those living in middle America don't have much use for shad (except for maybe catfish bait). However, if you do live near a coastal river, there is a good chance that it experiences a yearly run of American shad. Not only are these fish strong fighters, they make terrific fly rod targets. These tips will get you started in the shad game.

NO HATCH TO MATCH American shad do not eat once they leave saltwater and enter freshwater. All you really have to do is get something bright and shiny in their faces, and it'll irk them into a biting. A dumbbell eye on a streamer hook wrapped in colorful chenille with a flashy tinsel tail is all you need.

DON'T PULL Shad won't chase your fly, so there's no need to strip or impart any action. Cast down current and across a likely run, keep your tip low, and let the fly swing. All it has to do in cross the face of a shad

swimming upriver and it'll get bit.

EASY DOES IT Shad have paper-thin mouths, so don't crank the drag down and lean into them hard. Fight light, let them run as much as they want, and you'll get them in the net.

145 FOCUS ON THE FEEDERS

You can improve your odds in sight-fishing by casting at the right fish. What do I mean? Say you've spotted three fish in a run. Two of them are essentially glued to the bottom, not moving much, while the third one is suspended halfway up the water column, weaving back and forth, eating naturally. That's your player, and it should be your target.

Viewing the process from below the surface, a scuba diver watched an experienced angler casting at a group of several fish, only one of which was visibly suspended in the feeding lane. Instead of dredging the run for the fish on the bottom, the angler lightened his weight so the flies would drift midway up the water column. Sure enough, that fish ate it on the first drift.

Too many anglers make the mistake of chasing the biggest fish they see. If that big fish is hunkered down, you're wasting an opportunity. Catch the fish that's eating, then add another split shot and frustrate yourself by chasing difficult-to-catch bottom dwellers.

146 BUCK THE WIND

Don't overload your fly rod with a heavier line to make longer casts into strong wind. Instead, try going one size lighter than the rod's recommended line weight. This will underload the rod, causing it to flex less and allowing you to cast a tighter line loop. The lighter line directs the energy of your cast toward your target rather than dispersing it over a wide arc, extending the cast's distance.

147 ONE-TWO PUNCH A PIKE

Northern pike may be the most aggressive gamefish you'll ever chase. Make two strips, and bang, your fly is inhaled. But sometimes these predators will charge and miss, or head-butt a fly without ever opening their mouth. The natural inclination of the angler is to set the hook on the first miss or butt. Thing is, all that does is rip the fly right out of the zone. The key to connecting when pike aren't eating on the first pass is maintaining zen-like calm.

After a flash or miss where the fish rolls around the fly, give the line one short strip and let it hang. If the pike is going to come back, the quick action after its first try should get its attention again. Hopefully it'll swing back for the take. If you're getting bumped but not connecting, stop moving the fly altogether and let it fall. This simulates a stunned baitfish settling to the bottom, and the pike will often whip back around and crunch it.

148 FLY CAST UNDERHANDED

This cast soothes a number of tricky flyfishing situations. It's a good way to cast into a wind. It'll slip a fly under overhanging brush. And it's a go-to cast for a bow angler situated where a traditional cast might bang the fly against a tall boat console or pierce a friend's earlobe. This approach reverses the loop in the fly line and throws it under the tip of the rod. Here's the drill.

STEP 1 Start with a side cast, with the rod held nearly horizontal to the water surface. Turn the rod grip almost 90 degrees so the butt rests against your forearm (A). This will give you added leverage.

STEP 2 Begin false casting. At the end of each forward (B) and backward stroke (C), lift the rod tip up slightly. This will form the upside-down loop.

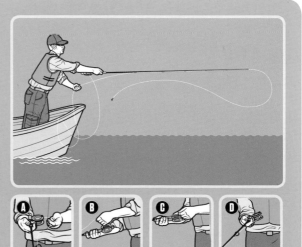

STEP 3 Deliver the fly with a forward cast powered with a strong flick-and-stop of the forearm, as if you were throwing a Frisbee (D).

149 STOP THAT CAST!

A smoothly accelerated forward stroke ending with an abrupt halt is key to both accuracy and distance. Done correctly, it'll add at least 20 feet to your cast. The stop is what makes it all work.

At the completion of the forward casting stroke (A), you stop your rod hand in an instant (B). The rod unbends, propelling the line forward (C), and the tip then also stops abruptly. At this moment, the loop forms in the air, and the rod becomes the anchor. The sharper the stop, the more energy is transferred to the unrolling line. Conversely, whipping the rod forward with no stop robs the cast of its power, no real loop forms, and the line will most often collapse in a pile.

Experienced casters sometimes "shoot" the line for extra distance, which means allowing the force of the unrolling line to pull slack through the guides. Here, again, the stop is critical.

Timing is crucial. If you brake too soon, with the tip held too high, the forward-moving line will collide either with the rod or with itself, creating what's called a *tailing loop*. And if you brake too late, meaning too far forward, your loop will be too broad and you'll lose distance. A few minutes of practice with various stop positions should make those differences self-evident.

Good casting doesn't rely on muscle; it's all about technique. Pushing a cast harder doesn't usually make it better, regardless of what tackle you're using. Adding a solid stop to your forward stroke takes minimum effort, but it does require a little thinking. You will fish better and have a lot more fun besides—this I can guarantee.

150 KEEP THE ARC

The trick to landing big trout on a river isn't tough to learn. Yes, you'll run into situations where a fish makes a sudden charge that snaps you off. But when I'm guiding beginners, I tell them that all they need to be concerned with, after the hookup, is keeping a steady arc in the fly rod, with the tip high. You need a strong, solid flex. If the fish wants to run, let it go, but keep the strong arc in the rod, and everything else will take care of itself.

ESSENTIAL FLIES: ROYAL WULFF

TYPE: Dry Fly
PRIMARY SPECIES: Trout

The Coachman is one of the most recognized dry flies ever, originating in New York's Catskill Mountains in the 1920s, and reputedly was a favorite pattern of flyfishing legend Lee Wulff. But he didn't care for its flimsy wings. He asked a friend to create a Coachman with a stiffer wing, and thus the Royal Wulff was born. That stiff split-hair wing makes it just as popular now as it was then. Nearly impossible to sink, the Royal Wulff shines on lumpy, fast water that often overwhelms or drowns more delicate feather-wing dries. It doesn't mimic a particular insect, but fish in faster waters just see a big target and rise aggressively to snap it up before it drifts away.

151 CAST IN TIGHT QUARTERS

When brush limits my back cast, I break out my lob cast. This little maneuver makes people look at me funny, but it get the fly where I want it to go.

STEP 1 Strip your line in until there is only about ten feet plus the leader in the water. Then pick it all up at once, right out of the water, and make a big, fast, clockwise, circular pass overhead. The reel is actually moving in a half-circle above your head—it's weird, I know, but do it anyway.

STEP 2 Next, stop the rod behind you, at the position where you would stop a traditional back cast. At this point, I'll fire all the line out with one forward stroke. It'll really launch a heavy fly or sink-tip line.

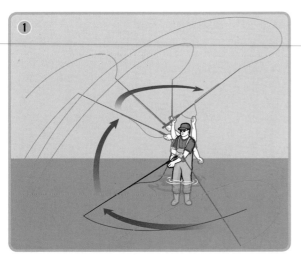

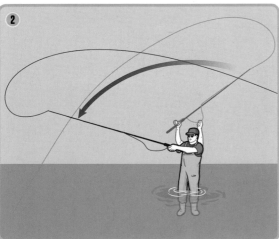

152 WIN THE END GAME

There are two main reason why people lose big trout. One is that they panic the second a toad eats their fly, and panic breeds mistakes. The other is that they just don't have enough experience with heavy fish to know what to do. These tips will help—as long as you don't panic.

MAKE NO SUDDEN MOVES When you've got a big trout on the line—a line in this game that's usually made of light tippet—don't make any abrupt movements. Every turn of the rod and crank of the reel should be thought out and executed slowly. Quick moves equal lost fish most of the time.

MOVE TOWARD SHORE Steer the fish out of heavy current by tipping the rod to the side and toward the shoreline. This works best when you are even with the fish's position in the river (not far upstream of the fish).

DUNK IT When you get the fish in slack water, stick your rod tip in the water and crank on the reel. You'll be amazed at just how easily trout will follow along when you do your reeling with the rod tip submerged. Before you doubt it, try it. You'll be surprised how many more fish this technique helps you land.

LIFT RIGHT When you reel the end of the line through your rod tip (leaving only the leader and tippet out), lift the rod, straight up, forcing the fish's head to break the surface. When the head is up, maintain that pressure, because the fish has no leverage, and you can slide it right toward the waiting net.

153 GET THE TUNA TUNE-UP

False albacore will give you a real run for your money on a fly rod, that is, if you can get a fly in front of them. These members of the tuna family swim in schools and will pop up and disappear in an instant. They move incredibly fast, so because you might only get a fleeting shot at a school, preparedness is the key.

STRIP IT OUT If you're standing on the bow with your line reeled in and your fly buttoned on the rod's hook keeper, you're not ready. As long shots are common in this game, have at least 60 feet of line stripped off the reel while you're searching for fish. Hold your fly in your non-casting hand, ready to toss overboard so you can start false casting the second you have a shot.

HAUL IT OR LOSE IT False albacore aren't going to give you two minutes to make false casts. You need to get that fly out there right now. This is where being a proficient double-hauler comes in very handy. A good double haul will help you get a heavy fly 50 feet or more in just three false casts, even in windy conditions.

TAKE THE LEAD Pay attention to the direction the school is moving, and land your fly ahead of the fish. You're not casting to the fish so much as trying to have your fly intersect their path at exactly the right time. False albacore move so quickly that it's not likely one will spin around for a fly that passes right behind its tail.

154 DON'T WIGGLE YOUR TIP

One of the biggest mistakes I see flyfishermen make comes when their leader gets wrapped around the rod tip during a bad cast. The first thing they do is start whipping and jiggling the rod, hoping the tangle will magically come undone. I'd say that 99% of the time, that only makes things worse, especially with a few split shot on the tippet. Taking the time to put your rod behind you and undo the mess by hand seems like a big pain, but in the long run, you'll get the fly back in the water faster than by doing the tip shake.

155 BECOME AMBIDEXTROUS

I can think of many situations where being somewhat ambidextrous as a caster can pay off in a big way. Say you're left-handed and fishing your way upstream along a left bank. When you want to pop casts around the bushes that protrude into the water (where the fish often are), it would be better to use your right hand than to reach across your body with your left.

When you're fishing with someone else from a drift boat, it's usually better to have the lines and flies outside the boat (off bow and stern) than swinging over the oarsman's head in the center.

We should all be able to switch hands. And we can, with a little practice.

First go ahead and try to cast with your off hand. It's probably going to be a mess. That's okay. Now do the same thing, only this time have your dominant hand hold onto the reel as you cast. Trust me, it will make a huge difference.

Why is that? What this really is, is our body and brain underscoring the point that casting is all about timing and tempo, much more than strength or power. When you put your dominant hand on the reel, you're syncing your brain (your brain is used to working with your dominant hand, which is why you are more "coordinated" and can perform fine motor skills better with it) with the casting stroke. You're letting your dominant hand offer "coaching" on starting and stopping the rod, tempo, and rod position, although the nondominant hand is still doing most of the work.

Take a few minutes to practice fishing this way every time you go out, and your non-dominant hand will require less and less coaching. You'll eventually be able to

take the other hand off the reel and cast normally. You probably won't ever cast with truly equal strength from both sides, certainly not in terms of distance. But you don't have to. If you're merely proficient and fairly accurate on your "off" side, even to no more than 30 feet out, you will improve your abilities to not only catch fish, but also fish with other anglers in tight confines.

ESSENTIAL FLIES: BLACK STONEFLY

TYPE: Nymph
PRIMARY SPECIES: Trout

It's hard to find a trout stream in the U.S. that's void of black stoneflies, but if you do, fish one of these flies anyway. They're dark, so they contrast very well in the water. Even if there are yellow stoneflies on the bottom, from a distance a trout will see the outline and profile of your black stone more clearly. These flies are a good universal pattern to drift in any run that calls for a nymph, but don't skip them in winter—some species of tiny black stoneflies hatch even on the coldest days. Swing one through a deep, slow hole, or the bottom of a tailout, during a sunny winter day, and you may get a heart-warming trout fight.

156 FLY CAST TO A MOVING FISH

Got the double haul down pat? Try a new challenge: Drop a fly in front of a moving gamefish, at 50 feet, with no more than two false casts. Here's a backyard drill for the redfish marshes and bonefish flats. For an authentic session, cast from atop a picnic table. It's about the size of a skiff's casting deck.

DOUBLE STACK Strip 50 feet of shooting line from the reel and stack it in large loose coils in front of your left foot (if you're a righty). If you shoot that line now, it will pull from the bottom of the stack and end in a tangle. In the crook of the pinky on your rod hand, grasp the line where it exits the reel. With your free hand, grab the line and pull all of it through your pinky, restacking the line so it will shoot tangle-free. Now, pick a target 50 feet out.

FIRE WHEN READY Pull 10 feet of that stacked line through the tip. Hold the fly at the hook bend in your reel hand and point your rod tip up. Fire a roll cast and release the fly after you snap the rod forward. Back cast with a haul, false cast with another haul, haul on your second back cast, and shoot.

157 PERFECT THE PARACHUTE CAST

The biggest trout hold in deep water, a situation that calls for heavily weighted flies. But simply adding more lead can be self-defeating. Heavy nymphs and streamers act unnatural underwater, which can deter strikes. Flyfishing guides know the secret to taking these trophy trout is to get deep with as little weight as possible. To do this, they use the parachute cast, which produces enough slack to let the fly sink unhindered by drag—you'll need only a small amount of lead to reach even the deepest fish.

STEP ONE Make a standard overhead cast, aiming for a point about 10 feet above the water.

STEP TWO Stop your forward stroke around the 12 o'clock position.

STEP THREE As the line passes overhead, snap the rod forward to the 10 o'clock position.

STEP FOUR Instead of straightening out, the fly line will hinge toward the water, dropping or "parachuting" the fly and leader vertically onto the surface.

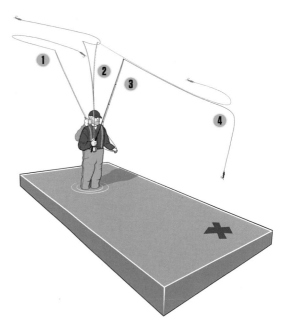

158 TIE THE BLOOD-KNOT DROPPER

Want to connect tippet to leader or fish a second nymph off a dropper? This simple splice comes in handy.

STEP 1 Overlap the lines to be joined by 10 inches.

STEP 2 Wrap the left-hand tag end five or six times around the

standing line, and then put the tag end back through the opening you're holding with your fingers.

STEP 3 Switch hands so your left thumb and index finger hold the opening. Use your right hand to make five or six wraps around the standing line with the other tag

end. Put it back through the same opening but the opposite direction.

STEP 4 Wet the knot with saliva, and then pull gently on the standing portions of the line. At least one of the tag ends must stick about 5 inches out of the knot for use as a dropper.

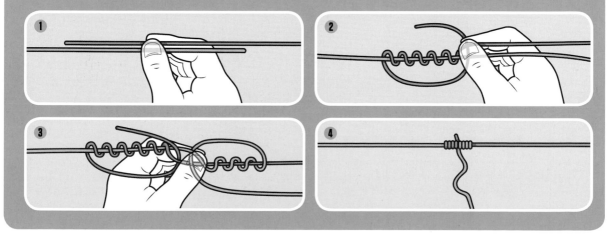

159 HELP CATCH-AND-RELEASE TROUT SURVIVE

While catch and release is a great practice, watching a fish swim away doesn't necessarily mean it's going to survive. If you're going to let your fish go free, you also need to take steps to ensure the healthiest release possible. These tips will help.

REDUCE THE STRUGGLE The sooner you release a fish after hooking it, the better chance it has of surviving. A two-minute fight on 4X is better for the fish than a 10-minute fight on 6X. We like to hear the reel scream, but cranking down the drag and learning to steer fish quickly to a reasonable landing zone isn't a bad idea.

NET CAREFULLY When a trout rubs around in a net, it depletes the slime layer on its scales, which protect it from disease. But I have seen fights take much longer when anglers fumble around trying to cradle a fish or grab it by its tail. Rubberized mesh nets are far easier on trout than uncoated surfaces, or fine nets that get caught in their gills.

REDUCE AIR TIME For a fish out of water, literally every second counts. Fish that were exercised but released without being held out of the water have an 88 percent survival rate; 30 seconds' air exposure drops it to 62 percent; at one minute, it is a mere 28 percent. Think about those numbers when you go to take that photograph of the big trout you just landed. Try to keep those shots to 10 seconds or less, if at all possible.

160 CAST IN THE WIND

If guide Rick Hartman of Harlingen, Texas, had to wait for the wind to die down before casting to a school of cruising redfish in the Laguna Madre, he wouldn't spend much time fishing. So, instead, he casts to limit the wind's effect.

"I hear people talking about casting under the wind," Hartman says, "but you can't really do that. What you can do is cast so a gust has less time to mess up your fly." Whether you're facing a headwind or a crossing breeze, your fly is going to be most vulnerable at the end of the cast. The trick to accurate casts in the wind is to keep your fly low.

"Your delivery stroke needs to unroll as close to the water as possible," says Hartman. "Instead of having to drop over 6 feet to the water, your fly should only have to drop a foot."

To finish near the surface, your back cast must end higher than usual. One of the keys to good casting, Hartman notes, is that the back and forward casts should unroll in planes that are 180 degrees apart. "You're tilting the entire plane so your back cast is higher and your fly ends up lower. Do this right, and it will drop in front of the fish before you have time to worry about the wind."

STEP 1 Stop your back stroke around the 12 o'clock position.

STEP 2 Maintain a 180- degree arc between back cast and forward cast, but rotate it forward so your fly unrolls a foot above the water.

STEP 3 Finish so the fly is exposed to the wind as briefly as possible.

WRIST Use as little wrist as possible to keep the loop tight.

161 HAVE A LOW-WATER GAME PLAN

Catching fish in low, clear water is one of flyfishing's biggest challenges. In these conditions, fish are ultra-spooky, so you can't just wade in and start flailing around as you would during normal flows. Try some of the sneaky tricks here.

BACK IT UP You know that run you love to stand on top of and high-stick nymph in April? In August, you might need stand to way back—15 feet or more—from the money spot, because just your shadow or a slight vibration in the ground can send fish packing.

TIE THE LONG KNOT Fly line slapping on the water can crush all hope of hooking up during low flows. Plan on using a 10- or 12-foot leader—or even 15-foot in some cases—so that little if any fly line ever touches the water near a prime holding zone.

LOSE THE WEIGHT You may have a conehead Woolly Bugger that trout can't blast fast enough when the water's up, but as levels drop, that deep pool might not be so deep. If that's the case, the loud plop of a heavy fly will do more harm than good, so re-tie your favorite patterns sans lead cores and weighted heads.

162 MASTER THE STEEPLE CAST

When a fly caster's back is literally against the wall, and the trout are rising, the caster has two options. One is the roll cast, but the maneuver can be splashy and not always accurate. The second is the steeple cast, so named because the rod tip lifts the line straight to the sky—like a church steeple. At short ranges, the steeple cast is easy to do and the angler's best bet for making accurate presentations.

GET A GRIP Your biggest risk for fouling up a steeple cast is overcocking your wrist on the back cast. To avoid that, straighten your index finger along the top of your grip (A). As you lift your cast, point your finger at the sky.

LOAD THE ROD LOW In tight spaces, use the water surface to create line tension and load the rod. Start the back cast with your rod tip pointed at the water (B), and line fairly taut.

ADJUST THE CLOCK The classic fly cast is often described as moving the rod tip between 10 and 2 o'clock. With a steeple, the back cast is an "up cast" that stops at 12 o'clock (C). Wait for the line to extend above the rod tip before you stroke forward, or the line will be impossible to shoot.

POINT YOUR SHOT Finish the cast at 3 or 4 o'clock (D) with a gentle flick, pointing your index finger at the spot where you want your fly to drop.

163 TAKE A KNEE

Whenever I catch a large fish while wading, I make the effort to kneel in the water when posing for a photo. If I'm in swift current, I'll keep the fish in the net and move to softer, shallower water if it's close by. If the fish wriggles out of my hands, it won't fall far and won't hit nearly as hard as it would if I were standing. I can also quickly dunk it and let it catch its breath if need be. It's an easy way to further reduce stress on the catch. If I'm fishing on a boat and there's a net handy, I'll ask someone to hold the bag below the fish just out of the photo frame. This way, if the fish falls, it won't smack down on the hard deck.

164 TIE AN IMPROVED TURTLE KNOT

This knot makes a straight connection through the hook eye that won't cause a small fly to cant or tilt unnaturally.

STEP 1 Thread the leader through the hook eye, and form a loop around the leader behind the fly.

Pass the tag end twice through the loop, forming a double overhand knot that also serves as a simple slip knot.

STEP 2 Hold the loop in your left hand and pull on the tag end with your right hand to tighten the double overhand knot. Now pass the fly through the loop.

STEP 3 Tug the main leader portion to seat the knot on the fly's head right behind the hook eye. As you tighten, adjust it with your fingers. Trim the tag end.

165 LOSE THE TAILING LOOP

A tailing loop occurs when the fly and leader dip below your line on the forward cast, usually causing a tangle. It is to a fly caster what a slice is to a golfer: an all-too-common predicament caused by a simple mechanical flaw.

The vast majority of tailing loops are caused by overpowering or "punching" the rod on the forward stroke. It's human nature. The trout are rising; you're making your false casts and you have a nice loop going. All you need is that extra 10 feet, just a little more oomph, and dang! Bunched up again.

When you overpower the rod, you flex it too much and actually end up shortening its length in midstroke. This changes the path of the tip and the line, causing the tailing loop.

How do you fix this? Try imagining that you have a tomato stuck on the end of a stick, and you want to fling that tomato into a bucket, say, 20 feet away. If you whip the stick, you'll end up splattered with red mush. But if you gradually fling the tomato off the stick, you might get it there. It's the same deal and same feel with the fly cast. The motion must be a gradual, controlled acceleration to an abrupt stop.

If you have trouble developing this feel, practice in your backyard. First, tilt the rod sideways and cast from waist or chest level on a flat plane in front of you so you can watch the line (A). Start with short flicks of line. You should see and feel good U-shaped loops as well as bad tailing loops (B). Eventually the good loops will become uniform, and you'll be able to lift that cast overhead, still feeling how the line shapes (C). Once you get the feel for this, you'll stop tailing, your loops will get tighter and your casts will go farther.

ESSENTIAL FLIES: ZEBRA MIDGE

TYPE: Nymph
PRIMARY SPECIES: Trout

Although you can find Zebra Midges in a fairly broad variety of sizes, it's the tiny ones—size 20 or smaller—that are the most lethal type. This pattern imitates a Chironomid midge, which lives in silt and mud in most lakes and streams. What's most important about these midges is that they hatch year-round, making the Zebra a must-have pattern during the coldest months. Presenting these micro morsels often requires the use of fine tippet and the skill to detect subtle strikes. Landing a big trout that has this little hook in its mouth is also no easy feat. But despite the challenges, sometimes these nymphs are the only things that will draw a strike when the going gets tough.

166 BE A TWO-TIMER

The practice of tying two flies to one leader has actually been around for well over a century, but came back into fashion a decade or so ago. Originally, "dropper" referred to the top fly because it was "dropped" directly off the main leader on its own short piece of line. Today, anglers reverse that order, tying dropper flies on an 18- to 24-inch section of smaller-diameter tippet, attached to the bend of the first fly's hook with an improved clinch knot.

Although the combinations of flies you can use are very nearly infinite, typically the first fly is a large dry, and the dropper is something that sinks or is too small to be seen on the surface. The large fly acts as a strike indicator for this second fly.

"Fly locator" may be a better description than strike indicator, though. Sometimes your top fly will sink like a bobber when a fish takes the dropper, but if the short section of leader between the two flies isn't drawn up tight, he can spit it out again without ever disturbing your indicator. That's why it's a good idea to set the hook whenever you see a rise or boil near your top fly. You can more easily fish small, hard-to-see patterns if they hang behind larger, more visible dry flies, and you also enjoy the added advantage of having two hooks in the water instead of one.

167 DO THE PANFISH CRAWL

Developed to work wet flies on still water, the panfish crawl is a retrieval technique all fly anglers should have in their back pockets, as they can use it to give flies a different action in a variety of situations, and it really helps bring flies with newer undulating materials to life. After laying out a cast, grab the fly line just ahead of the reel with your stripping hand. Alternating between your pinky finger and forefinger, quickly gather the line into your palm, turn your wrist down, and then drop the slack line out of your hand. This achieves a slow popping action with the fly as you advance it forward and automatically imparts short pauses. The tactic works great for wet flies on lakes and ponds, but try using the crawl to bring a bunny-strip streamer through a slow eddy, skate a foam hopper across the surface, or bounce a shrimp fly for bonefish or red drum on the flats.

168 GET HANDS-ON

Everybody needs a quick measuring device to check things like fish lengths or leader specs. The handiest is your own hand. Measure (and memorize) the distance between your pinky and thumb when your fingers are spread at their widest, for example, and then use that dimension to accurately estimate length.

169 PERFECT YOUR PAIRINGS

Casting two flies at once isn't as hard as it sounds. Just use a slightly slower casting stroke, which will open up your loop a little (a tight loop is more likely to foul up when you're using a dropper). And fishing two flies is simple, too. I usually use a basic dead drift, unless I'm working a hatch of active insects like caddisflies, in which case adding a twitch or skitter may draw more strikes.

I fish these rigs in Cheesman Canyon on Colorado's South Platte River. This is famously technical water, where large wild trout can get infuriatingly selective to tiny flies. The trout might appear to be taking bluewing olive duns, but they could actually be eating cripples,

emergers, floating nymphs, or something else entirely, like spent Trico spinners floating flush with the surface. Because the rise forms often look alike, you're sometimes reduced to just trying different patterns until you connect.

I've learned to tie on a large dun as my top fly and leave it there, changing the trailer until I find something that the fish are feeding on. For one thing, at some point trout usually start eating the duns, so I like to have one out there. For another, the white-winged parachute pattern that I favor makes it much easier to fish the flush-floating or slightly sunken fly behind it that's hard enough to see when I'm tying it on, let alone when it's out on the water.

170 AVOID DOUBLE TROUBLE

I've always hated to foul-hook fish, and it can happen when you're fishing a dry-dropper rig. A trout goes for your top fly, and you miss him then snag him in the belly with your submerged fly. You can avoid this by making sure that the length of the line between your top and bottom flies is never less than 18 inches. Other fishermen have told me that they need 22 to 24 inches, possibly because they set the hook harder than I do.

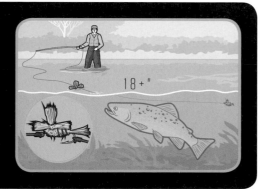

171 JOIN THE BOARD

A stand-up paddleboard (SUP) is portable, fairly inexpensive, and lets you access places you could never get to with other watercraft. SUP fishing can be incredibly rewarding, but bad planning or lacking a couple of key pieces of gear can make the difference between fighting the wind or fighting fish all day. So whether you are on the salt, the river, or your favorite still water, remember these factors.

THE ELEMENTS SUPs are light weight and ride high on the water's surface, so currents and wind can play a big role in your day. Make sure you are taking into account the wind, currents, and tide when choosing your fishing grounds. And remember that you will have to paddle back to where you put in, and you may be working against the elements.

ANCHORING I always carry a small anchor with me when I'm SUP fishing. I often paddle to a fishy spot and anchor up. This enables me to spend more time fishing without having to focus on getting into position. Let's say you are drifting through a hot spot and break a fly off. It's a great idea to delicately drop an anchor and retie so you don't miss more opportunities in a prime spot.

LINE MANAGEMENT This is always an important issue. You can use a stripping mat that lies at your feet and collects your line as you retrieve your fly. Some anglers use a stripping basket they can wear around the waist; it's really a matter of choice. When it's done correctly, you are ready for the next cast. And when you hook a monster and the run is on, your line will slide smoothly through the eyes of your fly rod, knot free.

STORAGE You have two basic options: attach your gear to your SUP deck rigging in a dry bag, or carry your gear on your back in a waterproof pack. Either way, make sure that your gear is quickly accessible and that you can reach it comfortably from your paddling position. Having all your essentials within reach will aid in easy fly changes, or in switching to a sinking line when the fish are deeper than expected.

172 JAM IT

A jam knot is the fastest-tying of all knots for attaching a leader to your fly line. It's essentially a square knot in the fly line that interlocks with the leader loop. When pulled tight, the fly line jams against itself within the loop. A nail knot is more streamlined and thus superior, but will take more time to tie—time you could spend fishing. If you're in a hurry, the jam knot is a great quick fix, especially if you're targeting smaller fish that won't overstrain the connection.

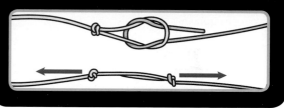

ESSENTIAL FLIES: KRYSTAL SPINNER

TYPE: Dry Fly
PRIMARY SPECIES: Trout

When adult mayflies die in the air and fall to the water's surface—known as a spinner fall—trout go on a feeding frenzy. What makes this scenario difficult for a fly caster, however, is imitating a dead bug. Most dry flies mimic a live insect drifting down the river. You might think that if you were to throw one among the feast of dead bugs, it would still get eaten, but quite often, trout will snub the offering. What they won't refuse is a Krystal Spinner. Available in many colors and sizes, the flat, splayed wings of these flies perfectly imitate a dead caddis or mayfly. You should have a variety of them on hand for that evening when the river is blanketed in bug carnage. It could be the only thing that will get bit.

173 PERFECT THE PITZEN KNOT

Besides not working equally well with all types of line, knots also don't perform alike with different diameters of the same line type.

This is especially true in flyfishing, where trout anglers in particular often deal with extremely fine tippet materials and very small flies. So I tested some line splices and terminal knots made with fragile 5X and 6X nylon tippet material.

I tested three knots, all commonly recommended for tying on small flies, for tying 6X tippet to a tiny size 18 dry-fly hook.

Interestingly, the results were close to a three-way tie. A 6-turn improved clinch knot had the same strength as the Pitzen knot (sometimes called the 16-20). An Orvis knot (sometimes called a Becker) came in at 94%. I chose the Pitzen knot because I think it's by far the easiest to tie. If you already like one of the others better, by all means stick with it. Winner: Pitzen Knot (5-turn) Strength: 97%

STEP 1 Extend about 8 inches of line through the hook eye and loop the tag end back on itself as shown. Hold the loop end and standing line with your right thumb and index finger.

STEP 2 Use your left hand to make five wraps toward the hook eye.

STEP 3 Put the tag end back through the upper loop. Pull on the tag end and hook to tighten the knot around the standing line.

STEP 4 Pull the standing line to tighten the knot to the hook eye.

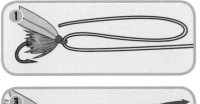

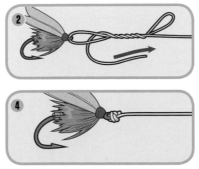

ESSENTIAL FLIES: SALMON EGG

TYPE: Wet Fly
PRIMARY SPECIES: Trout, Steelhead, Carp

It's hard to classify a salmon egg fly as a true fly at all. Fact is, it doesn't imitate any insect or baitfish, and yet this simple craft pom-pom threaded onto a hook accounts for incredible numbers of big fish. From Alaska to the shores of the Great Lakes, brown, rainbow, and steelhead trout that share rivers with spawning salmon gorge on salmon eggs. Even in streams and rivers void of salmon, trout will instinctively recognize a salmon egg as food. Stocked trout can't get enough of them, but wild trout also gobble them up, especially during colder months when natural forage gets scarce. I'd argue that salmon eggs are also the number one most productive carp flies. At any given time, a carp is less likely to be chowing down on something specific than just "tasting" anything it comes across that could be food. Not only do salmon eggs imitate berries (which carp love), they just look like, well, edible morsels worthy of a taste.

174 TIE A TIPPET TO A LEADER

Fly anglers often add a strand of 6X tippet to the end of a 5X leader while fishing small flies. Tippet strands sometimes break off when you strike a fish too hard, and tippets need replacing as multiple fly changes shorten them..

The 4-turn surgeon's knot, which is most commonly suggested for tippet connections, broke at only 84% of the unknotted 6X line strength. The old-time Blood knot did 81%.

This year I'm switching to the Seaguar knot—exceptionally strong for a splicing knot in this case—instead of the surgeon's knot I've relied on for many years. The Seaguar knot is also substantially easier and faster to tie. Just make sure that all the strands are evenly aligned as you begin tightening, at which point the knot should assume a twisted figure-8 shape.

STEP 1 Overlap the leader and tippet and form a loop.

STEP 2 Turn the loop 3 times.

STEP 3 Pull the ends through the loop.

STEP 4 Tighten evenly.

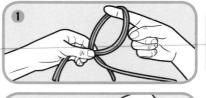
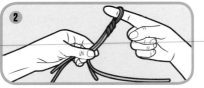
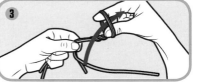

175 MIX IN METAL

Knowing how to tie line-to-line connections is necessary for many aspects of flyfishing, particularly for splicing a length of tippet to the end of your leader. These splices, however, can also become weak points that will break if strained too hard. If I'm drifting egg flies for steelhead or salmon, I forgo flyfishing "correctness" and use a small metal barrel swivel instead of splicing, as these brute fighters will pop a blood knot or uni-to-uni-knot connection with one shake of their heads. These days, barrel swivels are available in sizes so small that they won't add any weight to your line, and they create a much stronger connection point between leader and tippet than splice knots.

176 MIMIC AN ESCAPING CRAYFISH

Big trout can't resist the stop-and-drop flight path of a fleeing crayfish. Pro guide Landon Mayer perfected this retrieve while targeting largemouth bass, but it works just as well in a cold stream. Use a weighted pattern, such as Jan's Trout Crayfish, for best results.

STEP 1 With the rod tip pointed at the surface—or submerged as deep as 6 inches in the water—feel for tension on the fly. Strip in 1 to 3 feet of line in a single, abrupt motion that lifts the fly off the stream bottom and into the water column, like a crayfish trying to escape a predator.

STEP 2 Pause long enough to feel tension from a strike or until you no longer feel the fly as it settles back on the bottom. The drop often puts up a little puff of sand, just like a crayfish hitting the dirt.

STEP 3 Repeat the abrupt strip. When a fish hits, set the hook with a pinch-lift strike: Pinch the fly line against the cork handle with your index finger, and lift the rod hand sharply to a 45-degree angle.

177 PRACTICE PROPER BASS POPPING

Flyfishing for bass is a slow-paced antidote to metal-flake run-and-gun tournament style of fishing. It won't always offer the most or the largest bass, but it's relaxing in the way bass fishing used to be, and that's the basic appeal.

Sometimes, though, it's too relaxed. Catching bass on a surface bug is so often thought to be so simple a process that too much gets taken for granted. Leaders that are too light land floating bugs off target. Sloppy line handling produces fewer strikes, and impatient retrieves keep bug and bass from making contact. Pay just a little more attention, and you'll take more bass with surface bugs.

The biggest mistake most people make is holding the rod tip a few inches above the water. That leaves a short curve of slack line between it and the surface. When they strip a few inches of line to work the bug, they use up the force of that strip in shortening the slack, and the fly moves only a little. If a bass does strike, that sag sometimes means you'll miss the fish.

The rod tip belongs right on the water's surface when you're retrieving. With no slack line, if you make a 6-inch strip, the bug moves 6 inches. The retrieve is completely controlled, and you can work the fly more effectively.

178 MAKE IT A SLOW DANCE

With line control and the proper leader in check, you still need to find the right rhythm for a retrieve. Usually, that means slow. Some bass will smash a surface bug when it first hits the water, and aggressive fish may nail a fast-moving popper. More often, though, a suspicious bass will eyeball your bug for a while before doing anything.

Of course, if a standard slow retrieve isn't working, by all means try speeding your bug across the water. There are days when bass want bugs moved to a hip-hop beat, but

more often it's poppers played to a slow waltz.

Countless times in clear water I've watched the gentle splat of a landing bug bring a curious bass swimming over for a look. The bug sits still. So does the bass, just a few inches underneath, as if it's waiting to see what will happen next. After what seems like an eternity—actually about 20 or 30 seconds—I give the bug a gentle twitch, just enough to wiggle its hackle and rubber legs. Most of the time, that's enough to bring on a gasp-inducing strike.

179 USE THE RIGHT BASS LEADER

Even the best retrieve won't help much if your bass bug lands off target. Flies for largemouths tend to be bulky and air-resistant. A bass-taper floating line of 8-weight or greater helps in accurately casting them because of its exaggerated weight-forward bias, but that's only part of the solution. Leaders are just as important and are typically neglected.

A poorly designed bass leader will fall back on itself as you complete the final cast, or it may flop to the left or right as the cast straightens. In any case, your bug will land a foot or two off target, instead of being inches away from that shoreline stump where the bass are.

I solve the problem by cutting about 18 inches off the forward end of a new 8-weight bass line so that the forward taper ends more abruptly. Then I use a nail

knot to attach 3 feet of stiff, 40-pound-test monofilament (.025-inch diameter). Finally, I attach a common 7½-foot knotless, tapered bass leader (.023-inch butt diameter) using a blood knot, and cut about a foot off the leader's 12-pound-test tippet end. The combination of stiffer butt and shorter tippet does a better job than most off-the-shelf leaders in turning a big bug over at the end of a cast.

Make sure your surface-bug leaders are nylon and not fluorocarbon. I've seen some newer fluorocarbon products labeled as bass tapers, but fluorocarbon sinks more readily than nylon and will drag your floating bug underwater as you retrieve it.

180 FIND A DAMSEL IN DISTRESS

Damselfly nymphs rank high on the aquatic menu: available year-round but most helpless when struck by the urge to emerge. But damsels don't hatch on the surface—they head for dry land: downed timber, tules, or reeds above the waterline; rocks or docks; or the shoreline itself. There they shed their skin to become airborne. If you see cast-off shucks and note the presence of adult flies, you're in the right place.

As they head to shore, most damsel nymphs crawl along the bottom. In water 4 feet or shallower, use a floating line, an unweighted or lightly weighted fly, and a 9- to 12-foot leader. Cast perpendicular to the shore, let the fly sink for 10 seconds, then begin a slow, steady retrieve. Inch the fly back to shallower water to imitate a natural insect's path. Count longer on each cast until you touch bottom, then back off to keep your fly snag-free. Do the same in deeper water with a sink-tip or full-sinking line.

Some nymphs swim to shore on or just below the surface, triggering the violent, take-and-turn boils of every angler's fantasy. Target these trout with a floating line and an unweighted fly. Damsels appear to swim swiftly, but it's mostly shoulder-shrugging, butt-wiggling motion, with frequent stops and little forward progress. Imitate this using 8- to 12-inch strips, pausing between pulls. Stay sharp; trout frequently grab a fly when it's motionless.

On gusty days, freshly hatched adult damsels may be blown into the water and picked off. But it's not a bankable occurrence—I've witnessed it once or twice in 20 years—and unimportant to fishermen.

Marabou Damsel   *Spun Wool Dragon*

181 SINK THAT DRY FLY

Fish long enough, and eventually you'll encounter a situation where you see bugs on the surface, fish rising, and, no matter how hard you try, you can't get one to eat your dry fly. It's positively maddening, and you'll go through every fly in the box. Quite often, however, it's not your flies, but how you're interpreting the fish's feeding behavior.

What looks like surface eats to you could actually be the ripple and splash created by the trout as they snap up an emerging insect just below the surface. In that case, you can start playing around with wet flies and nymphs, but before you do that, try sinking your dry fly. I can't count how many times I've been mired in frustration, only to let my dry dip below the surface, and pow! In many cases, a sunken dry is the best match for the live bugs that are just about to break the surface, and unlike nymphs and wet flies, they'll only submerge an inch or two, which is often the sweet spot.

182 WAIT FOR THE WEIGHT

When a trout smashes a mouse fly in the dark, the explosion can stop your heart, and instinct will make you set right away. That's a mistake. Because you can only hear the hit and not see it, you have no idea if the fly is actually in the trout's mouth. It takes will power, but wait until you feel the weight of the fish before swinging.

183 CATCH HEAVY TROUT ON LIGHT TIPPET

The trout stream is transparent and the hatch consists of supersmall bugs, so you've tied on a hair-thin 7X tippet. You're landing plenty of small trout, but suddenly a 22-incher sips the fly. How do you keep it on and get it to the net? According to Joe Demalderis, a trophy trout guide, carefully.

"Nothing can be sudden," he says. "Everything has to be done easy, starting with the hookset. You want to gently lift to set. If you swing hard, it's already over. The key is to manage your line and keep the pressure on without doing anything jarring. When the fish gets on the reel, loosen your drag and keep your hands off. If the fish wants to take line, let it go. Whether you're wading or in a drift boat, chasing the fish is a must. When it's time to net, try to gently lead the fish into a bag that's already submerged. Don't take any sudden swipes, because if you hit the tippet it'll break."

If you panic, you have no chance. People are afraid of light tippets, but 7X is a lot stronger than you think. Demalderis tells clients to tie their 7X to a bush and slowly bend the rod. They'll bend it almost in half. But if they whip the rod fast, the tippet snaps. Try to stop a fish by choking off the line or changing directions suddenly, and it's over.

It's a balancing act, and if you do one tiny thing wrong, you risk losing the trout. Most mistakes happen just because the angler is panicked and does something too abruptly.

184 CONQUER THE BASIC CARP PRESENTATION

Got no respect for carp? Try stalking them in shallow water, and get ready for a big surprise. These ugly fish are wary and smart, and frequently hit 20 to 30 pounds. The key to fishing for carp in 2 to 4 feet of water is to go slow and easy. If you splash or stumble, they'll spook. Here's how to do it right:

STEP 1 Cast in front of one of the fish.

STEP 2 Noting the direction the carp is moving, lead the fish by 2 to 4 feet when you cast.

STEP 3 When the fish sucks up the fly, the take will be hard to feel. Hold your rod tip right down on the water and keep a straight line to the fly. That way you'll feel a little tug when the carp eats, and you can set the hook.

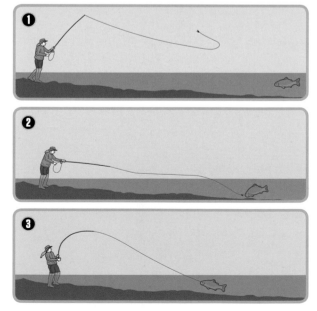

185 SWING A CURRENT SEAM

I learned to swing fish on a Southern shad river. Neither my buddy nor I could afford a motorboat, so we anchored our canoe behind river boulders and hurled homemade lead-core lines. Our shad darts swung into current seams that trailed downriver. But swinging is mainly a flyfishing technique that can be deadly on trout and smallmouth on any river if you do it right.

FLY BASICS Pick your pattern—Zonkers for trout, crayfish flies for smallies, or Clousers for stripers. Cast down and across into the fast water. As the line swings into the seam, adjust depth with the rod tip. (A high rod tip puts tension in the line for a slower sink rate, and vice versa.) As the cast straightens, point the rod tip toward where the line

disappears. Let the fly dangle there for a count of three, and then retrieve line using short strips or longer pulls.

THE CROSSHAIRS Target specific lies by allowing the fly to drift into a position so the swing carries it into a feeding lane slightly upstream of a log or boulder. Drop the rod tip sharply, and the fly could fall right into a fish's mouth.

HOLD YOUR GROUND Rather than tromping downstream to swing the next part of a run, increase your cast length incrementally to cover more water below you. If fish are spooky, you may have a better shot at connecting on a long-run swing than disrupting the water closer to the fish to swing on a short line.

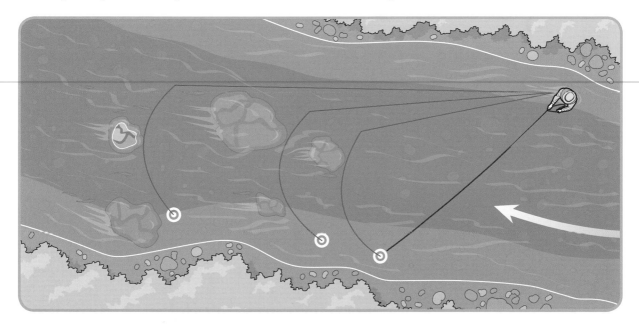

186 MAKE EASY MEASUREMENTS

Maybe you don't care about measuring 95% of the fish you catch, but when you stick that occasional big dog, you might want to count the inches. If you're not carrying a tape, just lay the fish down the length of your rod or net and note the spot where the tail ends so you can measure later. I actually pre-notch my net handle at the 20-inch mark. Even if I don't end up with an exact measurement of a fish, if the tail crosses the notch, I at least know that I have a trout over 20.

187 STRIKE SILVER

You're on a skiff with a fly rod, watching a big tarpon cruise your way. You make a solid presentation. The fish starts to track. Then the gills flare, its mouth opens and sucks in the fly, you raise the rod to set—and completely whiff. Lifting the rod the second a tarpon eats is a rookie mistake, but with a little discipline and a cool head, you'll rarely miss the stick. Here's the drill.

STEP 1 When a tarpon heads your way, don't panic. Keep your rod low and pointed straight at the fish. Resist the urge to begin stripping before you think the tarpon sees the fly. Once it keys in, let its initial reaction dictate how slow or fast you move the bug. As a general rule, I'll pause if the fish chases; if it stops tracking, I'll strip a little faster.

STEP 2 When the tarpon eats, keep stripping with a slow, steady pace. The point of the hook must be touching the inside of the tarpon's mouth before you strip-set. If you don't wait until you feel the point make contact, there's a good chance the fly is just floating around in that big mouth. The instant the tarpon feels tension, all it has to do is spit, and it's game over.

STEP 3 When you feel resistance against the fish's mouth, strip long and hard. But be warned; this will more than likely send the tarpon into a frenzy. Maintain tension on the fish by keeping a solid grip on your line as it slides

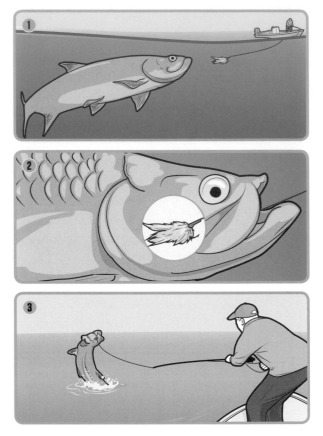

through your fingers onto the reel. Do all of this with a low rod angle to put a deep bend in the butt of the rod, which is where all the power lies.

188 STRIP-SET THE TOOTHERS

When a pike or muskie opens its maw and aggressively inhales a fly, it might seem like there's no way it won't get stuck. Truth is, between their roof teeth and incredibly bony mouths, these species are actually rather tricky to jab. Combine that mouth hardness with the thin, flat jaw structure, and a strip set becomes imperative. Striking with a low rod angle gives you the best shot at planting to hook, and provides much stronger hook-driving power than a high rod angle. If you lift the rod right after the eat, there's a very good chance the fish will just open its mouth and spit out the fly.

189 AVOID LOOSE ENDS

The first thing a tarpon will do when you stick it is take to the air. If you can get through the first set of jumps, your chance of landing the fish increases exponentially. To put the odds in your favor, use a stripping bucket to hold your loose line. If you've got all your running line lying sloppily around the deck, there's a much better chance it will tangle around cleats, feet, or hatch latches when the tarpon bolts. And if it does, you can kiss your fish goodbye.

ESSENTIAL FLIES: FOAM BASS BUG

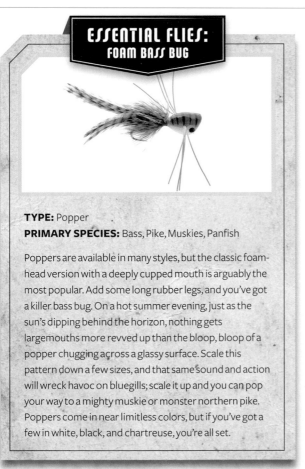

TYPE: Popper
PRIMARY SPECIES: Bass, Pike, Muskies, Panfish

Poppers are available in many styles, but the classic foam-head version with a deeply cupped mouth is arguably the most popular. Add some long rubber legs, and you've got a killer bass bug. On a hot summer evening, just as the sun's dipping behind the horizon, nothing gets largemouths more revved up than the bloop, bloop of a popper chugging across a glassy surface. Scale this pattern down a few sizes, and that same sound and action will wreck havoc on bluegills; scale it up and you can pop your way to a mighty muskie or monster northern pike. Poppers come in near limitless colors, but if you've got a few in white, black, and chartreuse, you're all set.

190 GET HITCHED

Whether you're tying up a fly leader for trophy muskies or rigging up to cast flies at tuna, adding a section of doubled line to the butt or shock tippet of your leader increases strength. Developed by saltwater big-game anglers, the Bimini twist was once the only trusted method for creating a double line, but man, is it a pain to tie. Many anglers these days have adopted the spider hitch for doubling up. The knot is strong and can be tied with any diameter line. And unlike the Bimini, a spider hitch is easy to tie while fishing. In 12 years of tuna fishing, a spider hitch hasn't failed me yet.

❶ **DOUBLE DOWN** Fold the line back on itself to create a doubled line. Make a second loop in the doubled line near the base by putting the looped tag under the standing section.

❷ **WRAP IT UP** Pinch this small loop between your thumb and forefinger. Wrap the length of doubled line loosely around your thumb and the small loop five to seven times.

❸ **PULL IT OFF** Next, pass the doubled line through the small loop. Slowly pull the doubled line, allowing the wraps around your thumb to peel off.

❹ **TIGHTEN UP** Once all of the thumb wraps are free, grab the doubled line and main line and pull sharply in opposite directions to cinch the knot. Trim the tag end.

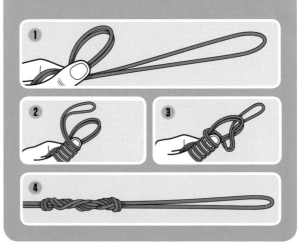

191 IF IT'S BROKE, FISH IT

I've spent a lot of time observing anglers on rivers, and one thing I see often is a habit of only targeting the most likely looking pieces of water. Guys will walk a mile to reach a nice deep, juicy run, but stroll right past hidden gems on the way. The reality is that almost any break in the current has the potential to hold a fish—be it a small soft spot behind a lone rock or one short seam of slower water in the middle of a raging run. Is it easier to drift a run with a long sweet spot? Absolutely, but these are also the places that get pounded. Some of my biggest trout have come from little one-off pockets only big enough to shelter a single fish. These nooks might take more strategy in positioning and presentation to target, but the pay out can be worth it, especially on crowded streams.

192 DRIFT A FLY WITH A DRY LEAF

Dark, gnarly undercut banks often hold the biggest trout in the stream. But getting a fly under those banks, and deep enough to prompt a strike from a monster trout, requires expert fly casting and a precise presentation. Or a leaf. Here's how to use fall foliage to float your fly into the perfect position.

STEP 1 Hook a weighted streamer or nymph fly, such as a Woolly Bugger, to the outer edge of a dry, buoyant tree leaf.

STEP 2 Carefully sneak to a position about ten yards upstream for the undercut bank you're looking to target. Strip off a few feet of line, and ease the unconventional rig into the current.

STEP 3 Pay out line as the leaf drifts to the target area. As it approaches to within 2 to 3 feet of the hole, give the line a sharp snap back with your line hand to rip the fly from the leaf. Your weighted streamer will drop into the current, which will carry the fly under the bank and down to that tucked-in trophy.

193 POP WITH CONFIDENCE

Catching anything from a pond largemouth to a striper in the salt on a popper is what those who love a surface explosion live for. Working these flies isn't very mysterious or difficult; try slow pops or hard pops until you get the kaboom! But there are a few little tricks that will make poppers a bit more lethal, and make casting them a bit less frustrating.

KEEP IT SHORT I don't care if your popper is made of foam, spun deer hair, or cork; every one of these materials makes these flies a pain to cast. Because they're very air resistant, poppers can be a chore to turn over on the final casting stroke. Using a short, stiff leader will help, but so will knowing your range limits. If the fish you're targeting are 50 or 60 feet away, either get closer or change flies.

GET LOOPY You can tie a popper to your leader with a clinch or Palomar knot and it will draw strikes. If you tie it on a loop knot instead, however, it will draw even more. I like to tie my poppers on a Rapala knot. This creates a small loop that the fly can slide on freely. This freedom of motion adds a little extra wiggle on the strip, but also gives the popper a second of extra shimmy when you pause, and sometimes that little subtle shake coaxes the crush.

FORGET FLUOROCARBON It's a fact that fluorocarbon leaders are all the rage in flyfishing these days, thanks to the way that the material pretty much disappears underwater, as well as its strength. But when it comes to popper fishing, you're going to want to stick with monofilament leaders. Fluorocarbon sinks, and while that's a plus when streamer fishing, all it's going to do to a popper is pull it underwater when you strip, severely marring the action.

194 ADOPT TUBE FLIES FOR TROUT FISHING

I really enjoy applying lessons learned in one style of fishing to another, and seeing what works. For example, I've thrown nothing but bonefish flies to carp in several years. One can argue that the "Czech nymphing" rig with weighted flies and a taut line is basically a bass drop-shot rig adapted for river trout.

On a recent salmon trip to Russia, we swung weighted tube flies. The advantage of this pattern is that the brass tube body sinks quickly and evenly. Unlike a conehead bugger or another weight-forward fly, this pattern doesn't dive nose-down in slack water. It sinks flat, and is consistent when you're sweeping a run. They're pretty simple to tie. And when you fish, simply thread your leader through the tube, and tie on a hook, which snugs into the flexible plastic sleeve at the back of the fly. They're easy to switch, adjust, and so forth.

I've been swinging tube flies for trout on my home

rivers since I got back. I reasoned that if a trout will eat a big Zoo Cougar or Autumn Splendor, why not one of these gaudy things? Trout do. Big time. Cast at the bank, let it swing through the run, and the big browns will pound this thing.

195 CATCH TROUT WITH A MUDDLER

The Muddler Minnow is one of the most versatile flies ever tied. Here's how to make it work for you on the surface and below.

Ⓐ LET 'EM RIDE My favorite way to dry-fly fish a Muddler is to skate it. Apply a little grease, then cast it downstream at a 45-degree angle. When the current grabs the line, it will pull the fly along, creating a wake as it sweeps toward the center of the river. This antagonizes trout. When they see that fly ripping along—just like a mouse or a crippled baitfish—large fish will attack it.

Ⓑ LET 'EM SWING The classic way to fish a Muddler is to swing it, imitating a sculpin. Use a sink-tip fly line to get the fly a foot or two under the surface. Cast at a 45-degree angle and land the fly tight to the bank. Mend once upstream, point the rod tip at the water, keep tension, and let the fly sweep along. After every cast, take two steps down so you systematically cover the water.

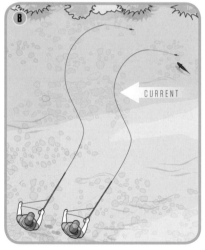

196 FISH THE THIN RED LINE

Sunset Amnesia line is pretty inexpensive—less than $5 a spool. Though it's intended as shooting line, it's a great tool for nymphers who want an extra visual cue when a trout slurps their beadhead. When tying on a fresh leader, clip away the pre-tied loop on the top end. Splice a 6-inch piece of 20-pound red Amnesia to the leader, and then connect the other end of the Amnesia to your fly line. Now you have a highly visible built-in strike indicator. As you drift, watch for ticks or stops in the red line. When you see one, set the hook.

ESSENTIAL FLIES: EPOXY SCUD

TYPE: Wet Fly
PRIMARY SPECIES: Trout

Scuds are tiny crustaceans that thrive in waters across the country, and make up to 20% of a trout population's annual diet in some areas. High in protein, scuds help fish grow, but the willingness to feed on them depends on what else is available. Scuds often take a back seat in waters rich in bug life, but you can be sure at some point in the season they become the main course when temps drop and bugs become scarce. Trout also gorge on scuds in midwinter, as they might be the only food source available. Fish them close to the bottom like a nymph in deeper water, or swing them just below the surface through shallow runs and riffles like a traditional wet fly.

197 MASTER THE MEND

The key to the perfect drift lies in mending your line: Basically, you have to keep your fly line upstream of your dry fly (or strike indicator when you are nymph fishing). Once the fly line gets downstream of the fly or indicator, it will grab the current and cause the fly to drag. Usually that's game over, and you lose.

An ideal mend will involve lifting the fly line from downstream, and then placing it upstream, but without moving either the fly or the strike indicator. The most common mistake, even among people who understand the importance of mending, is getting herky-jerky and trying to whip the line with the rod from chest level. Just wiggling your flies around for the sake of mending defeats the entire purpose.

Fly rods are built 8 feet long and over for an important reason. When you start the mend, you lift the rod tip just high enough to pick the fly line off the water, but not so much that you end up disturbing the leader (1). Next, with your rod tip straight up, swing it across your face from downstream to upstream (2). Then, you gently lay down your line to the upstream side of your fly or indicator (3). Also, in some cases, in faster water, you might want to kick that rod over with more force.

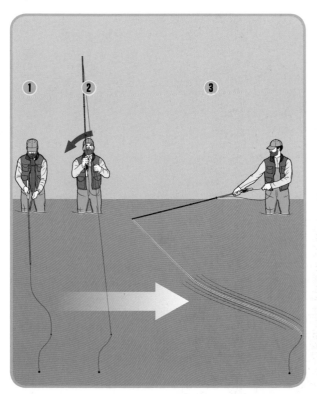

198 MEND IN MIDAIR

When there's fast water between you and a target fish, don't make a straight cast, because the current will grab your fly line and drag your fly. For a more natural presentation and a cleaner drift, you should make a reach cast—essentially mending your fly line in the air before it falls to the water. Here's how to do it.

STEP 1 Measure out as much line as you think you need by false casting away from the target. It is difficult to shoot line and reach at the same time, so your distance should be extra precise.

STEP 2 As you cast, the line will turn over on the forward stroke (A). As soon as all of the line unfurls in front of you, reach your casting arm in the direction the current is coming from (B).

STEP 3 Make the reach with the rod tip still pointed at the 2 o'clock position (C). Not stopping the rod, or dropping the rod tip as you reach, defeats the purpose and fouls the presentation.

STEP 4 In ideal conditions, you want your casting plane to be a couple of feet above the water's surface, so everything unfurls, the line moves upstream, and the fly falls gently on target.

199 DON'T FEAR THE REAR

There is a common misconception that if you're the guy stuck in the back of the raft or drift boat, you're going to catch fewer fish than the guy up front. If you're both casting dry flies, that might be the case, but I'll be the first person to volunteer to take the rear, because it has its advantages if you play your cards right. When streamer fishing, the guy up front often wakes the fish up and gets them interested, but it's the second fly the gets bit. If the front angler is casting dries, back him up with a nymph. If a trout rises to his fly and refuses, the fish may take a shot at your nymph as it swims back down to its holding position.

200 REACH FOR SUCCESS

One of the most useful presentations in the fly angler's repertoire is the reach cast. The two variations presented here deliver the line across the stream at an angle; the portion in the fastest current is placed farthest upstream, buying it some additional "free-float" time and delaying drag on the fly.

Say the target is in a slow flow across from you, beyond a band of faster current. Make a conventional overhead cast. On the forward stroke, as your rod reaches the 11 o'clock position, shift the direction of motion 90 degrees, swinging the tip upstream through a big quarter-circle. As you do so, reach the rod as far upriver as you can, ending with it held parallel to the water. The line now forms an angle, from the rod tip upstream and then across and down to the target.

To cast across a slower current to reach a faster one, simply swing the rod in the opposite direction and reach downstream.

STEP 1 Work out enough line to extend past the target. The cast angle effectively shortens the range, and overshooting the mark compensates.

STEP 2 End your forward delivery with a high rod tip for maximum upstream reach.

STEP 3 As your rod reaches the 11 o'clock position, swing the tip upstream, and drop it parallel with the water's surface.

201 MAKE A FIGURE 8

A short, braided-wire "bite" tippet can prevent cutoffs from toothy critters such as pike, bluefish, or barracuda. The figure-eight knot is a really easy way to attach a fly to light- to medium-weight braided wire. Note that this knot is for braided wire only, not solid wire or heavier cable.

STEP 1 Feed a few inches of wire leader through the hook eye, bringing the tag end forward and down to form a loop.

STEP 2 Bring the tag end under, then up and over the standing portion, forming a second loop and starting to create what looks like a numeral 8 on its side.

STEP 3 Put the tag end back through the first loop—entering from the far side and exiting on the side closest to you—creating a finished figure eight.

STEP 4 Grab the tag end with pliers. Pull hard on this end only, while holding the standing wire, to tighten the knot. If you pull on the standing wire, it will kink in front of the eye.

STEP 5 Trim the tag end of the wire, but not too closely. Leaving a short piece that you can still grasp with pliers will allow you to untie the knot more easily. Just grab the tag and push it forward.

202 GET AN INDICATOR EDUCATION

There is much debate in the flyfishing world over the use of strike indicators for nymphing. Many anglers—guides in particular—feel they are musts for beginners. Much of the reason is that indicators reduce the learning curve, because they cut out the need for a nymphing skill set that can take years to master. Instead of learning the traditional method of managing your line so you can *feel* the bite, an indicator provides a big, bright target that will *show* you the bite. Some purist anglers feel that the indicator method is dumbing down the sport, and over time, the art of traditional nymphing will be lost.

What I believe is that a strike indicator has a time and a place based on the situation, but it's certainly not every time and every nymphing situation. Every flycaster, in my opinion, should know how to nymph without an indicator, because certain scenarios will arise when having the ability to do so will catch more fish. There will also be runs—perhaps one with a very short zone or back eddy—where an indicator will make it easier to present the flies and see the strike. In this case, you're using it as a tool, not a crutch.

203 DRIFT AND LIFT

Casting down- and across-stream with a pair of small, weighted nymphs (one as a dropper) was the time-honored method decades before indicators evolved. By mending or stripping line in the current, you can precisely control the speed and action of the flies. You can fish blind in the absence of rising fish—or present flies to actively feeding trout.

Taken a step further, the same tactic becomes what was called the Leisenring Lift, named for the fabled Pennsylvania wet-fly artist of the 1930s. Cast and mend the line, giving your rig time to sink (1) before it reaches either a rising fish or a likely lie. As fly and fish converge, tighten your line slightly (2) so the nymph starts rising to the surface, much like a hatching insect (3). Strikes, when they come, can be vicious. Two weighted nymphs, such as a Gold Ribbed Hare's Ear and a Pheasant Tail dropper, work best with this method.

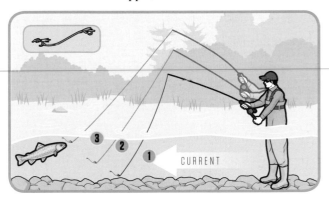

ESSENTIAL FLIES: FOAM BEETLE

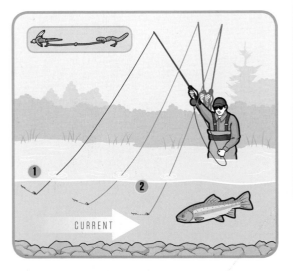

TYPE: Terrestrial
PRIMARY SPECIES: Trout, Panfish

The Foam Beetle has a lot going for it. It's a pretty tough fly to sink regardless of water type or speed, its dark silhouette helps it stand out when viewed from below, it makes a nice splat when it hits the surface, and it's hard to find a fish that won't eat it. Bluegills will slurp this fly almost any time of year, but in late summer, it's a trout killer. Even if there is a significant hatch taking place, trout get tuned in to land-based bugs falling in the water during the dog days, and a juicy beetle is hard to resist. It'll catch trout located just about anywhere in a stream or river, but if you can get it drifting tight to a bank of tall grass, or under low-hanging tree branches, you won't find many trout in late July through mid-September that won't rise to take a shot.

204 TRY HIGH-STICKING

You can duplicate the effectiveness of indicator fishing without using an indicator—instead, try the high-sticking approach. The typical rig is a pair of weighted flies, with a small split shot between them. Wade to the edge of a deep riffle or run, and flip the flies upstream (1). Follow their downstream drift with your rod held high to keep most of your line off the water (2), thereby avoiding drag. When a trout takes, you'll feel a tug or see the line move.

To fish a deep riffle or run, rig a No. 16 Beadhead Prince Nymph with a No. 14 San Juan Worm as a trailer, and put a split shot in the middle Like most traditional nymph fishing, this takes some skill, of which you can be proud. Nobody brags about watching a bobber.

205 SURVIVE THE STEELHEAD JAM

If there is a logjam or root snarl nearby, guaranteed a steelhead will run for it the second you set the hook. If you end up hooked to a red-hot chromer bolting for cover, the situation may turn sour no matter what. but to up the odds of getting the fish out, resist hitting the brakes. It's instinctive to lift the rod and rear back to try to stop the fish from getting under the wood, but if the hook doesn't pop before the fish hits cover, the line will likely rub and break as soon as it meets the log. Instead, drop the rod tip into the water and keep some side pressure on the fish. A low angle of line entry raises the chances that the line won't rub on the cover; if you're very lucky, it'll pass under the logjam and clear. This may at least keep you tied to the fish longer, and every second you're connected gives you more time to keep the pressure on, hopefully forcing the fish out.

206 GO SHOOTING FOR CHROMERS

Fall steelhead anglers typically cover water with cross-stream casts until a fish hits. Instead, try putting the fly right in front of the fish.

GETTING DOWN Pattern choice matters, but presentation is the real key. You need to put the nymph or egg 4 to 8 inches above the bottom; this means adding weight to your line. An unweighted fly moves more naturally than a weighted one, so try a slinky weight attached to the leader butt, instead of split shot. The setup lets you easily change the weight as river conditions dictate.

DEAD DRIFT When water temperatures dip below 50 degrees, dead-drift a nymph on a 9½-foot (or longer) 7- or 8-weight rod with a small-diameter shooting line (A) instead of a traditional weight-forward floating fly line. The small line allows for quieter entry of the flies on the cast (no line slap to spook fish) and offers less resistance in the water, so it's easier to get a drag-free drift. Don't false cast. Simply pick up the line and shoot it directly upstream (B). Casting with the added weight is smooth and effortless. This is a great way to work a tree-choked stream that routinely snags back casts.

Pros suggest an 8- to 10-foot butt section ending with a bead and barrel swivel (C). A slinky weight slides freely on the butt section via a snap. Tie a 3- to 6-foot leader to the swivel; onto this, knot a green chartreuse Caddis nymph. Run 17 to 24 inches of line from the eye of this fly, and add a Stonefly nymph. The long, light tippet offers little water resistance and sinks quickly.

207 MATCH A STEELIE'S MAIN COURSE

When reproductive urges drive their migration, steelhead often show amazing indifference to everything you cast. A study by California's Department of Fish and Game on the Lower Mokelumne River, however, offers some aid in approaching picky steelhead.

Researchers checked the stomachs of 179 steelhead up to 20 inches long and found (in rough descending order): aquatic insects and nymphs (mostly caddis pupae and larvae); eggs (chinook, steelhead, sucker); baitfish and fry; crayfish; bird feathers; mammal hair; and two mice. Steelhead ate in proportion to availability. Prey size remained the same as they grew; bigger fish just ate more, by muscling in on runs with access to the richest drifts.

If fishing is slow, instead of using a big, flashy bait or fly, think actual seasonal forage. Use a smaller fly or bait (try a single egg, instead of a yarn cluster), focus on the best runs, and keep on casting until you find the money pattern.

208 DO THE CHUCK 'N' DUCK

Adding four big split shot ahead of a nymph takes the sexy out of fly casting real quick. But when you are faced with a deep, dark hole that might be home to a massive brown trout or steelhead, sometimes you just have to suck it up and dredge. Getting that much lead to the top of the pool without smacking yourself in the back of the noggin takes skill. Master the chuck-and-duck cast, and you'll get to score more fish and suffer fewer welts.

STEP 1 False casting is what you have to avoid, so start by feeding line straight downstream with the rod tip held high to stop the weights from snagging on the bottom until you have enough length to reach the top of the hole you're trying to fish.

STEP 2 In one fluid motion, swing the rod over your downstream shoulder to get the line swinging in an arc over the water behind you. Keep the line tight so it stays straight and extended. If the line collapses, get ready for a thump to the cranium.

STEP 3 When the line reaches the 1 o'clock position, hunch down, bow your head, and then bring the rod straight over your body, pointing the tip exactly where you want the rig to land.

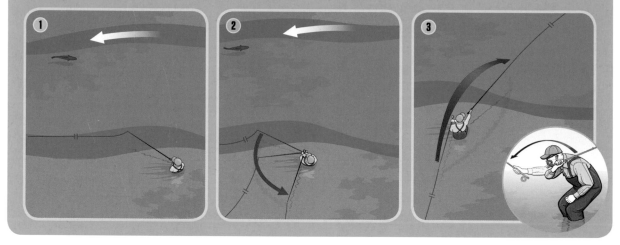

ESSENTIAL FLIES: GRIFFITH'S GNAT

TYPE: Dry Fly
PRIMARY SPECIES: Trout

I call Griffith's Gnat a necessary evil. Though you can find them in a range of sizes, the most common—and most productive—start at a tiny size 20 and only get smaller from there. They can be a pain to thread onto your tippet, they can be a nightmare to see drifting on the surface, but these midges are downright deadly. Their dark color and wispy appearance help them imitate a single midge or a small cluster of midges. Regardless, if you trout fish long enough, eventually the day will come when the fish are rising to bugs so tiny, only a Griffith's will make the play. As many midges continue to hatch during colder months, these flies are key to capitalizing on winter hatches. Just remember to play every fish you hook on a Griffith's lightly, because those delicate little hooks love to come unglued.

209 CASH IN ON SUMMER'S MONSTER HATCHES

If I could only flyfish one month per year, it would be June. That marks the emergence of the biggest aquatic insects on the stream—two, three, and four times the size of their spring predecessors. With the water still cool, the trout go on the prowl. In some regions, the hatches often occur right as dark falls, just when the largest brown trout begin feeding. Here are the hatches that bring out the big boys.

BROWN ALL OVER Like other burrowing nymphs, brown drakes require sand and a fine gravel substrate. Their hatch can be sporadic and long-lasting, which probably explains more than anything why they remain under the radar for many fishermen—and why an oversize March Brown is never a bad fly to choose when you're unsure what pattern to tie on in June.

GANG GREEN With their inch-long size and their barely developed wings, green drakes struggle to take flight, flapping those wings constantly—and making a serious impression on fish below. Medium to slow runs and pools produce the best fishing. Twitching the artificial insect while it drifts drag-free can lead to an immediate if temporary end to your worldly cares. Green drake spinners return to the water three days later to lay eggs. Flights appear as distant speckles in the twilight, eventually gathering into swarms over the river. Elegant, with white bodies and black wings and tails, the coffin-fly spinners drop down at evening in concentrations that bring up the largest trout in the river. Get into position early and wait until the fish begin to reveal their locations before casting.

HEX SIGNS The Michigan caddis is the largest mayfly on the continent. This is a meaty 1½-inch yellowish-brown Hexagenia nymph, so fat that it can molt up to 40 or 50 times. It squeezes out of its burrow in silt or clay-bottom stretches of slow water, usually around dark, and leaves its shuck, and the biggest brown trout in the river are waiting. Get into position early. Don't forget to bring your headlamp, but use it only if you stick yourself; light spooks fish. Some anglers pre-tie imitations on tippets so as to avoid needing their lamps to re-tie. As with all nighttime fishing, try to fish close and, when possible, watch the patch of water where your fly might be. The feeding can continue long into the night, and the main challenge is to avoid ripping the fly away. Calling a one-Mississippi count after a splash, or waiting until you feel the strike, can help you slow down.

STONE GIANTS Beginning life as a slow-moving nymph, the salmonfly is the brontosaurus of the stonefly world, reaching up to 2½ inches in length and looking fierce, but in fact eating only the plant detritus it finds beneath rocks. After creeping along the stones in an apparent daze, the black stones form herds and crawl to shore. Unlike the mayflies, they hatch on land at night. The flies mate within two days, and the females return to the water to drop off their eggs. Any stoneflies that aren't dropping eggs stay on land—or try to, anyway. But since there are so many of them, a good number end up in the drink. Some of the biggest fish hold near banks where they can get the first shot at this free buffet. The hatch moves upriver, and the best fishing is at the early points.

RIVER GOLD If the plant-eating giant salmonfly nymph is the brontosaurus of the stonefly world, then the beautiful 1½-inch golden stone, with its powerful mandibles, is the Tyrannosaurus rex. Golden stoneflies share their life and hatching patterns with the salmonfly, with which they overlap on some western waterways. The best places to fish any dry stone—golden or salmonfly—are in the deep, fast slots near shore and beneath trees and bushes. Many fishermen overlook these spots as they have no wading or room for a back cast.

210 READ THE WEATHER

Summer is a great time to fish for trout, but it's also a season that can encompass a wide range of weather conditions. Here's how to adjust your game depending on what Mother Nature has in store.

MUGGY WEATHER Brown trout are most active at night during the hottest part of the summer. After dark, toss large flies that push water (such as a size 2 Muddler Minnow).

WINDY CONDITIONS Windblown terrestrials collect in the lee of cutbanks. Fish small ants, or a hopper dry with a size 16 Hare's Ear nymph on 12 inches of 5X tippet tied to the hopper's hook.

HIGH PRESSURE Mayflies are often active on cool days with little wind. Check for spinner falls between 8 a.m. and 10 a.m., and then fish a nymph in the riffles.

IN A SUMMER STORM Trout feed aggressively during the initial increase in stream level, when the current is washing prey downstream. Run to catch the first rise of water and throw a streamer.

211 KICK OFF WITH TRICOS

Tricos are diminutive mayflies that hatch in August in trout streams nationwide. It's some of the year's best fishing, but you'll have to get up in the morning to catch it. The spinner fall is most important and usually happens when morning air temperature reaches 68 degrees. Check the weather forecast the night before. Note: a stiff wind prevents the spinner fall entirely.

Imitative fly sizes range from 20 down to 28, on tippets from 6X down to a cobweb 8X. Such fragile tippets spook many anglers, but tie a rigged leader and fly on your rod, hooking the fly to a branch. Step back, let out 20 feet of line, and start pulling as if fighting a fish. Increase the pressure until the tippet breaks. It'll surprise you just how hard you can actually pull with a fine leader.

When the day's Trico activity dwindles, switch to terrestrials. Grasshoppers, ants, and beetles all peak in activity on stream margins on hot, muggy August days.

Keep in mind there's more to fishing terrestrials than plunking a giant hopper next to the bank. On heavily pressured rivers, including many in the West, a size 10 or 12 hopper often outfishes the bigger foam-bodied versions that the trout have seen more often.

Time of day can make a big difference also. As a hot afternoon turns to cooler evening, terrestrial insects become less active along the stream banks. Trout feeding patterns change, too; a dry caddis or mayfly imitation will typically start to outdo terrestrial flies as the sun dips to the horizon.

212 CHECK YOUR DOUBLE TIMING

Two-fly rigs allow anglers to present double the meal options to discerning trout. The best fly pairings, however, are no given. Trout streams and trout feeding behavior are dynamic. What works in the morning can just as easily strike out in the afternoon. Check your watch, and try these three killer combinations when the time is right.

MORNING Tie a No. 6 weighted stonefly nymph to a 3X leader. Next, add 2 feet of 4X tippet to the bend in the nymph hook, and finish with a trailing No. 12 caddis pupa. Drift this combination below a strike indicator behind rocks and in eddies where natural nymphs are stirring. A large and small offering gives trout options prior to any hatch activity starting. Choose a stonefly in black or brown, as dark colors show better contrast in low light.

MIDDAY As the sun gets higher, trout switch to surface feeding and eat both live bugs and dead mayflies that have fallen back to the water after mating. An easy way to present both options is to fish a No. 10 Irresistible with a No. 18 Adams a foot in tow. Clip the hackle off the bottom of the Adam so it sits flat in the film like a dead mayfly spinner. The bulky Irresistible not only draws strikes, but it helps you keep track of the tiny Adams' location during the drift.

EVENING Low light brings big trout out of hiding. They may be interested in eating bugs, or they may attack the smaller trout still sipping on the surface. To fool these toads, strip a No. 6 yellow Marabou Muddler with a No. 12 Leadwing Coachman bringing up the rear by 14 inches. The streamer will move plenty of water to get a meat eater's attention, and the large wet fly will imitate drowned aquatic insects that require less work to eat than snapping live bugs off the top.

213 BUDDY UP

Sightcasting to carp, trout, or bonefish by yourself is fun, but it's never a bad idea to bring a buddy. Two sets of eyes are better than one, especially when one set acts as a dedicated spotter. The angler in the water always has low-angle sight limitations, but a friend on a high bank, skiff poling platform, or bridge usually has a better view. The spotter can tell you whether you need to cast more left, right, longer, or shorter. He can also tell you how the fish is reacting to your fly. If you hook up, it's a sweet team effort.

214 RUN A SEARCH PARTY

If I get to a river and see no bugs hatching or fish rising, I run a search party rig. Tie on a heavy black Woolly Bugger, and trail a small light-colored nymph 10 to 12 inches behind it. Tie the tippet that holds the nymph to the bend in the Bugger's hook to dead-drift, strip, or swing while offering the fish two food size options. Often, the large streamer grabs their attention, but they clobber the nymph bringing up the rear. No matter which fly they eat, this rig will help you find elusive fish fast.

215 MAKE THE SEASON'S END MEMORABLE

"Trout streams gurgled about the roots of my family tree," naturalist John Burroughs once wrote, and so it is with me. I was born and raised within view of a lovely trout brook, where I learned the magical promise of opening day in spring. The only trouble was the corresponding thought of a last day when trout season would end in fall.

Many catch-and-release areas are open year-round, so the concept is a little outmoded. But many trout rivers still are seasonal. The last day is melancholy, like a wake for an old friend. But I still find that heading out on that day is a ritual to relish, and requires some careful choices.

Small bluewing olive mayflies are usually the season's last hatch, sometimes well into October. Hatches are most intense in the afternoon but pose a problem: They're small flies—from size 20 on down to 26—requiring a 7X tippet. To fish this hatch, I pick a long, slow, flat pool where I can most easily control the drift of a small fly on a long, fine leader. The olives hatch in faster water, too, but fishing such a small dry on broken water is more difficult.

After years of experimenting, I'm down to two basic fly patterns. One is an RS 2 Emerger that I can fish damp right in the surface film or drift just under the surface, avoiding most of the floating leaves. The other is a BWO dry tied with a small buoyant CDC wing and no regular hackle; I fish this more on top, and gently sipping trout take it more often than anything else I've found.

Around 5 p.m., the sun is low on the horizon and the day develops a chill. The hatches quickly taper off to nothing, and trout stop rising. I watch this happen and wish the day would not end. Inevitably, it does.

But on the drive home I am consoled by an immutable fact: We are now one day closer to the next opening day.

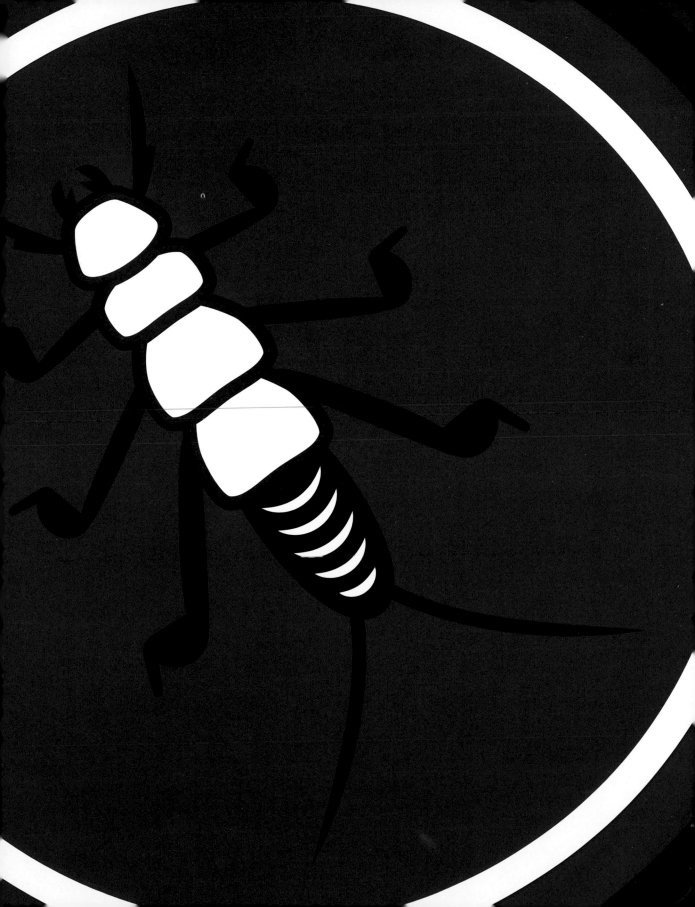

I AM ADDICTED TO CATCHING BROWN TROUT.

They are my favorite freshwater species. If I had my way, I'd cast giant streamers for them every time I hit the water, because in my opinion, this tactic statistically produces the biggest specimens. The reality, however, is that you have to recognize when your method of choice isn't going to work. You have to be able to adapt. If I wasn't just as fluent in presenting a grasshopper to a rising brown, or versed in swinging nymphs in the colder months, I wouldn't catch nearly as many of these fish.

Having a working knowledge of how fish behavior, location, and feeding habits change based on time of year, time of day, and the weather is crucial for success in flyfishing. Likewise, always remember that the hookup is only the beginning of the battle. The tactics in this chapter come from some of the best guides and fly anglers in the U.S., and they'll help you become well rounded in everything from finding your favorite species, to making it chew, to putting it in the net.

216 PROSPECT A TROUT POOL

Pools on a trout stream may vary some in size, conformation, and peculiarities, but all share the same basic anatomy. Understanding that structure is the key to finding and taking fish. Don't charge in without a plan. Instead, carve the water into separate, fishable portions. Work systematically from the tail of the pool to the head, and from near water to far.

BANK WATER From the outside seam to the water's edge. Good from late spring through fall, this strip hits its peak from midsummer on, when overhanging vegetation offers shade and an abundance of terrestrial insects.

TAIL The most commonly overlooked and undervalued section. It holds nice but spooky trout when light is low—in the early morning, in the evening, and on overcast days, primarily late spring through fall.

LOWER LIP The downstream edge of the pool's deepest part. The bottom rises abruptly at this lip, and trout lie just ahead of it.

SEAMS Where the tongue current meets slower water on either side. Often marked by a foam or bubble line, it's a prime feeding area all day long. Large trout do hang in the seams, but look here mostly to rack up numbers.

① Keep low and stay above the fast water. Use a dry-and-dropper combination to work the tailout fish. Begin at the near bank and fan casts across to the far side.

② Stay just behind the lower lip and cast, quartering upstream. Gradually lengthen your casts, working across the lip.

③ Comb the band of current from the soft water in front of you to the inside edge of the seam. Don't cast into the tongue current from here; you'll get instant drag on the fly.

④ Fish the flat all the way out to the seam. Then work to the upper lip, still keeping your fly on the inside edge of the seam. Finally, search each finger of current spilling through the riffle.

⑤ Walk the bank to the tail, and wade quietly into position, disturbing the water as little as possible. Stay in the slower water, ideally about one rod's length away from the seam, which will help you minimize drag. Work across the gut from seam to seam.

EDDY Formed where current breaks around a point of land. Bigger is better, but even an eddy the size of a turkey platter can hold fish. These are most reliable after early summer.

THROAT The narrow section of water that runs into the pool. Unless there's visible cover on the bottom—boulders or shelves—don't bother. Swift current over a smooth streambed won't hold fish.

8

9

TONGUE The main flow of current through the pool. It creates the seams and transports food.

7

RIFFLE Created by a shoal at the inside of the throat. Any current over a foot deep can hold big surprises. Broken, well-oxygenated water draws fish in hot weather. The riffle and flats below are a good high-water bet.

GUT The sweet spot. Trout stack up in this deepest part of the pool from late fall to spring, making it the top choice for winter fishing. During summer, you'll find fewer trout here but generally they're the largest.

UPPER LIP The upstream edge of the deep part of the pool. The current tongue slows as it drops over the upper lip into deep water; trout tuck up behind this shelf to feed.

6

4

6 As you wade to this position, begin covering the far bank by quartering downstream and shaking slack into your cast. It's easier to control drag this way than by casting upstream from lower in the pool. Place your fly as close to the bank as possible.

7 Continue wading toward the upper lip, working the tongue with quartering-upstream casts, and the far bank with quartering-downstream casts. Finish by searching the outside edge of the rock shoal, the lip, and across the tongue to the edge of the eddy. Then walk back to the tail.

Replace the dry-and-dropper with a tandem-nymph rig. Fish positions 5 through 7 just as you did before.

8 Cross the stream, staying well behind the eddy fish. Use a dry-and-dropper again, concentrating on the bank side of the eddy.

9 For a stream too big to cross, tie on a streamer. Cast, quartering down at the far bank, and let it swing around below you. Hit the eddy first. Take two steps downstream, and repeat until you reach the tail.

217 IDENTIFY TROPHY WATERS

How do you know when you're looking at a potential trout goldmine? These simple rules of thumb can help you be sure you're casting in the right place.

OXYGEN Native trout thrive in streams with high oxygen levels. Likewise, stocked trout are more likely to hold over in waters with good oxygenation, and a few key factors in producing it are water speed and how the current is broken. Riffles, plunge pools, bottlenecks, and waterfalls all help oxygenate water, especially if the bottom is rocky. A stream with good current in spring that turns into slow, featureless puddles in summer isn't likely to house a local toad.

COLD WATER Both stockers and native trout have been known to tolerate pretty high water temperatures, but colder is always better. Spring creeks maintain cooler temps year-round; well-shaded stretches of freestone streams can provide lower temperatures, even in summer. If local streams get low after spring, find a topographical map and look for stretches with the steepest elevations on each side, as less water-warming sunlight will hit them.

BUG LIFE To survive, wild and native trout need aquatic insects. Stockers have a better shot at holding over in a stream with good bug life. Flip some rocks and check for stoneflies, or keep an eye out for emerging caddis and mayflies. If you find some, note the size and color, tie or buy some matching patterns and return in the evening when hatch activity should peak. You'll know quickly if there are trout around.

218 DE-FUNK AND RE-FUNK YOUR CARP BUGS

Carp have terrible eyesight. With that in mind, so long as your fly looks like something they think could be food, you're in good shape. However, carp have an incredible sense of smell, and more often than not, if one snubs your offering, it's because it wasn't digging the odor.

Human scent alone is unnatural to a fish, but if you factor in the aroma of gas from fueling the truck, sunblock residue, or mustard from your sandwich, it's not difficult to accidentally turn your fly into a total turnoff. Adding fish-attracting scents to flies is somewhat of a taboo, but when it comes to carp, it can be a necessary evil.

At minimum, rub your fly in the silt, mud, or algae that's in the water you're fishing before making the first cast. This helps mask human scent, and gives the fly a neutral odor. If there are berries present along the bank, and you're using a berry fly to match them, don't hesitate to squeeze some berry juice on your bug. And if you really want to play dirty, soak your flies in the liquid found in a can of corn.

ESSENTIAL FLIES: CRAZY CHARLIE

TYPE: Streamer
PRIMARY SPECIES: Saltwater, Carp

You'd have a very hard time finding a flats fisherman who doesn't have a heaping helping of Crazy Charlies in his fly box. While you'll find endless varieties of bonefish flies on the market, none is more widely known or consistently productive than this simple shrimp imitation. If you've got a few in white, tan, and light pink, you've got everything you need to dupe bonefish anywhere on the planet. Provided you make a good leading cast out in front of feeding bones, short strips along the bottom get this fly puffing sand, and the fish will home right in. In recent years, crafty anglers have also started tying Charlies in colors that match crayfish, and using the same bonefish presentation on muddy freshwater flats to best behemoth carp.

219 DUNK A SPOON FLY

Spoon flies are exactly what they sound like; patterns tied with holographic material that mimic the flash and action of a metal spoon, which is one of the all-around most versatile and deadly lures in fishing. Anglers that needed a secret weapon for finicky seatrout and redfish originally created spoon flies, but these patterns aren't just at home in shallow saltwater. Looking to dredge a giant smallmouth or brown trout out from under a cut bank? When other more traditional patterns aren't making the play, swing or high-stick a spoon fly with a few split shot ahead of it in the sweet spot. The current will give the fly action, and the flash will draw out the big boys.

220 PICK POCKETS FOR TROUT

In fast-moving streams, fish use obstacles to avoid strong currents. These boulders, ledges, and snags also help you stay out of sight. So make like a heron and snatch fish at super-close range.

"In mountain stream pools, you don't need a 30-foot cast," says George Hunker of Sweetwater Fishing Expeditions in Lander, Wyoming. "I like 3 feet of line out of the top guide. With a 9-foot rod and a 9-foot leader, I can put the fly where I want it and keep everything else out of the water." His fly: a size 14 Stimulator. His spot: a short waterfall into a deep pool. "I like to present the fly right at the seam edge where the pool starts to run." Keep a close eye on your fly.

If they're not taking it up on top, go subsurface. Fish in this environment can't resist a big meal staring them in the face. Cast to the head of the pool and let a weighted fly roll through the turbulence. Make another cast or two, and then move on. "There's no reason to beat a dead dog," Hunker says. "Hit as many pockets, inside edges, and little slow spots as you can."

For the heftiest stream trout, work what Hunker calls "the eye of the pool." It's a big-fish haven in the eddy on the inside of a stream bend. Between the eddy and the bank, look for a section of slower, deeper water. That's the eye. Drop a Parachute Adams above the slack water so that your fly rides the very inside edge of the seam, and get ready.

Here's a pro tip: Sleep in. "It's difficult to catch fish first thing in the morning in these snowmelt streams," Hunker explains. "We fish banker's hours." When the water warms, insect activity peaks, and it stays high until the afternoon cooldown.

221 DELIVER A WOUNDED DRY

Still-water spots like lakes, ponds, and glassy spring creeks can offer epic summer dry-fly action. They can also be terribly frustrating. You can match the hatch perfectly, tie on what you think is the right bug, lead the trout just so...and still get refused. When this happens, most anglers are quick to change patterns, yet almost nobody thinks to do the right thing—which is to change the character of your bug, rather than the bug itself.

In flat, calm water, trout have ample time to scrutinize your fly and are inclined to go after the easy pickings whenever they can. They key on natural bugs that are struggling at the surface—the ones that are unable to spread and dry their wings or shed their shucks. These insects are most vulnerable, and the smartest anglers always turn to cripple patterns—which float high enough for the angler to see but leave a tantalizing chunk of body suspended just below the water surface.

Just about every fly shop will have cripple variations of the most popular patterns, such as Hendricksons, Green Drakes, and caddis flies. Of course, you can tie your own. Tie the dry as you normally would, except wrap the hackle at a 45-degree angle, so when the hackle rides flat on the water, the tail end of the fly drags below the surface.

222 MAKE A SEINE

Collecting live aquatic insects so you can match the hatch is easy with a pocket seine. You can make your own cheaply.

STEP 1 Cut a 1 x 2-foot piece of fine-mesh netting—the lighter its color the better.

STEP 2 Cut a 3/8-inch wooden dowel into two 2-foot lengths.

STEP 3 Attach the netting to the dowels with duct tape so that you have a 1-foot-wide net between them.

STEP 4 Roll it up like a scroll, shove it into a vest pocket, and go.

223 DAPPLE A FLY

To work a fly in a log- and rock-jammed headwater creek, forgo the back cast and try the old dappling method. Using a bushy dry fly, fish with just the leader and a foot or two of fly line outside the tip-top. Sneak up on a pool, and drop the fly vertically on the water for a short drag-free drift. You can even dapple a fly by picking it off the water and plopping it back down, simulating a mayfly flittering up and down to lay eggs in the surface film.

GET SHOCKED

A common problem when swinging wet flies is missing strikes. On most takes, you'll be facing downstream at a trout that's facing upstream. When you set the hook, you may pull the fly out of the fish's mouth. You can try a "shock loop," a few inches of line hanging loosely between the reel and the index finger on the rod hand. If you hold the loop lightly and let it go when you feel a strike, the fish has time to take the fly and turn, so that when the line tightens against the drag of the reel, it's hooked solidly in the corner of the jaw. And the shock loop has the added benefit of absorbing the impact of a hard strike.

225 GINK AND SINK FOR SMUTTING TROUT

When you see fish that are porpoising without their snouts breaking the surface (some people call these "smutting" rises), but you don't see dry-fly duns on the water, assume the fish are eating emerging bugs beneath the surface. But noisy and gaudy weights and strike indicators will spook wary trout in slow, shallow currents. Modern anglers have hit on a virtually invisible and silent method, developed ages ago on the chalk streams of England, to catch such wary fish. Tie on a single Black Beauty midge nymph. Coat the 18 inches of tippet directly above the fly with Gehrke's Fly Xink to submerge the line. Then, holding your fingers in place to mark the spot, coat the next few feet of tippet and leader with Gehrke's Gink floatant. Cast the line 6 to 12 feet upstream from your target fish. That transition point on the tippet will bend abruptly

as the material dips below the surface. This creates a clearly visible dimple in the film, for a de facto strike indicator: When the dimple caves in, wobbles, or vanishes altogether, set the hook (gently), because that's your signal that the trout has taken the fly.

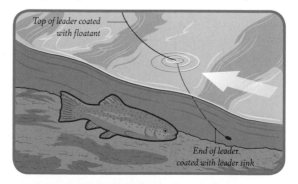

Top of leader coated with floatant

End of leader coated with leader sink

226 FIND YOUR RHYTHM

Pike and muskies are extremely smart hunters. They know how to ambush their prey efficiently, striking at the perfect time so they expend the least amount of energy. While this behavior can make them tricky to catch, you can also use it to your advantage. These toothy fish will actually calculate the rhythm of how their prey is swimming, noting when the baitfish pauses as it moves. When working big streamers for these fish, always make sure to use a repetitive cadence, such as two strips and a pause. Any pike or muskie tracking the fly will key in to that cadence, anticipate the next pause in the series, and strike when the fly stops.

227 DROWN A HOPPER FLY

Grasshoppers are like cheeseburgers for trout—fatty, juicy, and packed with protein. A languid hopper strike by a rising monster brown is always a thrill, but sometimes the fish just won't gorge themselves on a surface smorgasbord. If naturals are jumping off the banks but trout won't look at your fly, it doesn't necessarily mean they aren't eating hoppers. The smart trout wait for hoppers to sink below the surface before taking a bite.

To fish the hopper season most effectively, you must learn to fish those patterns dry—and wet (by which I mean drowned). Apply sinking grease to the hopper, and dead-drift it down a seam where you think trout are holding low. You won't need a strike indicator; when a fish grabs it, you'll feel it. Or let that waterlogged pattern swing out at the end of a run, a good foot or so below the surface.

The best way to fish drowned hoppers is to weight a leader with enough split shot to feel steady tension as your rig drifts in deeper, more turbid runs. Pinch on enough weight for it to drop like a rock, adding an extra BB. Below the weight, tie a gaudy hopper on 18 inches of tippet. If you feel the tension hiccup or lift when drifting, assume that a trout has taken the fly, and set the hook. It's an acquired feel, but this method often gets the biggest trout in the heart of hopper season.

228 PLAY IN THE NIGHT LIGHT

Lights that shine on the water night after night—whether they're on docks or bridges—are gamefish magnets. That's because light attracts small baitfish in salt- and freshwater, and predators know these hot spots provide easy meals after sundown. Here are the rules for playing in the glow.

SHADOW LURKING Gamefish won't often expose themselves in the brightest parts of the lit area. Focus your casts on the shadow lines where light meets dark. This is where predators sit in ambush.

USE THE FLOW If tidal or river current is also a factor in the lit area, assume any gamefish hanging around will be on the downcurrent side of the light. In this scenario, cast flies into the light, and let them drift or swim naturally into the darkness.

PULL INTO THE BLACK When you hook up, go heavy on rod pressure to try to keep the fish in the dark water. A struggling fish that runs around in the well-lit water is likely to spook the bait and alert other gamefish that something isn't right, reducing your chances of a second connection.

229 GET DOWN— SLIGHTLY

Chances are some of the trout you see rising in spring are feeding on emergers just below the surface—mayflies, caddis, or midges that remain an inch or two underwater while beginning to emerge as adults. That's where your emerger fly should be. To suspend your fly just below the surface, apply some floatant to your entire leader except for the last 3 or 4 inches of tippet. Most of the leader will float, keeping your fly just barely underwater and right where the trout expect to see it.

230 ENTICE A CARNIVORE

When you fish big articulated streamer flies, like the Sex Dungeon or the Stinky Mayo, you're not just fishing for any trout. You want "the one," the biggest brown in the river. Here are three ways to get him.

CREEP AND SWEEP Giant streamers shine when it comes to big browns holding tight to the bank. Situate yourself 25 to 35 feet off the far bank, and cast directly cross-stream tight to the edge. As soon as the fly lands, make a couple of big upstream mends. Once the fly has had time to sink, make three or four hard, fast strips. This gets the fly working upstream tight to the far bank for a few beats before it swings out into the main flow—and it's often right at this turn that a big trout smokes the bug. If not, take 10 steps downstream and repeat the process until you've worked the whole bank.

SPLASH AND DASH In pocket water, you're apt to be dropping the fly behind a boulder only 10 feet away, and the zone may be so short that you don't have time to strip. So just pull 15 feet or so of line off the reel and make short roll casts to the sweet spots. As soon as your fly smacks down, give it a few fast twitches with your rod arm. You're trying to mimic prey that is suddenly in the wrong place at the wrong time and wants to get out fast. This doesn't allow the trout much time to inspect your streamer, and the big profile makes for an easier target. A big brown may attack the second it hears the fly slap the water.

LOW AND SLOW Several newer patterns, like Rich Strolis's Head Banger, are designed to mimic sculpins, and you need to fish these flies right on the bottom. "I cast mine directly upstream with a floating line," says Strolis, noting that a sink tip adds too much weight. "Once it gets to the bottom, I'll strip it slowly, just enough to keep contact with the fly as it moves downstream." Working a streamer downcurrent on the bottom takes some getting used to, but Strolis says the trick lies in setting the hook on any stop or tick during the retrieve. Even big trout will just suck it up off the bottom, which can feel very subtle.

231 HOOK BIG BRONZE ON TINY BUGS

When most anglers think of smallmouth bass flies, big Hair Bugs, heavy Clouser Minnows, and weighted crayfish imitations usually come to mind. By and large, these patterns will always be top choices for smallmouths, but during the middle to late summer, these fish have a tendency to key in on tiny emerging insects, and when that happens, the entire game changes.

Instead of being able to use fairly heavy tippets drawing explosive strikes, smallies—even the big ones—will sip bugs with the subtlety of a little native trout. Problem is, when you hook a smallie on the light tippet needed to cast the flies that match hatching caddis and

mayflies, the bass is going to fight just as hard as it would if you stuck that fly on a streamer. Quite often, this results in snapped tippet and heartache.

The trick to besting a bronzeback after it has slurped a micro-bug is playing it incredibly lightly. I keep my reel's drag as loose as possible, and if the fish wants to run, I just let it go. Keep gentle side pressure on the fish to help steer it, but be careful not to jerk the rod or force the fish to turn. It may take much longer than normal to put the bass in the net, but going easy and taking your time is the best way to ensure that the tiny hook stays planted in the fish's lip, and that a forceful run doesn't straighten the hook right out.

ESSENTIAL FLIES: SNEAKY PETE

TYPE: Popper
PRIMARY SPECIES: Bass, Pike, Muskies, Panfish

Take a standard foam popper, flip the head around so the tapered end becomes the mouth, and you've got a Sneaky Pete. It's a simple change, but it creates a huge difference in how the fly behaves. Whereas the cupped mouth of a regular popper creates water resistance when pulled to produce its signature bloop, a Sneaky Pete glides and dances across the surface with much less noise. When stripped hard, it will even dive under the surface a few inches and pop back up. This subtler topwater presentation often draws more strikes than a loud, thrashing popper, especially if the water is low or very clear.

232 SUCCEED WITH ATTRACTOR DRY FLIES

There is a subtle difference between fishing with dry flies when you are matching a hatch, and fishing with attractor dry flies. With imitations of natural bugs, you want to mix in with the real things, and pinpoint your casts in very precise spots where the hatch is concentrated. With attractors, you want to space things out a bit, not only to cover more water, but also to keep the fish guessing.

Think of it this way. When you swing streamers through a steelhead or salmon run, it's very important to cover water. You cast, mend, let the fly sweep, and then step downstream. If you move too slowly, you telegraph to the fish that your fly is coming. Ideally, you want your fly to just "appear" and the fish to suddenly see it and decide to eat it. If the fish sees something slowly sweeping back and forth in the near distance, chugging its way downstream, that's not going to work.

The same applies when prospecting with attractor dry flies. You want the bug to "appear" in a pocket. So space those casts out more, and don't bang the same spot over and over with an attractor pattern. Even a foot or two can make a world of difference.

233 GO LOW AND SLOW

This is the ideal nymph-fishing technique for fishing deep, soft water near shore. Focus on current seams close to the bank.

Any length rod is fine. Use either a floating line with a 7½-foot 2X or 3X leader with a split shot, or a sink tip with a 3- to 4-foot 2X or 3X leader. The latter setup allows longer, strike-provoking pauses.

Tie on a Tunghead Woolly Bugger here. Flip the rig upstream and retrieve in 3-inch strips just faster than the current.

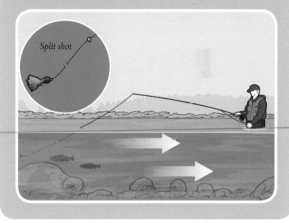

234 LOSE WEIGHT, NOT FLIES

High-sticking allows you to drift a nymph along the bottom through fast water 4 or more feet deep. Begin with a 9- to 10-foot, 6-weight rod, a floating line, and a 9-foot 2X or 3X leader, with nontoxic split shot pinched on a dropper from the Blood knot so as not to weaken the tippet. Tie on a Beadhead Stonefly nymph; fast water is the natural's habitat. The Beadhead Caddis Larva is a good backup, as it offers a solid silhouette that drops down quickly.

Sling the rig across and upstream; casting directly upstream can cause the shot to wedge between rocks. Gather line and raise the rod as the drift approaches— the shot should just tick the rocks—then lower the rod as it passes you. Keep the line barely taut, with the fly line above the water's surface if possible. When the line

stops, set the hook. If it's a snag, the weights should pull off, stopping you from breaking the entire rig.

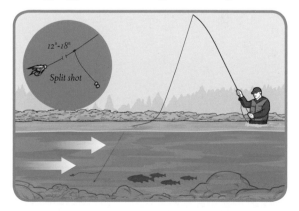

235 BOX IN A REDFISH

What makes redfish so appealing to anglers is not only that they grow big and fight something fierce, but they can also be sight-fished. Reds of all sizes thrive in shallow flats, backcountry creeks, and marshes, making them prime targets for fly casters. However, while these fish have keen senses of smell and hearing, their eyesight is fairly poor. That means your cast has to be perfect or a cruising red might cruise right by. When you lock your sights on a red, draw an imaginary 2-foot box around its head. You want your fly to land right inside that box. Too far left, right, in front, or behind, and you're liable to miss, but if the offering is in the box, the fish is going to see the movement and strike. And though some guides might beg to differ, if your cast is spot-on, what's tied to your line really makes little difference, because a red won't want anything that looks like forage to escape.

236 FORM A FLOAT PLAN

A float tube or kick boat offers great advantages when fishing lakes or ponds. The secret is to plan well and drift stealthily into place.

SCOUTING REPORT Watch the water and plan your path. Rings on the water mean that fish are eating bugs off the surface. Scout closely for fish clues, such as wakes and rise rings (A). Wakes indicate baitfish chases. Identify weedlines, areas with submerged structure, shallow flats, and foam lines that suggest wind-drive current breaks. Cast your fly where the fish is headed—not where you saw it cruising or eating off the surface (B). Here are where the fish you can't see are often holding.

SNEAK ATTACK Figure out which way the wind is blowing. Let the breeze push you along as you fish (C). You'll want to kick into place upwind from your target zone. But don't kick into casting positions; your feet should make long, slow, quiet beats to brake your momentum, and set you up for accurate shots as you drift along.

BRIGHT IDEA Consider the angle of the sun as you plan your approach.

Surface eaters are reluctant to point and feed straight into brightness, unless strong wind-driven currents are flowing from that direction. Be mindful of the shadows you create.

THINK AHEAD When in flat water, presentation really matters. Lead your fish and let the fly sit—more than you would in moving water. When you hook up, gently kick away from the feeding alley to move the fight to open water.

SILENT RETREAT After you've drifted through a zone, if you want to hit it again, gently kick out into open water well away from your target fish before going into "motor mode." As a rule, if you're kicking like a swimmer within 30 feet of the fish you're chasing, you're ruining your odds. And do all of your digging for tackle and rerigging at a safe distance from the fish zone.

237 SCORE WHILE YOU WAIT

Before the hatch, trout will be on the hunt for nymphs, which become increasingly active prior to the main event. If adults are on the water and the trout seem indifferent, they may be keying on nymphs as well. Drifting stonefly nymphs (which are poor swimmers) and twitching mayfly nymphs is the smartest way to score pre-hatch trout. Pond anglers waiting for a Hexagenia hatch often bring a rod rigged with a Maple Syrup nymph and strip it on a sink tip until the festivities begin.

238 BEAT THE TUNA DEATH CIRCLE

Catching any member of the tuna family—from bluefins to false albacore—on a fly rod is one of the sport's ultimate challenges. Not only is casting accurately to these fast-moving targets a test, but fighting them will give your arms a workout. What tuna species have in common is a propensity for diving, forcing you to work them back up from the depths during the final part of the battle. A big mistake anglers make during this stage is lifting the rod too high as they try to raise the fish. Tunas swim in what's known as a "death circle" as they tire, making loops around and around under the boat. The higher you lift the rod, the wider a circle it allows them to make, and the longer it will take to get them to the surface. Instead, make short six-inch pumps between taking up line on the reel. This will help keep the circle diameter tight, and force the fish up much faster.

239 FISH THE HIGHS AND LOWS

Fishing two flies lets you turn fluctuating water levels into an opportunity. The following fly rigs allow you to adjust your presentation to any level. With both rigs, strikes often come at the end of the drift. Drag causes the dropper to rise, simulating a hatching nymph and triggering a strike. When you're about to give up on the drift, be ready.

A HIGH-WATER RIG In more torrential waters, attach an indicator at the butt of a 3X leader. Tie a size 8 weighted Stonefly nymph to the end of the leader. On the hook bend, tie 2 feet of 4X tippet with an improved clinch knot. At the terminal end, tie on a size 12 Hare's Ear or a size 12 Sparkle Pupa. The leader should be 1 to 2 feet longer than the water is deep, depending on the current speed. Then, cast upstream and present the nymphs drag-free. When a fish takes, the indicator will twitch, hitch, or sometimes just stop.

B LOW-WATER RIG After water levels fall, begin with a size 12 Elk Hair Caddis. On the hook bend, tie 3 feet of 4X or 5X tippet with an improved clinch knot. At the other end, tie on a size 14 Caddis Pupa or a size 16 or 18 Beadhead Pheasant Tail. Cast upstream and present the flies drag-free. Set the hook if the dry fly twitches or disappears.

240 LEARN THE CZECH TRICK

Czech nymphing is all about feel. The basic premise is to use a short tippet system and tie a heavy fly at the end (the "point" fly) and a second fly on a dropper tag roughly 2 feet above that. You sneak up close to the trout and make short, pinpoint casts, and then lead the line downstream with the rod tip pointed at the water's surface. The point fly ticks and bounces along the bottom. When a trout strikes, you feel resistance—and set the hook. In many ways, Czech nymphing mirrors popular bass techniques such as tube jigging and using a drop-shot rig.

THE RIG Choose a long, supple rod, such as a Sage ESN 10-foot 3-weight. At the end of a weight-forward floating line, attach a 12- to 18-inch "sighter," which serves as a strike indicator (A). The sighter is made from a section of bright Dacron backing or red mono. Tie 5 feet of 5X tippet from the sighter to the dropper fly, which hangs on an 8-inch dropper, then 20 more inches of 5X tippet to the point fly. Your leader should be about 8 feet long.

THE FLIES There are many woven, weighted (often beadhead) fly patterns designed specially for Czech nymphing, but your favorite local patterns will do the job just fine. Try a size 8 Pat's Rubber Legs Stonefly as the point fly and a size 14 Graphic Caddis as the dropper.

HOW IT WORKS The key here is to move the rod tip with—or even slightly lead—the line as it moves downstream (B). The tippet should form what's known as a Lazy J (C) as the flies drift in the current. Because you are so close to the fish, you'll have to crouch down and flip short casts. It takes practice to hone the rhythm of leading flies so they sink to the bottom but don't get stuck.

ESSENTIAL FLIES: INCHWORM

TYPE: Terrestrial
PRIMARY SPECIES: Trout, Panfish

Lovingly referred to by many as "the green weenie," what an Inchworm fly lacks in complexity, it makes up for in fish-catching power. In spring and early summer, these tiny green wrigglers are dangling from trees almost everywhere in the U.S., and when they fall or get blown into the water, they have seconds to live. So potent is the inchworm in certain parts of the country that some flyfishermen consider the use of these flies cheating. You can dress an inchworm to make it float, but it's deadlier when drifted just subsurface under overhanging limbs. You can also slowly strip it back, imparting a little wiggle—a presentation fresh stocker trout can't resist.

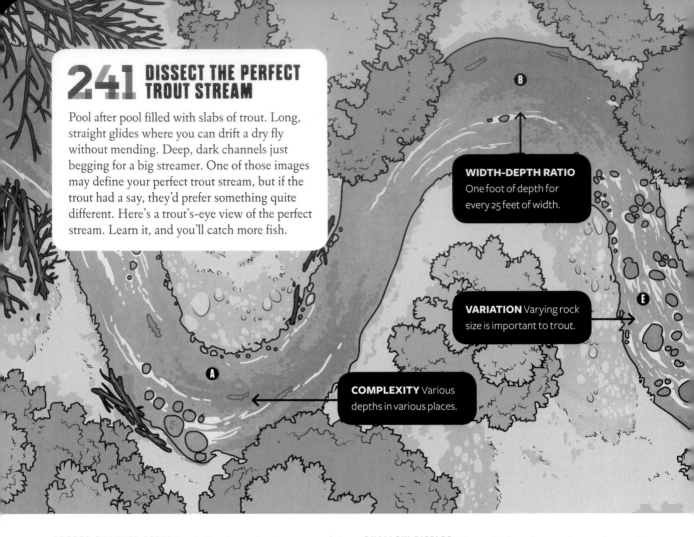

241 DISSECT THE PERFECT TROUT STREAM

Pool after pool filled with slabs of trout. Long, straight glides where you can drift a dry fly without mending. Deep, dark channels just begging for a big streamer. One of those images may define your perfect trout stream, but if the trout had a say, they'd prefer something quite different. Here's a trout's-eye view of the perfect stream. Learn it, and you'll catch more fish.

WIDTH-DEPTH RATIO One foot of depth for every 25 feet of width.

VARIATION Varying rock size is important to trout.

COMPLEXITY Various depths in various places.

PROPER CHANNEL FORM Look for channels that curve and vary in shape—deep on one side, and then on the other, and then in the middle (A). That generates the most biological productivity. Another vital channel-form characteristic is width-to-depth ratio. For every foot of depth, a stream should be no more than 25 feet wide (B). Narrow, deep channels lack photosynthesis necessary for insects to forage; wide, shallow streams get warm.

EVEN RIFFLE-POOL RATIO A perfect stream will have one pool for every section of riffle. Pools provide resting places, protection from aerial predation, refuge from high water, and overwintering habitat. Riffles provide food. If there are too many pools, the water slows and you get a lot of deposits which clog microhabitat. Too many riffles, and you have a sediment-starved area that eats away at itself. When you see a riffle followed by a primary pool and then a secondary pool, the secondary pool will offer a lot less. If there was a neon sign saying "Place Fly Here," it would be in that primary pool (C).

SHALLOW RIFFLES The majority of macroinvertebrates in a trout stream depend on algae for forage. But in riffles much deeper than 12 inches, ultraviolet light can't penetrate to fuel the photosynthesis that algae need to grow, robbing all those bugs of their primary food source. A stream with few riffles can't support a host of macroinvertebrates, and thus can't support many trout. Fish downstream from large swaths of riffles less than a foot deep (D). Deep pools adjacent to riffles in the 6- to 12-inch range are ideal. Riffle communities are food conveyor belts.

DIVERSE MACROINVERTEBRATES The perfect stream contains healthy populations from all five main macroinvertebrate orders—caddisflies, mayflies, stoneflies, riffle beetles, and midges. The complete suite of stream bugs ensures forage in the drift at all times. Use a small seine in riffles to examine what's in the drift. Only 10 percent of a trout's feeding habits are on the surface; the forage is on the bottom and in the drift.

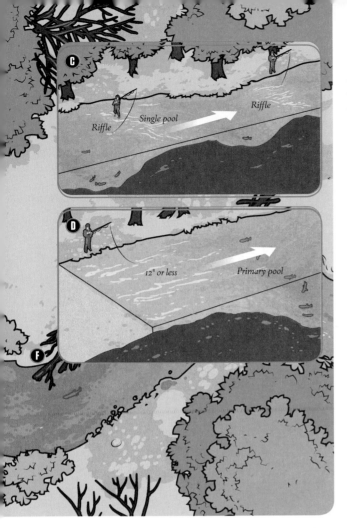

FISH DIVERSITY A lot of flyfishermen whack whitefish and suckers to eliminate competition for trout. But those fish provide ecological services to the stream, such as keeping algal growth in check and releasing nutrients to the system when they die. More important, as trout get older and larger, they prey increasingly on small fish. Juvenile whitefish, suckers, and other species are ideal nuggets of forage for big trout. Every little whitefish that gets munched is a juvenile trout that doesn't. In streams that have a diversity of species, approach pools and deep holding water with streamers to provoke large trout that might not be actively feeding but won't pass up an easy bundle of calories.

STREAM STABILITY Streams want to change, and a dynamic system is usually the most productive one. Still, a diverse, healthy, native community of riparian plants provides bank stability and contributes steady amounts of organic matter to feed macroinvertebrates. Chemical stability is important, too: a well-buffered pH that's close to neutral, a stream that doesn't get high acidity during

spring runoff. Headwater fisheries, for instance, often deceive. You see nice streams cascading over boulders, with great holes and riffles, but that water is flowing through highly tannic and acidic soils and over granite rocks, which means few macroinvertebrates or fish.

Instead, target stretches of stream flowing over sedimentary rock. Avoid banks where sod is falling into the water and channels that change drastically from year to year.

THE RIGHT TEMPERATURE RANGE Trout thrive in water temperatures ranging from 52 to 66 degrees. Brook trout prefer the lower end of that range; browns like the upper. When a stream's temperature remains relatively constant, fishing can be productive all year long. It may seem obvious that carrying a stream thermometer can help you determine optimum fishing conditions. But measure in more than one place. In many streams, temperatures vary from stretch to stretch.

VARIED SUBSTRATE Unevenly sized substrate is perfect for the bottom of a trout stream (E). Gravel enables successful spawning, stones create microhabitat for fry, midsize riffle cobbles increase bug productivity, and big boulders create holding areas for trout. If you find yourself wading on long stretches of fine gravel bottom or uniform cobbles, move along until you find a good assortment of rock sizes.

STRUCTURAL DIVERSITY Along with a wide variety of structural habitat in the streambed, there should also be woody debris falling in from the banks (F). Old predatory trout seek out broad boulders; smaller rocks shelter the smaller trout the big fish exile from the prime lies. Too much wood leads to silt and sedimentation. Not enough, however, and you lose the organic particulate matter that many bug species need to survive.

Look for diverse features along the bank and in the water — snags, sweepers, boulders, undercut banks, overhanging grass. Structure creates varying flow patterns depending on what's around it; the same boulder in two different places will create two different currents.

FISHABLE HABITAT Fishing behind structure, drifting through deeper pools, fishing a dry fly through a run, fishing riffle tailouts, accessing casting lanes, wading safely—these are all important factors in desirability. Wade, hike, or cross the stream so you can get into good casting positions. The more accurately you can cast into tight cover that other anglers can't reach, the better your catch rate will be.

242 TRY A FRENCH TWIST

The French have won six world flyfishing championships because they are masters of catching trout in the trickiest, most technically demanding conditions—clear, shallow water and slow-moving currents. When you find trout in these situations, and they are not eating dry flies, the best option is to throw light nymphs on a long, fine leader. The French have devised a rig for this scenario that works better than anything else. Their twist (literally) is a coiled, two-toned sighter, sometimes called a Curly Q. The sighter is actually at the end of a standard leader, making the total leader system very long—16 feet or more—which can make casting tricky. A deliberately long stroke and wide loop is necessary here.

THE RIG The same style of rod used in Czech nymphing works (see item 240) but you'll need to chop 5 feet from the tip of the weight-forward floating line. From the line, connect an Umpqua 9-foot Power taper leader (butt section at least 2X), followed by the Curly Q. The length of 5X tippet that extends from the Curly Q should be 2.5 times the water depth. The dropper fly hangs on an 8-inch tag, and the point fly is tied to 5X or 6X tippet 18 to 20 inches below the dropper.

THE FLIES Fish a size 16 (or smaller) tungsten Zebra Midge as the point and a size 18 Soft Hackle Pheasant Tail as the dropper. Egan's Frenchie is also a great all-around nymph for this tactic.

WHERE IT WORKS This rig is ideal in spring creeks and clear tailwaters—water where you know the fish are eating nymphs and emergers, but you think the splash made by a dry fly in a dry-dropper rig would spook most of your targets.

HOW IT WORKS Cast upstream and let the flies drift over your target fish (1). As the flies come downstream, lift the tip of the rod to gather the slack in the line (2). When a trout takes either fly, the Curly Q will stretch ever so slightly. Set the hook. The long leader makes the cast tricky, requiring a deliberately open loop. After the Curly Q starts to lose its memory, you can refreeze it into form, but once it kinks like a telephone cord, it is *ruiné . . . finis*!

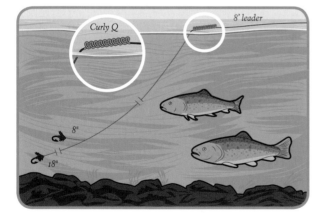

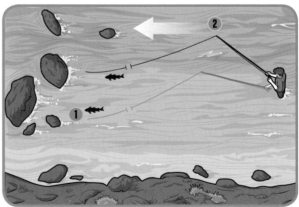

243 MAKE A CURLY Q

To make your own Curly Q for French-style nymphing, take a 24-inch section of Siman Bi-Colored Indicator and wrap it around a 3-inch finishing nail. Boil the line-wrapped nail for 5 minutes, and then freeze it for 24 hours. Make perfection loops on both ends. *Voilà!*

244 INCH A MIDGE IN STILL WATER

Abundant in virtually all lakes, chironomids, or midges, are one of the first insects to get up and moving in the spring. Neither strong nor fast swimmers, midge pupae make an easy target, even for lethargic trout in cold water. This long-leader technique matches up well to the pace of both predator and prey.

Rig a floating line with a 14- to 20-foot leader (the deeper the water, the longer the leader). Tie on a midge pupa pattern such as a Thread Midge, Disco Midge, or small beadhead midge. Add a yarn indicator 4 to 8 feet from the fly, and a few tiny shot a foot above the fly. Cast in water 4 to 10 feet deep, and count down for 20 seconds. Begin an agonizingly slow retrieve; just barely inch the fly along. Takes are subtle. If the tip of the line so much as pauses or twitches, give it the gas. If you snag or pull weeds, reduce the count on the next cast; if not, increase it. It's a painstaking but deadly technique.

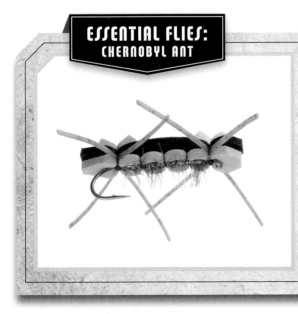

14- to 20-foot leader

Fly line

Split shot

245 MASTER THE SLOW RETRIEVE

When you're fishing the bottom of a pool, this method will increase the odds of success. Use a Tunghead Woolly Bugger with a sink tip or sinking line and a 3- to 4-foot 2X leader. Use any length rod. Shake extra line out of the rod tip so that the retrieve does not lift the fly off the bottom. To present the fly naturally across the floor of the pool, where the current is slow, don't add any split shot. In areas of slow or no drift, retrieve slowly via a hand twist once the fly reaches the bottom: Pinch the line between the index finger and thumb; roll the third, fourth, and fifth fingers ahead over the line; and repeat. The fly will crawl along at about 2 inches per twist. Strike at any resistance. Fan-cast the pool so you cover all potential holding areas.

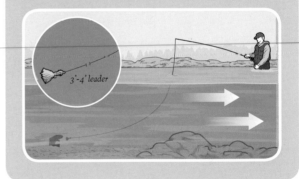

3'-4' leader

ESSENTIAL FLIES: CHERNOBYL ANT

TYPE: Terrestrial
PRIMARY SPECIES: Trout, Bass

The joke behind this fly's name is that it looks like an ant that fell into some radioactive goo. In truth, the Chernobyl Ant doesn't mimic anything in particular, though it does make an excellent grasshopper and salmonfly imitation. This bug, however, is less about matching an insect and more about making a splash. Its flat design causes it to slap down hard on the water, and the sound is like a dinner bell ringing for monster trout. A favorite among western flycasters in summer, the Chernobyl accounts for some of the biggest trout taken on the surface. Even during major hatches of smaller bugs, splat this fly in the right feeding lane and be prepared for an explosion—not a sip.

246 JOIN THE 20-20 CLUB

Catching a 20-inch trout on a size 20 fly is just about every fly angler's personal goal. This season, you're going to do it—and the midsummer Trico hatch that happens across the country offers the perfect opportunity.

The key to making a big trout eat a tiny dry fly lies in knowing when to drop your bug in the money zone.

Wait, and watch the fish feed. Focus on the trout closest to the bank, where the biggest ones love to sip. Usually, you'll discern a feeding pattern: fish eats left . . . fish eats right . . . pauses, then resumes. Sync up with the trout's rhythm, false cast, and, just before the fish should rise, drop that fly in front of him.

247 DRIFT AN IRISH DIBBLER

Using subsurface patterns for trout on lakes can be deadly, as fourth-generation Irish ghillie (guide) Neil O'Shea explains. The traditional "dibbling" technique involves showing the fish bright, attractor wet flies with a slow, methodical retrieve. This is a way of hooking curious, rather than hungry or aggressive, fish.

Dibbling is best suited for flat water—preferably in light wind-driven chop on overcast days when the trout are not dialed in on a specific hatch. Work it over structure, off points, in current lines, and especially near weed mats.

THE RIG Use a 9- or 10-foot 5- to 7-weight rod with a weight-forward floating line—or a sink tip for targeting trout 8 feet or deeper. From the fly line, tie a 6-foot 3X leader. This rig presents three flies—two are on dropper tags. From the leader, tie a 3-foot section of 6- to 8-pound mono tippet, leaving a 6-inch dropper tag. Attach another 3-foot section of tippet, again leaving a 6-inch dropper tag. The leader length is roughly 12 feet.

THE DROPPER CONNECTION You'll make the dropper tag from the "parent" strand of the leader (the section that extends from the fly line). Attach additional tippet, making sure that the parent tag end is 6 to 8 inches long. Clip the opposite tippet end close to the knot. To make the dropper stand out, wrap the strand once above the knot, and pull the end through the loop you form.

THE FLIES Stick with proven patterns: a size 10 Damselfly Nymph, followed by a size 14 Prince Nymph, and a size 16 Mercer's Poxyback PMD as the point pattern.

HOW TO DO IT Make a long, delicate cast and let the flies sink for a few seconds before starting your retrieve. You will want to make long, slow, consistent strips (1). Near the end of the strips, lift your rod tip toward the sky so the flies "emerge" to the surface (2). The trout, which will likely have trailed the rig out of curiosity, will grab a bug—just as it reaches the surface—often within short reach of the boat or shoreline.

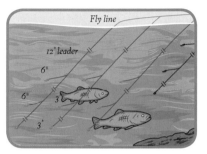

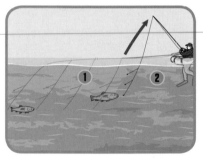

248 PICK A PICKEREL FIGHT

Flyfishing for muskies and pike has become very trendy recently, but anglers tend to overlook chain pickerel, the smallest member of the *Esox* family. These fish are found in more bodies of water than pike and muskies, and while a 10-pounder would be a giant, they exhibit the same behaviors as their bigger cousins. Best of all, you can use a light fly outfit and small streamers to catch them. They're great practice for their large relatives, as they ambush and track flies the same way—not to mention that their strikes are just as explosive. Cast an unweighted bunny strip streamer to log jams, lily pad edges, and potholes in shallow expanses of bogs, lakes, and ponds, and there's a good chance you'll find a pickerel eager to charge down your fly.

249 GAUGE UP FOR TARPON

Though tarpon are massive fish with massive mouths, small flies often score more silver kings than large patterns. These fish love small baitfish and marine worms, which presents a challenge for flyfishermen. Because tarpon have rock-hard mouths, a hook that's too flimsy won't penetrate the jaw, and if it does, it will likely bend out. The key to matching forage size and staying glued is not bigger hooks (which will make the fly look unnatural) but heavy-gauge hooks. Not only will small, heavy-gauge fly hooks stay pinned, but their extra weight will help flies fall faster, and getting a fly eye-level with a tarpon is critical for drawing more strikes.

250

USE OUTSIZE FLIES FOR OUTSIZE TROUT

Big trout lurking under cutbanks are cannibals that prey on smaller fish, and the best way to entice a strike is to offer them prey—an outsize fly that forces them to strike out of a territorial impulse. The wrinkle? Heavy tippets will spook these fish. You'll need to downsize to 4X tippet, quite a trick with a big fly.

The traditional advice is to use black in turbid water and light colors in clear water, but I've always had better results with darker flies—black, green, and brown. Woolly Buggers and Zonkers are effective, as are steelhead patterns. Use the largest fly you can handle on a light tippet.

As to tackle, a 9-foot, 5- to 6-weight rod works well. Load it with a weight-forward floating line—and, because you have the chance to hook up with a big trout, don't go with a cheap reel that has an indifferent drag.

Casting outsize flies on light tippets can feel like you're casting a bowling ball. The key is to mend the line immediately in order to reduce drag, and then make sure there's no excess slack as you drift the fly through the lie. When you get it right, hold on—the strike will be like a jolt from Jove. You won't be able to manhandle this fish, either, so get it on the reel and let the drag do the work. Since many cutbank fish head for an obstacle, expect a lot of breakoffs. It's just part of the game.

STEP 1 Make sure to throw an upstream loop to eliminate drag.

STEP 2 Continue mending line, but keep slack to a minimum so you don't lose contact.

STEP 3 Though the strike will be hard, set the hook softly.

251 SLAP THE HAMSTER

Smacking the fly on the water and causing a little commotion can get a trout's attention. The big, bushy fur-strip streamers often used for this inspired a fishing partner to dub the technique "slapping the hamster." Heavy patterns tied with lead eyes or coneheads work, but lightly weighted or even unweighted flies are often just as effective and much easier to cast, especially when you're casting all day. Be ready for the hit one or two strips after the slap.

252 FLYCAST TO A FICKLE POND TROUT

When conditions are perfect, one of trout fishing's signature endeavors is fly casting to brook trout rising to surface flies in a remote pond. But when the stars haven't lined up over the North Woods, Maine guide Kevin Tracewski has learned how to fool pond brookies. Here's the routine.

Anchor your boat fore and aft as far away from a structure, such as a suspended weedbed, as you can cast. Using a heavy sinking line, make a long cast. Strip out 10 feet of line and shake it through the tip-top guide. Drop your rod tip to the water—and do nothing. The line will sink to form an underwater L, dropping straight from your rod tip and then extending out toward the structure. Count down 10 seconds before starting a retrieve. The belly of the line will pull the fly through the sweet spot until it is nearly to the boat. If you don't get a hit, cast again and count down to 15 seconds before retrieving, and then count down to 20 and 25 on the next casts.

253 SECTION OFF YOUR STEELHEAD

Great Lakes tributaries from Wisconsin to New York experience tremendous runs of steelhead in the fall. These fish follow spawning salmon upriver, and then remain in the tributaries through the winter. Their feeding habits, however, vary by time of year and location in the tributary. Here's a quick look at what to cast where.

LOW RIVER	MIDDLE RIVER	HEADWATERS
The closer you are to the lake, the fresher the steelhead you're going to encounter. From early fall to early winter, steelhead in the bottom end of a tributary are the most aggressive, and as they haven't fully acclimated to eating salmon eggs just yet, these fish are the more likely to swipe at streamers imitating the baitfish they were feeding on in the lake. Once the water temp dips below 45 degrees, switch to egg flies in this stretch.	Steelhead in the middle range of tributary are usually keyed in to salmon eggs and flesh flies, although transient fish that are moving even further upriver will still take a shot at a streamer. Focus efforts in this zone on long-term holding water, such as eddies, slack pockets, and deep holes below riffles. Drift egg flies below indicators in slower runs, and tight-line bounce the bottom without a strike indicator in water with more flow.	Fish that winter in the high end of rivers will have been pressured by anglers during their journey. These fish are among the most finicky, especially once natural salmon eggs are no longer their main diet; they become more acclimated to eating natural river forage. Large stonefly-imitating nymphs and San Juan worms can draw more strikes late in the season than egg patterns. Downsize leaders and tippets.
LOW-END FLIES White Zonker, large yarn eggs	**MID-RIVER FLIES** Estaz eggs, medium yarn eggs	**HEADWATER FLIES** Large Prince nymphs, large black stonefly nymphs.

254 GO DOWNTOWN FOR BIG BROWNS

When big brown trout in streams swing at sizable streamers, they often miss. For a second chance, don't cast back at the boil. Instead, cast 5 or 10 yards downstream of where you saw the fish. Why? The trout is going to look for the lost bit of forage where the flow would naturally carry it. Think about it: Dazed prey that's under attack isn't going to swim against the current.

ESSENTIAL FLIES: FLESH FLY

TYPE: WET FLY
PRIMARY SPECIES: Salmon, Steelhead, Trout

Flesh flies might look like streamers, but these tan, pink, and orange pastel-tone chunks of marabou and rabbit fur aren't designed to imitate baitfish. They're supposed to look like chunks of salmon flesh. Therefore, dead drifting them with as little movement as possible is the go-to presentation. The various colors match meat in different stages of decay, and in any river where spawned-out salmon are dying and rotting, flesh flies are a must. Not only will living salmon eat the flesh of their own kind, carnivorous steelhead, rainbow trout, and brown trout in the same waters binge on the stuff.

255 RESIST THE URGE TO RECAST

We all have heard that "if at first you don't succeed, try try again." But that seldom pays off on the river—at least not in the context of firing off repeat casts within seconds at the same fish.

Let's say you make a nice presentation. The fly floats perfectly into the run. You see a fish move on the fly, maybe splash at it, but no dice—you've been refused. So what do most of us instinctively do at that point? We pick up the line and fire that fly right back at the fish. And when it doesn't eat the bug, we cast again, and again, and again.

I have seldom, if ever, seen an angler successfully beat a trout into submission. And yet, the most common presentation mistake I see— among newbies and seasoned anglers alike—is that repeat shot. Sometimes presentation has as much to do with timing as it has to do with placement, especially after a refusal.

To fight off the instinct to shoot again right away, try some tricks to slow things down. Recite the alphabet in your head, forward and backward, a few times. Sing a song. Go sit on the bank, take off your boots, and put them on again. Whatever it takes to create a pause of a few minutes.

Here's what I like to do whenever I see a fish that's interested enough to check out my bug, but unwilling to commit: I go to the bank, sit down, and change the fly. Remember, the fish refused for a reason. I figure that my pattern is pretty good, just not good enough. So I size down. Switch a size 14 dry fly to a size 16 or 18. Wait a few minutes, and go again. Give that a try, and you'll catch more on the second cast. I promise.

256 GIVE IT A REST

To understand how trout choose new locations in a stream, researchers tagged cutthroats and observed them responding to changes in the placement of artificial feeders and to the manipulation of stream flows. The transient trout always moved to the spots with the highest velocity, even if the water was shallow. The biggest fish would take the best spots and hold their position even when finished feeding—apparently so they wouldn't have to fight off challengers when the munchies returned.

So identify the quickest water in any given stretch, and be ready for a hit on the first cast. No response? Large trout don't miss much, and they'll have seen and passed on your offering (and probably those of other anglers, too). Rest the pool for a few minutes and drop down in size with a San Juan worm or a smaller streamer. It might just be the one changeup the trout haven't seen.

257 SPOT AND STALK WILD TROUT

The secret to catching big, wild trout often comes down to identifying a single target, and then dissecting the fish's feeding rhythm. Fishing as focused as this requires patience and stealth. Here's how the mix works.

Ⓐ STALK INTO POSITION On broken pocket water, the rippled surface allows a closer approach. Cast from straight downstream to keep your line out of mixed currents, but beware of small "lookout" trout that will spook into the head of the pool. If you're fishing slick pools or spring creeks, don't push too close. Anglers casting wet flies should post across and slightly upstream of the fish for drifts that keep the leader, tippet, and any split shot outside the trout's view.

Ⓑ MATCH THE RHYTHM Does your trout rise to every morsel of food, or every few seconds, or for every few drifting insects? Does the fish prefer prey off to one side, or directly in front of its snout? Does it slurp up a mouthful of spinners, or sip in singles? Pay attention to these patterns and factor them into your presentation.

Ⓒ CALCULATE THE ANGLES When fishing at close range, count down the cast, and put the fly 2 feet in front of the fish. A tighter cast will spook it. A longer cast could require too much mending to stay drift-free. If you bomb a sloppy cast or miss a strike, resist the temptation to fire out a quick cast to cover up your mistake. Give the fish time to settle back into a feeding rhythm.

258 SCOUT A TROUT RUN

The trick to catching more trout has less to do with perfect fly patterns and long casts, and more to do with knowing where the fish are and what they're up to. The only way to figure that stuff out is to sit down and watch. There are tricks to more effective run scouting. Here are five.

GET HIGH Seek a vantage point above the river, such as high on a bank, even up in a tree. Once you get to the high ground, you want to keep a low profile, and not go jumping around so you will stand out and spook fish.

PUT THE SUN BEHIND YOU This trick dramatically increases the risk you'll cast shadows on the run, and shadows spook fish.

FIND GOOD GLASSES Finding one pair of all-around polarized glasses that you trust is better than toting around 10 different tints for 10 situations.

DON'T BE FOOLED Learn to identify what is *not* a fish. The sooner you eliminate the distractions, the easier it is to tell what the real fish are doing.

BE SURE When you see a fish rise, don't barrel right down into the river. Watch it happen again. Then slowly slink into position. The more you understand why fish are behaving a certain way, the easier it is to catch them. You can't capture the "why" with one glance.

259 SIT STILL

I've done some of my best trout fishing while sitting down. That's because I try to watch a piece of water for a while before actually starting to fish. By the time I've sat for 10 to 20 minutes, many of the trout I may have spooked on approach have resumed their normal activity. I might see their sides flashing golden down deep as they feed on bottom-dwelling insects. Or I might eventually see some gentle rises, noting carefully exactly where they happened. So by the time I get around to fishing, I have a pretty good handle on what the trout are doing at any particular place and time. The trout, in essence, have taught me how to fish.

There's a lot to be said for sitting still.

260 UNCOVER DARK SECRETS

When the sun is shining, that big, mean brown trout you've always wanted to hook is likely under a big, mean undercut bank. Good luck yanking it out. Once the sun goes down, however, that fish is going to move. Tagging studies have shown that large browns in rivers will travel up to 4 miles per night. Tweak a streamer to fool them.

USE A BULLET In the dark, you just want to lay out your fly and start your swing without worrying about mending or sink time. If you slide a $\frac{1}{16}$-ounce tungsten bullet weight on your tippet and peg it at the nose of your streamer, there's no question; it's in the zone on the entire pass.

FLY BY NIGHT Though any dark, bushy sculpin streamer is a good choice for a nighttime quest, the new Schultzy's S3 Sculpin is packed with different furs and feathers that will increase flutter in the water, beef up the silhouette, and make more noise on the retrieve.

RING A BELL When it's time to rig up, slide a 6mm red glass bead ahead of the tungsten bullet weight. Tungsten is a hard metal, so when you strip, the bead will click against the weight and amp up the sound element.

ESSENTIAL FLIES: BANGER

TYPE: Popper
PRIMARY SPECIES: Saltwater, Pike, Muskies

Anglers often use this pattern, since it's larger than other poppers, for striped bass, redfish, bluefish, and bluefin tuna. Stouter rods are needed for firing this fly given that it's so air resistant—but the effort is worth it, because its loud pops and the long bubble trail it leaves in its wake have the ability to call ocean-roaming gamefish in from a distance. It will do an equally fine job with freshwater heavyweights like pike and muskies.

261 CATCH A BREEDER

Breeders are an early-season trophy, large female trout, typically 2 to 5 years old, weighing 3 to 8 pounds, that hatcheries no longer use for egg production. They have served their time, if you will, so the hatcheries release them into streams and rivers, where they become trophies worthy of some serious parking-lot bragging rights.

While you don't have to be an elite angler to score a big breeder, a bit more planning and strategy than you'd put into a normal stocker hunt can increase your chances of hooking into one. Here are some insider hints from Jim Sciascia of the New Jersey Division of Fish and Wildlife, a devoted fly fisherman.

SCOUT IT OUT Visit the river you plan to fish before the season opens to figure out exactly where hatcheries stock fish. Look for easy access points close to roads, where stocking trucks and workers can reach the water. "Breeders don't want to fight heavy current," says Sciascia, "so if there's no deeper, slower water right at the stock point, you already know any breeders released there will have moved up- or downstream."

LOOK CLOSELY You might then assume any breeders in an area will flock to the closest big, deep hole, but they are often content to sit in a small depression or eddy big enough for only one fish. That's why you shouldn't pass up any pockets or short runs that have just a bit more depth than the main river.

DON'T DUMB DOWN "Breeders are often released during the first round of stocking prior to the opener," notes Sciascia. "That gives them more time to acclimate to the river." By the early season, breeders will have had plenty of opportunity to feed on natural forage. That's not to say they'll never eat something that looks like a hatchery pellet, but don't expect a breeder to grab the first salmon egg fly that drifts past.

262 SIGHT-FISH SPOOKY TROUT

Anglers often forget that a trout's eyes are on the sides of its head and not pointing forward, like human eyes. Thus, the fish's peripheral vision is far more effective than ours is. And yet, when we see a fish laid up or sipping in calm, clear water, we always try to sneak in for that cast from the side. When we get just about close enough...poof, the fish darts away and we wonder why.

When you're fishing in calm water, the most important tip is to keep a low profile. The No. 1 factor that spooks fish is shadows, which allows them detect motion in their vicinity. I cast from my knees—and from the bank—whenever I can.

I keep my boots as dry as possible, because even the smallest wakes and waves will put feeding trout down. I try to position my body so that I'm not casting my shadow (and the shadow of my fly rod) directly over the target. Never false cast directly over the target fish.

When you present the fly from downstream, you want the leader to cover the fish, but not the fly line. Imagine your target is about 2 feet above the water surface, so don't drive a cast that splashes down with force—you want it to gently fall from the sky. The calmer the water, the more you must pause between casts. If the current is moving at a snail's pace—maybe 2 feet per second—I might wait two minutes between casts. And I will probably change the dry-fly pattern if I am reasonably sure the fish saw my bug the first time around.

There are many moving parts to sight fishing in calm, clear water. And there's nothing more frustrating than blowing up as all those thoughts pass through your mind at the moment of truth. So before you even cast, take a minute to pause. Watch the fish. Calmly make your plan, and then visualize it all coming together.

Just be sure to do that behind the fish's field of vision, preferably while sitting down or kneeling.

263 FIND A TROUT IN THE DARK

Bushy streamers that splash and gurgle are the typical nighttime flies of choice for trout fishermen. For something different, when you have the best pools to yourself on a quiet night, try catching big browns and rainbows on dry flies. At night, color doesn't mean anything. It's all about silhouette. Tie on a slightly larger size than you'd use during the day, with a white wing for visibility. Anchor in a slow pool just before dark. Once your eyes adjust, you'll be able to pick out rises.

This is unlike a daytime approach. Don't try to lead a trout at night. When you see a dimple on the surface, cast right to that spot. To make it easier, target fish rising 30 feet away or less, and fish on nights with plenty of moonlight. You might not know exactly where your fly is, but the goal is to land as close to the rise as possible. In the dark, it's difficult to determine whether you overshot or undershot the fish. If you lay out and see the dimple again, just lift the rod instead of setting. Either the fish will be on or it won't. If it's not, you just lay out again to the same spot.

264

PLOT A LATE-NIGHT STALK

Nighttime fly casters should find a run with no large rocks, few overhanging limbs, moderate depth, and uniform current that'll allow them to back cast and swing a streamer with little obstruction. If the run also has a slight depth increase along the bank, even better. Position yourself 6 to 8 feet off the bank and stay put.

A Cast down and across at a 45-degree angle, gradually increasing distance to cover more water.

B Don't strip or twitch. Keep the tip high and line tight, letting the current sweep the fly across the run. This swing will draw a reaction strike from fish cruising through the main current.

C When the line straightens out along the bank, violently strip the fly upcurrent. Any trout that is already holding along the bank, or moving in to use the softer bank current to make its way upstream, will deliver a crushing blow.

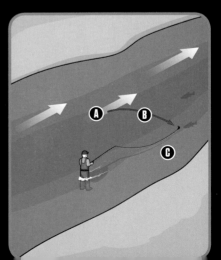

265 DON'T GET GLUED TO THE BOTTOM

While carp are primarily bottom feeders, it's a misconception that they only eat food sitting on the lake- or streambed. In reality, a carp's mouth is designed to both suck food off the bottom and eat food at eye level in the middle of the water column. Some carp anglers only look for fish grubbing in the mud, but moving fish can actually be easier to catch. Always carry a few small strike indicators on carp quests so you can suspend your flies in front of roving fish. If carp are on the move, they can easily swim right over a berry fly lying on the bottom since they're not keyed in to grubbing at the moment, but a berry hanging right in front of their noses is much harder for them to miss.

266 CAST INTO THE GRASS

Here's a common scenario: You see a trout rising on the other side of the river. Between you and the fish, the current is strong and deep, and the fish seems to have its nose practically glued to a point of land that's sticking into the river.

Oftentimes, even if you make a reach cast (in effect, mending your line in the air), or immediately mend your line after the fly hits the water, the current is still going to grab your fly line, create serious drag, and rip your fly out of the strike zone. Do that a couple times, and, after the fish sees the fly behaving strangely, it's not going to take long for it to swim off. Game over.

Instead, you can use the shoreline to your advantage, assuming the bank vegetation is short grass and moss. Last time I was in this situation, I intentionally shot a cast that stuck my fly on the grass on the point. I aimed at the grass, and hung it up on purpose. With the fly in place, I made a huge mend of the line. Just as I finished the mend, I gave the line a quick jerk. The fly popped free, and I got about a one-second drag-free drift. That proved to be enough, as the fish indeed ate the fly.

This move works better when the sun hitting the side of the fish. If the sun is behind you, the shadows you create will usually ruin the approach. Also, understand that there's a reason this fish is rising so tight to the bank... it's probably eating terrestrials. So this trick works best with ants, beetles, and hoppers.

In any case, it's a long shot, a last resort. But heck, if you're like me and you snag the opposite bank often anyway, why not use that to your advantage?

Do remember that you are better off casting a few inches too long than you are to cast short. And sometimes, the perfect shot that lands in the water is actually too short.

267 SAY SÍ TO THE SPANISH COMBO

Spanish nymphing uses a heavy weighted fly on the point and leads the flies through a run with the rod tip pointed at the water. The leader in this technique is very long—15 feet or more—and, rather than feel, you are relying on a sighter that is relatively far from the end of the fly line to tell you when to set the hook. Spanish flyfishermen created this nymphing technique to help them catch the notoriously elusive *fario* (brown trout) in Pyrenees mountain streams. They found that the extra-long leader is the key to avoid spooking the fish.

This technique is especially effective in the tailouts of runs, in slow, deep water, and in spots where you have to reach across fast or deep water into a seam where rainbows and browns are holding.

THE RIG The ideal rod for Spanish nymphing is a 10- to 12-foot 3-, 4-, or 5-weight. Use a weight-forward floating line and a 3X to 5X 9-foot tapered leader. Spanish anglers tie a two-tone sighter to the end of the leader. Make the sighter by splicing two 12-inch sections of Sunline Siglon F mono together with Uni knots or a Blood knot. Below the sighter, attach 4 feet of 5X tippet and leave an 8-inch dropper tag while adding 2 more feet of 5X for your point fly.

THE FLIES Try a size 10 Conehead Woolly Bugger on the point and suspend a size 18 Flashback JuJu Baetis on the dropper.

HOW IT WORKS Cast at a 45-degree angle upstream (1), and then follow the flies with the tip of the rod as they move downstream. With such a long leader, back casting is almost impossible, so lift the rod high at the end of the drift, letting the current load the rod (2), and lob the line back into the target zone. Keep your eyes focused on the sighter and set the hook on the slightest stagger, change of direction, or pause. The key to effective Spanish nymphing is choosing a point fly that is heavy enough to tick the bottom but not so heavy as to hang up on every drift. For that reason, anglers switch point patterns often—usually run by run.

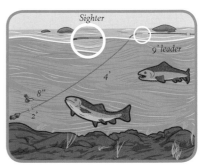

ESSENTIAL FLIES: FOAM ANT

TYPE: Terrestrial
PRIMARY SPECIES: Trout, Panfish

Ants are everywhere. Bug spray in your kitchen kills some, while others experience death by trout when they fall into rivers and streams. Don't expect to tie on an ant pattern often, but do expect to run into a situation somewhere down the line when ants are the money bugs. It often happens in late summer or early fall when streams are low and hatches minimal. Maybe the fish aren't interested in blasting a big beetle or hopper, but they'll gladly rise to gently sip an ant. A good ant pattern sits low in the water like a real drowned ant. Whenever possible, buy ants with brightly colored posts or dots on their abdomens, as all-black ants can be tricky to see on the surface, especially in low light or shade.

268 LET THE BIRDS COME TO YOU

Chasing flocks of birds diving over bait that striped bass, bluefish, or false albacore are pushing up really gets the adrenaline flowing, but sometimes fishing a "bird blitz" is a real challenge. If the school stays put, you can sit on one feeding frenzy for hours, but quite often, these gamefish species pop up, feed quickly, and dive back down. If that's happening, don't try to run to each newly formed flock of diving terns and gulls. Pay attention to the general direction in which they're are moving and run a good distance ahead of them. You're better off waiting for the fish to spring up in casting range than trying to move in tight and fast, spooking them with engine noise. Though it takes some willpower not to gun it to each pod of busting bait, sitting still can get you more fish in the long run.

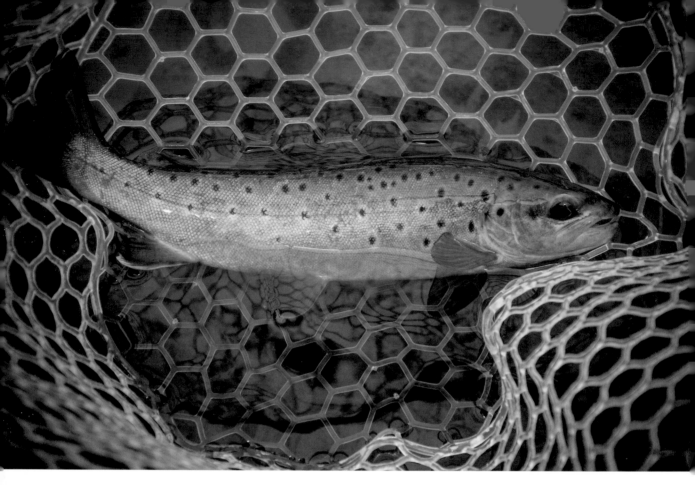

269 DO THE WET FLY SHUFFLE

Swinging wet flies can be a pleasantly old-school way to fish between hatches, but when caddis and mayfly nymphs are milling around in preparation for an impending hatch, you're missing out if you don't give this method a shot.

PICK YOUR FLIES My standard fly for this kind of fishing is a lightly weighted size 14 Hare's Ear soft hackle. This is one of any number of flies that don't mimic any insect in particular but, by virtue of being a medium-size drab shape with legs, could pass for just about anything. These and other simple wet flies and soft hackles—the Brown Hackle Peacock, the Muskrat, the Starling and Herl, the March Brown, and the Leadwing Coachman—have been catching fish for centuries.

STEP, SWING, STEP Start with an across and slightly downstream cast, followed by an upstream mend. Let the current swing the fly down and across the river on a tight line until it hangs straight below you, and allow it to

hover for maybe 30 seconds. Then take two steps downstream and do it again. Fish the water in roughly 3-foot-wide stripes, so virtually every trout in the river sees your fly. This way, you can cover vast amounts and types of water, stopping only to go around logjams, beaver dams, and other fishermen. The method works especially well in faster or more broken water. Fish don't see the fly coming—it's just there and gone in a second or two, and they'll often grab it out of pure instinct.

GO HEAVY These strikes can be vicious, so you should tie on a slightly heavier tippet than you'd use for dry flies or nymphs, anywhere from 3X to 5X, depending on how murky the water is. Since I'm usually anticipating a hatch, I will generally attach that tippet to the end of a standard dry-fly leader nail-knotted to a floating line. If you want to start imitating surface bugs, just add some finer-diameter tippet and tie on a dry fly. If you want to get deeper, tie on a weighted version of the wet fly or nip on a single small split shot.

270 CATCH A KILLER

Large browns don't behave like small ones. Monster trout fishing is a game unto itself, and many of the standard rules of trout fishing—like perform perfect "dead drifts" with spot-on mayfly patterns, or twirling lures through pocket water—do not apply. Here's how to adjust your tactics to suit the prey.

SMALL BROWNS	VS.	TROPHY BROWNS
Juvenile brown trout eat frequently and typically focus on invertebrates such as worms, aquatic nymphs, and smaller insects.	FORAGE	Large brown trout eat fewer, larger meals. They key on calorie-rich foods such as baitfish, mice, leeches, and nightcrawlers.
Smaller brown trout are in tune with natural fly presentations.	ATTRACTION	Motion on a fly often piques the interest of a large brown.
Smaller browns feed at various times, including midday.	FEEDING TIMES	Large browns feed in low light, often in the dead of night.
Small browns cling to "ideal" trout habitat where insects are plentiful. You will occasionally find these fish sharing the riffles with rainbow trout.	LOCATION	Large browns can survive and thrive in sections of the river with warmer water and fewer insects.
Small fish will forgive almost any casting faux pas. If you see a fish strike at your lure or fly, miss, and then come back, assume it's small.	SPOOKINESS	You won't fool a monster brown trout if you make a bad cast. Large browns will shut down entirely if they sense any of your movements.
River currents influence smaller brown trout as the battle ensues.	FIGHTING ABILITY	Current doesn't affect a hooked big brown very much, and it will head for cover.

271 START A FRENZY

Having a slow day on the trout or smallmouth river? Here's a dirty trick. Post up 30 to 40 feet above a likely run and start quietly and gently flipping rocks. The sediment underneath will flush down into the run, bringing aquatic insects with it. Wait 30 seconds after flipping, and then swing a nymph into the sweet spot.

272 DON'T WASTE THE GOOD STUFF

Saltwater species such as bluefish, jacks, and Spanish mackerel can be downright gluttonous eaters, so when you get yourself within in fly range of a pile of them, you can literally hook up on every cast. These fish will attack bait so ravenously, they pay little or no attention to what they're eating; if it moves, they chomp it. Because of this behavior, and because these fish have teeth, it's not worth casting expensive or painstakingly tied flies into the fray. I keep a handful of simple, sparse patterns handy specifically for encounters with these species. A hook dressed with a single clump of white bucktail is usually enough to draw a strike. I've even put strips of an old white T-shirt on hooks with super glue, and they wiggled just enough that monster bluefish trashed them. At the end of the day, your arms will be sore, and you won't be crying about losing $50 worth of flies.

273 ICE OUT A TROUT

In early spring, when ice is melting, ponds and small lakes are a great place to fish. And, with oxygen confined to the surface layer, most prey is in depths of less than 10 feet. Trout are rarely far away. When so many trout are within easy casting range, the most effective tactic may be to fish from the bank. Start early, because the period during and just after ice-out can be absolutely hot. It's essential that you cast in the right places. This illustration shows you where.

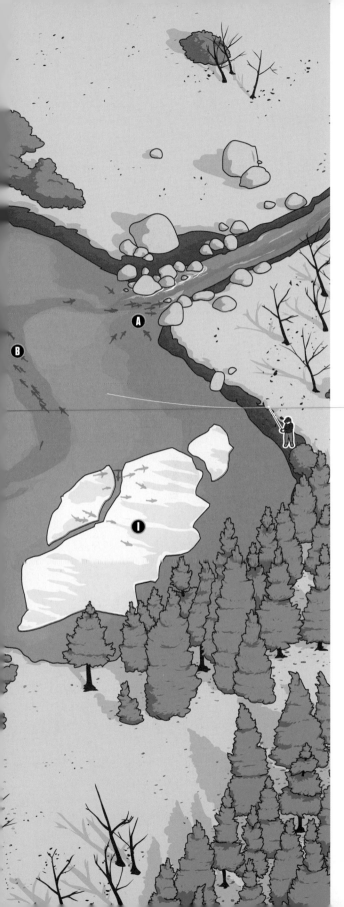

A **INLETS** Rainbows, cutthroats, and baitfish stage off inlet mouths prior to spring spawning. Hit these spots with streamers or egg patterns. Fish may also drop back into outlets, so try there as well.

B **CREEK CHANNELS** In stream-fed, man-made, still waters, look for the old creek channel cutting through a shallow flat. This deeper water offers trout a natural ambush point. Hang a nymph in the middle, or ply the edges with Woolly Buggers, Muddlers, and Zonkers.

C **WEEDBEDS** Aquatic vegetation dies back in winter, depriving insects of cover and exposing them to trout. Work dragonfly nymph patterns, scuds, or sow bugs just above the dead weeds.

D **DEADFALLS AND TIMBER** Downed wood is a magnet for insects, bait, and trout. Fish it with a white Zonker or Woolly Bugger on floating line. This is also an excellent place to slow-crawl a midge or leeches pattern below a strike indicator.

E **SHALLOW BAYS** You can prospect skinny-water bays—the first areas to warm up in the early spring—with leech, weighted nymph, or Water-Boatman patterns. Look for cruising trout and cast well ahead of their line of travel.

F **MUDFLATS** Bloodworms, bright-red midge larvae, inhabit the soft, silty bottoms on the flats. Rig a small San Juan Worm or red Copper John under an indicator, and ride it just off the bottom.

G **NEW GROWTH** From shore, cast out in open water beyond the new growth of reeds, tules, or rushes. Use a strip-and-pause retrieve with a floating line and a damselfly nymph, Gold Ribbed Hare's Ear, Prince nymph, or leech pattern.

H **BARS AND MIDWATER SHOALS** Work these structures by casting from shallow water to deeper. Rig a floating line with a 12- to 14-foot leader. Count a fairly large (No. 8 to 12) midge larva or pupa pattern down to the bottom, and then use a glacially slow retrieve.

I **ICE SHEETS** As the thaw begins, look for open water between ice sheets and the shoreline, particularly in shallows adjacent to deep water. Cast baitfish imitations onto the ice shelf, and then drag them into the water and begin their retrieve.

274 GET A SPRING ON STREAMERS

One of my favorite ways to fish for trout is by throwing streamers, especially in the early spring. Whether you're in a boat or walking down a bank, there's nothing quite like that big tug you get when fishing those bigger baitfish and leech patterns for trout. Just don't fish it like you would in the middle of the summer or early fall. Here are eight tips that are sure to help improve your fishing with the big bugs next spring.

SLOW DOWN When water temps are colder from snowmelt and early season rain, fish are less aggressive and won't move nearly as far to eat. Vary your retrieve speed and go much slower than you would later in the season.

GET DEEP Use a sinking-tip type of line or very heavy bugs. This makes casting a bit harder, but will pay dividends in terms of getting your fly in front of more fish that are willing to take a look.

In the spring, you need to get your bugs down in the water and fishing upstream is a great way to do this. Throw a quartering cast upstream. Right after your fly hits the water, give it a huge mend, which will let your bug get down to where the fish are. This will work with a sinking or floating line.

DEAD-DRIFT BUGS I know, this runs counter to what you do most of the time with a streamer, but it can have a deadly effect in the spring when fish are less apt to chase down a baitfish. Try dead-drifting with a sinking line and a natural-material leech pattern.

GO NATURAL Use or tie streamers that utilize natural material such as rabbit, marabou, or peacock. Typically, when you're fishing these flies at a slower pace, this type of material gives a more realistic action and just moves more at slower speeds. Use streamers with heavy weight like tungsten heads or lead-core bodies.

LINE UP Try fishing two streamers in-line with each other. I like to use something I call salt and pepper—one darker and one lighter. This gives you two advantages: One, you can use the lighter color to verify the location of your streamer and attract fish. Two, you're giving the fish an option—if the fish doesn't like the darker pattern, it might go for the lighter, and vice versa.

USE FLUOROCARBON Fluorocarbon is more abrasion-resistant and it sinks a bit better when you're throwing these types of flies. Many times in the spring, the water is dirty and sizing up is a good option as you lose less fish and fewer expensive flies when underwater snags are more difficult to see. Yes, you might forgo a few fish because of the larger tippet, but if a fish is committed to a streamer, it's probably going to bite it anyway.

KNOT IT RIGHT Use a nonslip Mono loop knot (see item 275) to tie on your streamer. It's a stronger knot and gives the fly a much more natural presentation when fished at slower speeds. It basically allows the fly to move more freely than if you tied it on with a simple clinch knot.

275 TIE A NONSLIP MONO LOOP

To get a lifelike presentation, you want your flies to be able to swivel, and not sit too close to the knot. Try this knot.

STEP 1 Make an overhand knot in the line about 10 inches from the end.

STEP 2 Pass the tag end through the hook eye and back through the loop of the overhand knot.

STEP 3 Wrap the tag end around the standing part five or six times.

STEP 4 Bring the tag end back through the overhand knot, entering from same side it exited from before.

STEP 5 Moisten the knot, and then pull slowly on the tag end to cinch the wraps loosely together.

STEP 6 Pull the loop and the standing line in opposite directions to seat the knot, and then trim the tag end.

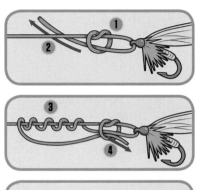

276 LIFT AND LOWER

Never overlook shallow runs between deep runs in early spring for big trout, especially when water levels come up and increase the depth of those shallow runs a bit. In these spots, try an in-line double fly rig, consisting of a Finnish Raccoon Shad streamer 18 inches below a size 10 Beadhead Pheasant Tail nymph. Cast upstream and allow the flies to sink, but don't strip the line. Instead, gently lift the rod, and then lower it to give the flies an enticing crippled action. Trout often strike just as the flies begin to rise in the water, or immediately after they begin to fall.

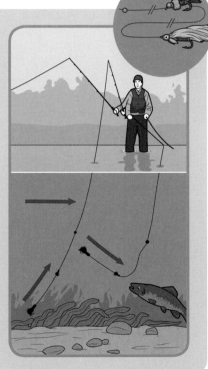

277 SWIM A SPRING

If you're fishing still water in the early spring, use a thermometer to locate springs, which can produce water 10 degrees warmer than the rest of the lake. Submerged weedbeds are thicker in these areas, and trout will cruise them while feeding on aquatic insects. On a 20-foot leader, tie a light soft hackle on a dropper on top, a lightly weighted nymph on a dropper in the center, and a heavy nymph at the end. Make an open loop cast parallel to the weedbed (1) and swim the flies toward you very slowly (2). Gently twitching the rod tip from side to side, pausing and repeating, will trigger strikes from following fish.

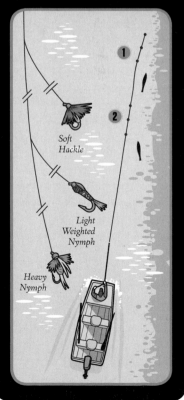

Soft Hackle

Light Weighted Nymph

Heavy Nymph

278 FISH AN EARLY-SPRING POND

Some of the spring's best flyfishing can be had on those faster-warming ponds and small lakes while rivers are still a little chilly. Fishing flat water can be technically challenging, but it doesn't have to be, because you can use a wide variety of techniques to score. Here are my favorite approaches.

STAY DRY You may see a mayfly or two in early spring, but the predominant still-water bugs now are midges, which can provide fabulous dry-fly action. Just don't make the mistake of trying to match these tiny insects exactly with microscopic patterns. Midges like to cluster, and trout love a "meatball" of bug protein. Try a Griffith's Gnat or a Grizzly Cluster in size 18 or 20. Use a light tippet, starting with 5X or 6X and working smaller if necessary. You don't want to make much surface commotion, so cast only to rising fish. Imagine your target 3 feet above the surface: Cast to that spot, and your fly will fall gently onto the water.

GET DOWN Trout eat most of their food below the surface, especially at this time of year. That's why nymphing can be deadly. Focus your attention on vegetation and

structure, such as timber, rocks, and inlets. Don't mess with heavy weights or strike indicators. Cast to your target, let the fly sink, and then work the fly with deliberate 2-inch strips. A size 16 soft-hackle Pheasant Tail or Hare's Ear usually gets the job done. Sometimes, for whatever reason, spring trout prefer darker flies. I always carry a few black AP nymphs in my box.

GO UGLY You don't expect aggression from early-spring trout, but the right streamer fly can bring it out in them. Try a tandem rig. Start with a large, white attention-getter, like a size 10 Zonker. Tie a foot or so of tippet onto its shank and add a trailing "stinger" fly, like a size 12 black Woolly Bugger. With a floating line, your leader should be at least 6 feet long. With a sink tip, you can go down to just a few feet. Be sure to let the flies sink after your cast. Then mix up your retrieves until you figure out what works. Trout often turn on the bright fly, then inhale the dark one. You can set the hook when you see a flash or boil and experience some heart-pounding spring action. Or you can wait to actually feel the strike and have all that excitement . . . plus land some thumper trout.

279 SHARPEN YOUR SKILLS WITH 'GILLS

Most anglers, myself included, have the bluegill to thank for getting them hooked on the sport. Unfortunately, many fishermen forget about this introductory species after they graduate from dipping worms and bits of bread on the shore of the local park pond. That's a mistake, because not only are bluegills a blast on a light fly rod, but catching them hones your casting and presentation skills, which can help you catch more of the "grown-up" species you've come to enjoy.

While bluegills will eat almost any wet or dry fly, there is arguably no more enjoyable way to catch them than with small foam poppers. These flies are fairly air resistant, forcing you to cast with a bit more oomph. It's a great excuse to practice your double haul, which will come in handy the next time you need to deliver a bigger popper to bass, or a bulky streamer to trout.

As bluegills are typically plentiful and aggressive, they provide the perfect opportunity to experiment with retrieve styles that may help you figure out how to work a fly for another species later. Keep changing up from letting the popper lie still, to imparting a subtle pop every few seconds, to rapidly chugging it across the surface. Take note of the conditions and which retrieval method scores the most fish. I guarantee you'll be able to use that information later for a more substantial target.

280 CUT SOME SLACK

In high, murky spring water, big trout often hole up in slow-spiraling eddies. Contrary to popular belief, these fish will frequently face downstream in the slack water created behind boulders and other structure. Nymphs that incorporate some purple material or that have flash backs are highly visible to trout in dirty water. Fish them on a 10-foot leader, starting at the outside edge of the eddy (1) and gradually working toward its center (2). Cast upstream and allow the fly to dead-drift. Take up the slack as the fly drifts back toward you (3), watching the line for subtle bumps and stops.

Flash Back Nymph

281 FIND HOT TAIL (RACE) ACTION

Mid- to late summer is the perfect time to fish for trout in the tailraces below dams, as those waters stay much cooler. Here's what you need to know.

KNOW HIGHS AND LOWS The rate of flow from the upstream dam (A) dictates the location of tailrace trout. When the river is low, trout will locate in riffles, behind rocks, and around submerged moss beds. They range further from cover when foraging for minnows and crayfish, and they will rise to take insects off the surface. When the water rises, trout gravitate to the bank and stick tighter to larger pieces of cover, rushing out to grab passing prey.

BE LEVELHEADED In low water, tailrace trout can be spooky; approach them by wading from downstream (B), which makes for fewer ripples and less bottom disturbance. Once you're within a long cast of your target, make several presentations from different angles before going to another spot.

PAY SOME DAM ATTENTION The trout bite can be fast, happening within the first 30 minutes after the dam's turbines kick in. The rising water sweeps insects off the bank and churns up bottom debris, exposing sow bugs and crayfish, so be ready when they start generating bites. (Note: A tailrace can rise high very quickly. Return to shore on the shallow side for safety.) High water can mean a shot at a trophy trout for anglers drifting in a small boat (C). Make accurate casts upstream, and retrieve the fly past your target so it barely ticks the log or rock they're hiding behind.

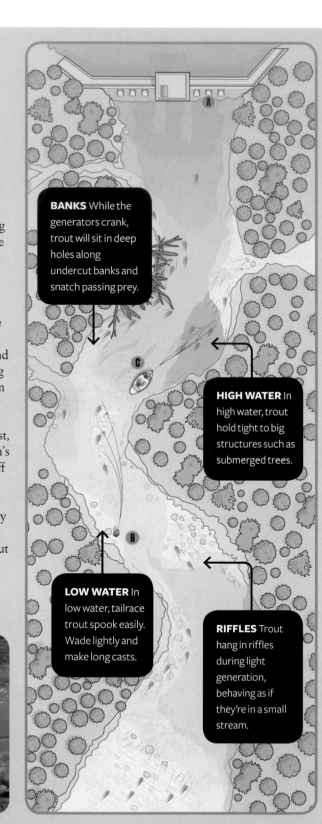

BANKS While the generators crank, trout will sit in deep holes along undercut banks and snatch passing prey.

HIGH WATER In high water, trout hold tight to big structures such as submerged trees.

LOW WATER In low water, tailrace trout spook easily. Wade lightly and make long casts.

RIFFLES Trout hang in riffles during light generation, behaving as if they're in a small stream.

282 PLAY TO A PEACOCK'S AGGRESSIVE SIDE

Whether you're casting to peacock bass in South Florida or on the Amazon, understanding how to capitalize on the aggressive nature of these fish will put more of them in the net. Success largely boils down to making them mad. These three tricks will help you get on a peacock's bad side.

GO GAUDY Peacock bass are reaction strikers. If they can see it, they'll hit it. With that in mind, make sure you give these fish something to see. Streamers in chartreuse, pink, orange, and bright yellow often draw more strikes than more muted tans, olives, and browns. Don't worry so much about matching natural forage as about giving them a target they just want to kill.

MOVE WATER Leave your little trout and smallmouth streamers at home. For peacocks, you want flies with lots of flutter and vibration. Patterns tied with long rabbit-strip tails and lots of marabou feathers work well. Wide-profile hair heads put out a lot of vibration, as well as giving flies a nice side-to-side twitching action on the strip.

KEEP WORKING If a peacock bass misses your streamer, the worst thing you can do is stop moving it. In fact, after a miss, you want to strip even faster than you were before. You need to make the fish think its food is getting away, and an uptick in speed after a miss tends to aggravate peacocks.

ESSENTIAL FLIES: ADULT DAMSEL

TYPE: Dry Fly
PRIMARY SPECIES: Bass, Trout

The damselfly—which is essentially a dragonfly—isn't something you'll tie on often, but it's good to have one on hand for those magic days when all the bass in the river or pond get cued up to eating these speedy buzzers. It usually happens on lazy summer afternoons when the air is extra-thick with dragonflies that keep swooping and dipping and occasionally landing on the surface. Bass and trout are highly adept at tracking these bugs in the air, and then smashing them when they touch down. A dead-drifted damsel will catch fish, but since these bugs are always on the move, try skittering the fly across the water to mimic a dragonfly that's injured and just can't seem to take off.

283 KNOW WHEN TO BE DULL

In general, anglers tend to tie or buy streamer flies with some flash. Without question, that flash can be a major advantage in high or stained water. However, when the water is very low and crystal clear, too much flash can actually be a detriment, spooking far more than it attracts them. This is especially true of wild trout in small spring creeks. Though not as appealing to the angler's eye, always carry a few simple streamers in muted colors that have no flash material. Sometimes these boring patterns do a better job of imitating natural forage in clear water and can spell the difference between a fish eating and bolting.

284 HAVE A BROWN-TROUT SUMMER

In summer months, brown trout in rivers and streams are opportunistic ambush feeders, both day and night. Knowing which part of the river they head to during the four distinct feeding periods is the key to selecting the best fly for that time period.

A MORNING

FISH MINNOW IMITATIONS NEAR STRUCTURES In the cool early hours, insect activity is less intense, and a predatory brown trout is more likely to hunt small baitfish such as sculpins and creek chubs. Confine your casts to deep pools with structure like sunken tree stumps and weeds. Use a sink-tip line and cut your leader down to 5 feet with a 2X tippet. Tie on a streamer, such as a white Zonker or a Muddler Minnow, and add a BB-size split shot above it. Cast so your streamer will pass close to cover.

GEAR TIP A white Zonker fly is most effective in clear streams, where its light color and slowly oscillating tail matches natural baits

B MIDDAY

FLOAT A TERRESTRIAL On summer afternoons when there isn't a prolific hatch going off, brown trout hunt for terrestrial insects. Focus on grassy undercut banks and overhanging logjams where these bugs drop in the water. Fish upstream to keep your shadow outside the fish's field of view, and use attractor patterns that replicate ants, beetles, and grasshoppers. (You can also suspend a nymph from a tippet tied to the dry.) If you'd rather score aggressive reaction strikes, strip a jointed leech pattern.

GEAR TIP The Amy's Ant pattern is a hot "prospecting" fly, and it's buoyant enough to float a suspended Copper John nymph effectively.

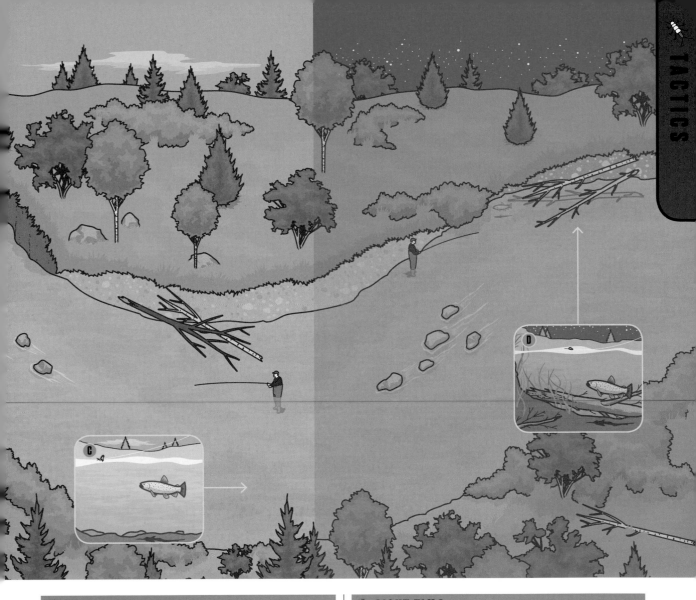

C EVENING

FISH A BIG-BUG HATCH Summer afternoons and evenings will trigger hatches of the largest mayfly species, such as brown, gray, and green drakes, as well as various stonefly species. This can lead to terrific fishing, because big browns simply cannot resist sipping bugs from the surface. Crouch on the bank and survey a run for rises. Big fish will be glued to the banks or in deep pools with current seams. Fish upstream and time your casts to fit the natural feeding rhythm of the fish.

GEAR TIP A Green Drake Cripple pattern, which appears more helpless as it rides low in the water, will get eaten when other patterns won't.

D NIGHT TIME

THROW A MEATY MOUSE Look for a deep, slow-moving run adjacent to a grassy bank or brushpile. Position yourself on the bank, or as tight to it as your back cast will allow, and then cast a surface-riding mouse fly toward the middle of the current. Strip it back with erratic twitches. The fly should look like a panicked mouse swimming for the safety of shore. When a brown hammers the fly in the dark, your fishing world will change forever.

GEAR TIP With any mouse pattern, aesthetics matter less than action. Hair bodies that displace water and tails that wiggle catch fish.

285
BAIT AND SWITCH A BILL

Flyfishing for sailfish and marlin isn't really flyfishing in the traditional sense. You're not casting to fish that are swimming past, but rather using hookless lures and baits on conventional rods to tease them into fly range behind a moving boat. Still, for those that want to say they've hooked a billfish on the long rod, it definitely involves some skill. While you might be lobbing flies more than casting, timing is everything, and this game is usually a two- or three-person operation.

As soon as a billfish pops up behind the teaser, you need to get your fly in the water. Don't wait until the mate or a second angler starts reeling in that teaser to draw the fish closer. The idea is to get your fly in front of the fish's face just as the teaser it's following is quickly ripped away. If you're slightly late with your delivery, the fish may dive without ever seeing the fly.

ESSENTIAL FLIES: FLASHTAIL WHISTLER

TYPE: Streamer
PRIMARY SPECIES: Pike, Muskie, Saltwater

Although largely associated with flyfishing for toothy pike and muskies, the Whistler is equally at home in the saltwater angler's fly box. The fly is fairly sparse, yet long, making it easy to cast while still simulating a big baitfish with a wide profile. It delicately flutters with just the slightest strip, and its pulsing, flashy tail grabs the attention of aggressive visual feeders. Large bead-chain eyes (which whistle during the cast) allow it to get below the surface quickly, but they won't cause the fly to sink too fast. This is important when targeting pike hanging over thick weedbeds or barracuda cruising the edges of grass flats. Bring a lot, as the fish will chew them to bits.

286 DROP AND WIGGLE FOR BRONZEBACKS

When you're choosing streamers for smallmouth bass, the amount of wiggle a fly has on the fall is important. While these fish are happy to track and blast a streamer you're steadily stripping through the water column, sometimes what triggers more strikes is the action when you stop the fly and allow it to drop. Opt for a jointed streamer with marabou feathers or rabbit strips in the tail, and a heavily weighted head. When you pause, the head will cause the fly to fall fast as the tail flutters away. A tick in the fly line lets you know a bass has grabbed the pattern on the descent.

287 STAY WITH YOUR TROUT RIVER THIS FALL

On moderate-gradient rivers, fall brings fewer hatches and smaller flies, mainly bluewing olives and midges. These insects demand small imitations, from size 18 down into the 20s, as far as you have the courage and eyesight to go. You need 6X to 8X tippet, and, on glassy water with spooky fish, leaders of 12 feet or longer.

Trout won't move far for tiny bugs; you must place your fly precisely in the feeding lane, a move best made with a downstream presentation. Station yourself upstream and slightly to one side of a rising fish. Aim for a spot about 3 feet above the fish and 3 feet beyond the far side of its feeding lane. Stop the rod tip high on the forward delivery so the line falls to the water with some slack. Immediately lift the rod and skate the fly toward you, directly into the drift line. Then drop the rod tip to give slack and float your fly right down the pipe.

Always check out bankside eddies, especially after a hatch. Drifting insects collect in these backwaters and circulate on conveyer-belt currents past hungry mouths—like those you see in some sushi bars. Look closely for trout snouts dimpling the surface film. Don't let the tiny rise forms fool you.

Migrating browns stick primarily to the main channel, intermittently holding up in the slow current behind submerged obstructions and along deeper or rocky banks. Holding fish are scattered, and you can search the most water by casting upstream, parallel to the shoreline. Drop a streamer a few inches from the bank. Alternate dead-drifting the fly with twitches imparted by the rod tip, stripping in line to control the slack. Make five or six casts and move on. Browns in the channel are traveling upriver; the best way to intercept them is by working downstream, swinging a streamer. Begin at the head of a deeper run, off to one side of the channel. Cast across the current, and take an upstream mend to let the fly sink. Let your streamer swing on a tight line, following it with the rod tip until it's directly below you. Take a couple of steps downstream and cast again, continuing through the run.

 HOOK MORE RISING FISH

Instead of setting the hook when you see a fish take your fly, wait until you see your leader move. Fish often roll to sink a fly, and then take it on a second pass. Giving yourself that extra moment will allow you to confirm that you have a solid hit and not a passing swipe.

289 PICK A FALL MEAT FLY

Specific patterns are generally less important in fall streamer fishing than they are in dry-fly fishing. The flies should be big, however: sizes 2–4 for larger waters, sizes 6–8 for smaller streams and creeks. Olive, tan, brown, and yellow are top fall colors. Black and chartreuse produce as well. You can do fine with three basic designs.

BUGGER-STYLE FLIES Especially effective are ones with rubber legs, such as the Autumn Splendor or Rubber Leg Crystal Bugger.

Autumn Splendor

Rubber Leg Crystal Bugger

FUR-STRIP FLIES Be sure to include a few in conehead style: The Double Bunny, Bandit Leech, and Kiwi Muddler are all good choices.

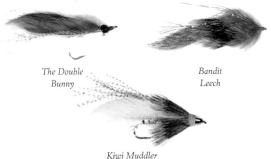

The Double Bunny

Bandit Leech

Kiwi Muddler

SCULPIN PATTERNS Serious trout-slayers include the Woolhead Sculpin, Matuka Sculpin, and Zoo Cougar. Some fishermen have even taken to using big saltwater patterns like a No. 2/0 Lefty's Deceiver, which measures 6 inches from tip to tail.

Woolhead Sculpin

Makuta Sculpin

Zoo Cougar

Lefty's Deceiver

290 FISH AROUND THE LEAVES

Autumn is probably my favorite time to fish. Rivers are typically low. Crowds have thinned. Trout are active. And the brightly colored leaves create a stunningly beautiful backdrop. The only problem is, a stiff breeze can blow all those pretty leaves into the river, making it harder for a trout to spot your fly. A few tricks will work in this situation.

FIND A SEAM First of all, I like to look for eddies near where fast water meets slow water. Trout like those hard seams, where leaves collect in a line, because that's where the bugs are also collecting. So if you find that comma-shaped line of leaves, and cast into the clear water right next to it, there's a good chance you will coax a trout to chase your fly, even a dry fly. In this case, the leaves actually help you pinpoint the cast.

STAND OUT Use flies with colors that don't match those leaves. In leaf-clogged water, I've done well with a Royal Stimulator with a peacock herl body and a band of red floss, and, as a dropper nymph, a blue Psycho Prince. Trout often hit blue and purple nymphs all day long.

TRY STREAMERS Think about it. A trout sees flecks and globs of plant matter washing by all day, but suddenly, out of its peripheral vision, it notices something darting in the other direction. You might have to pick leaves off a streamer every few casts, but it's worth it.

291 LUCK INTO A LAKER

Lake trout spend most of the year in the deepest, darkest parts of large bodies of still water. To catch them, conventional anglers lean on heavily weighted lures, lead-core trolling lines, and downriggers. By and large, lake trout aren't associated with flyfishing, but every spring, nature provides a brief window of opportunity for the fly caster to tie into one of these line-peeling brutes.

During the winter, when there is ice on a lake, lake trout gravitate to the upper portion of the water column to feed. Ice fishermen routinely hook trophy specimens in as little as 4 feet of water. When the ice breaks up in spring, lake trout tend to mill around in the shallows—just as they did under the ice—for a fleeting few days or weeks. Getting a fly in front of these fish before they retreat to the depths is all about making sure you're in the right place at the right time.

A good lake contour map comes in handy, as you want to identify any points where shallow flats butt up against slopes that drop off quickly into deep water. Lake trout

will hold in the deep water, but slide into the shallows to grab a quick meal. Ideally, you want to wade to a spot that allows you to cast into deep water, and draw the fly back into the shallows.

To entice these meat eaters, you want to present a big meal. Beef up to a 9- or 10-weight fly rod with a intermediate sinking line that can handle throwing double bunny-strip streamers measuring up to 10 inches long. These flies mimic smaller trout, which are a favorite forage of big lakers. Flies with a wide-profile head can up the ante, as they'll move more water and create more vibration for the fish to detect.

While it's possible to find early-spring lake trout feeding shallow any time of day, low light periods are prime. Since throwing the heavy rods and large flies that entice these fish is taxing, try not to burn yourself out by lunch time. Save your energy for the last few hours of light from the setting sun, or get up at zero-dark-thirty and attack at dawn.

292 DON'T KNOCK THE WHITEFISH

To most fly casters, nymph-stealing whitefish are nothing but pests. When one strikes, you'll think you've tied into the trout of a lifetime, only to be foiled again. I say embrace the whitefish. They get a bad rap, but each one you catch makes you a better nymph angler. Pick through enough hard-fighting whitefish, and you'll be more in tune to feel the subtle tap, or set on the slightest stop of an indicator, each time a fish slurps a nymph. And one of those times it'll be that big brown trout.

293 DEODORIZE FOR PERMIT

Ask any flats fisherman which skinny-water species is most challenging on the fly, and 99% of time you'll hear "permit." These fish are super-spooky and extra-picky about what they eat. Permit have an incredible sense of smell that allows them to sniff out crabs buried in the sand. It also gives them ability to catch the slightest whiff of sunblock or saliva on your fly from biting the tag end of your knot. Some fly-tiers are so sure unnatural smells cause the most permit refusals, they won't use any glue or cement on their patterns. Others will let their flies soak in sand and saltwater for a day before fishing. Since you may only get one or two shots a day at these fish, minimizing unnatural scent on your flies is definitely worth the effort.

ESSENTIAL FLIES: MOUSE RAT

TYPE: Hair Bug
PRIMARY SPECIES: Bass, Trout, Pike, Muskies

If you think mouse flies are gimmicks, think again. Not only do largemouth and pike go crazy over a helpless rodent that accidentally falls in the water, giant brown and rainbow trout blast them with a vengeance. You can find a wide variety of mice in fly shops, but those made of spun deer hair—like the Mouse Rat—are proven classics. Are you going to tie one on every weekend? Not likely. But it's smart to have a mouse on hand for that evening on the trout stream when the hatch is over, the sun is gone, and the big fish that haven't moved all day come out to play. Likewise, when darkness falls on your bass bite, cast out a mouse and swim it across the surface with long, slow strips. Listen for the attack, wait until you feel weight on the line, and then drive the hook home.

294 SKATE A PINK POLLYWOG

While silver salmon are quick to strike streamers and egg fly patterns, some of the most fun you'll ever have catching them is on topwater flies. Getting them to eat off the surface is a rare treat, and the fresher they are in the river from saltwater, the more apt they are to rise. It's not impossible to get a silver to hit a bass popper or slider, but by far the most popular salmon surface bug is the Pollywog. These deer-hair and foam creations are most often tied in pink or orange, and are closely related to mouse flies. Gently rake one across the surface with slow strips, and if the silvers in the run are feeling frisky, they'll pile onto this hot pink hunk of hair. Overcast days are typically more productive for topwater silver action than bright sunny days.

Catching a muskie on the fly is a Holy Grail achievement for many fly casters. Above all else, it takes drive and the willingness to keep going after them despite failed attempts at getting one of these finicky goliaths to actually open its maw and eat your streamer.

One choice you can make that will increase your odds of hooking a muskie is spending more time on rivers than lakes. While lakes produce plenty of 'skis, prime holding lies are not as easy to pinpoint as they are in moving water. Just like brown trout or smallmouth bass, muskies tend to hang at ambush points. Here's how to identify them—but getting a fish sitting on one to chew is up to you.

DAM SEAMS Directly below dams, you often find fast-moving, frothy, confused whitewater. This washing-machine effect disorients the smaller fish that muskies eat, and the current pushes this forage to the softer seams on the sides of the dam outflow. Work streamers from the whitewater into the soft spots (A).

BACKWATER EDDIES Muskies are not huge fans of holding in direct current, so any spot on a river where a pocket of calm, still water forms is worth a cast or 20 (B). Not only do these calm spots allow muskies to rest easy out of the flow, eddy currents associated with slack pockets often funnel forage in like a buffet line.

CURRENT BREAKS Literally anything in a river that breaks the current and creates a calm spot could be home to a muskie. The more broken the current, the larger the soft spot and the more likely a toothy is waiting in ambush. Large boulders are good, as are wing dams, but big fallen trees or logjams are often the real money (C).

CREEK MOUTHS Confluences of feeder creeks or tributaries provide muskies with a constant food source (D). Not only do fish flush out of the creek into the main river, but certain species, such as rainbow trout, will swim up tributaries to spawn.

INSIDE BENDS Sharp bends in a river deflect the main current to the outside of the turn, which usually creates a soft spot on the inside of the turn (E). Muskies hold here, waiting for forage riding the main current to pull in for a rest.

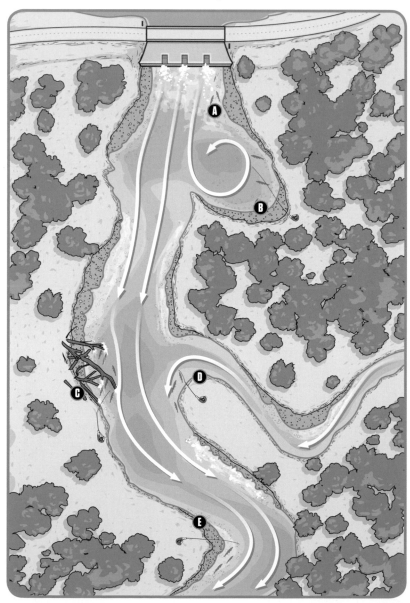

296 LAND YOUR DREAM MUSKIE

You've made 9,999 casts, and on lucky number 10,000 the muskie of your dreams shoots out from behind a submerged tree and hammers your fly. Now is not the time to panic. If you can remember these rules, you'll put your trophy in the net.

STRIKE LOW The biggest mistake anglers make when a muskie hits is lifting the rod to set the hook. The points rarely dig into its bony jaw, and you'll watch it swim off after spitting your fly. Strip-set, strip-set, strip-set, strip-set! A low strike angle will help drive the hooks home.

STRIKE LOW, AGAIN You remembered to strip-set and now the fish is pinned...or so you think. Go ahead and strip into the beast a few more times. Quite often, the fly material gets caught in a muskie's roof teeth. You think your fly is glued, but a few head shakes later, out pops the streamer. A couple more strip-sets should provide deal-sealing insurance.

FIGHT SIDEWAYS You want to really keep the pressure on, and keep the fish "hammered," as muskie nuts say.

To do that, fight the fish with the rod parallel to the water and bowed up hard with side pressure. If the fish pulls right, your rod should bend left and vice versa. The goal is to not give the fish any slack, which lets it run and roll and increases the chances that it will come unpinned.

ESSENTIAL FLIES: TARPON BUNNY

TYPE: Streamer

PRIMARY SPECIES: Saltwater, Pike/Muskies

Even though tarpon are huge fish, it doesn't take a complicated fly to fool them, and nothing proves that point better than the Tarpon Bunny. Widely hailed as one of the most effective tarpon flies ever created, the original pattern consists of nothing more than a rabbit-strip tail and body, and some marabou or schlappen feathers tied on an extra-strong hook. The pulsing, undulating action drives tarpon wild, especially when they're feeding in areas with current that let the fly breathe with minimal line movement. When stripped fast, it will also do a number on giant pike in freshwater.

297 CATCH A STONE-COLD TROUT

As a teenager, my box of go-to winter trout flies consisted of exactly two patterns: pink San Juan worms and orange salmon eggs. I was caught up in the misconception—as are many anglers, I think—that when the water's freezing cold, there are no bugs hatching, so I'd better drift something colorful that will look to a sluggish trout like an easy-to-get, protein-rich meal. I realized I was wrong one sunny afternoon in January as I sat on the bank of New Jersey's Pequest River, where thousands of tiny black stoneflies were crawling on the snow. I wasn't carrying a nymph box, but I managed to dig an ant pattern out of the bottom of my pack. I sunk it, swung it downstream to a riffle, and tied into a small rainbow trout within five sweeps of the run.

I decided then that black might be the new Day-Glo pink. Now, I never hit a stream after November without carrying some black stonefly nymphs in sizes 18 and 20, which have scored me some nice trout on days when my fly line practically froze in midcast.

Though your gut may tell you to fish a stonefly with split shot under an indicator, as you would in spring, I've found that subtler presentations often fool more trout in winter. Look for shallow riffles that transition into deeper, slower tailouts, and drift a stone on a light tippet, using only the weight of the beadhead to gain depth. Winter stones are tiny, and the current can carry them more quickly. Trout willing to feed at all this time of year will move around in the water column a bit to snatch a meal.

And if you have trouble letting go of your eggs and worms, you can have the best of both worlds with some tweaks at the vise. I started tying pink beadheads on my stones instead of gold or black, and replacing the traditional black split tail with iridescent orange marabou. You get some wiggle and a little bit of bacon-and-eggs color, but you're still matching the natural forage.

298 UNDERSTAND THE SNOWFLY'S LIFE CYCLE

"Stoneflies in the Capniidae family only hatch in the winter, even on the coldest days," says Robert Younghanz, a Colorado trout-fishing guide and aquatic entomologist. "They're jet black to help them absorb heat from the sun, and they don't fly. They mate right on the snow. It's the only significant insect fauna in winter, and you can find them in rivers from coast to coast."

While these little stones can hatch on any river on any given day, even large hatches will not trigger frenzies among trout in cold water with their metabolisms already slowed. Given that the stones are a natural winter food source that fish across the country universally recognize, however, trout may be quicker to eat them than to pursue a worm or egg. If you're going to try to take advantage of this winter hatch, you do need to keep an eye on the weather forecast.

"These stoneflies will mate on a cloudy day when the air temperature is in the teens," Younghanz says. "But big hatches will happen during ideal conditions. Bright sunny days are best, and if they coincide with a window where the temperature climbs into the 30s or 40s, all the better."

Field & Stream editor-at-large and FlyTalk blogger Kirk Deeter points out that many of his fellow diehard western winter trout bums tend to overlook these bugs in favor of tiny midges, and that's a mistake. "I think the little black stonefly is effective because it's a contrast bug," says Deeter. "In winter, when light is less direct and intense, I believe fish key on shapes and profiles as much as anything, and a dark, distinctive bug like a stonefly is going to get noticed. And at that time of year, when a trout's metabolism is slowed, they aren't going to chase some big chunky insect. That's probably why the little black stonefly is so deadly."

299 POP BY SPECIES

Poppers come into play when you're chasing a wide variety of species, and, regardless of which one you're after, nothing is more fun that watching the water erupt as one of these flies gets sucked off the surface. Here are some tricks that drive popper eaters crazy.

LARGEMOUTH BASS If you're working a popper through flooded grass or lily pads and it gets stuck, don't yank it with all your might. Give it some short, gentle tugs. The slight movement of the vegetation often gets a bass's attention, so it'll remove the popper from the snag for you.

SMALLMOUTH BASS In low light, tie on a black popper and pull it across the surface with slow, gentle strips instead of hard jerks. The color creates a better silhouette for bass to see from below, and the subtle swimming action mimics a juicy mouse trying to swim to safety.

PIKE Whenever you're casting a popper for pike, try to avoid having any slack in your line when the fly lands.

The sound of the bulky bug hitting the water is often what triggers a pike to strike, and it can happen so fast, you won't have time to pick up the slack and get tight.

REDFISH Between their poor eyesight and a downturned mouth, redfish have a habit of missing a popper on the first strike. If that happens, give the fly a short pop and let it sit still. It won't move out of the fish's narrow field of vision, and the redfish will get its mouth around a fly that's not moving much easier than one that is.

STRIPED BASS Stripers feeding on a school of live bait can get so keyed in to the real thing, it's hard to get them to hit anything artificial. The trick is to give your fly a different sound and vibration than the live bait, which will all sound alike swimming together underwater. Cast to the outside of the bait school and work your popper erratically, constantly changing the amount of pops and lengths of pauses.

300 BANG SOME BUCKETMOUTHS

Bass are found in every U.S. state except Alaska. They eat readily, and you can fish them for most of the year. With flies like Umpqua's Game Changer and Schmidterbait, it's never been easier to target these fish with the long rod. Here are five tips that should help you catch more bass on the fly.

SLOW DOWN Fish slowly with a topwater bug. I'd say nine times out of 10, the fish ate it when I wasn't paying attention to my popper. This tells me that I ought to slow it down and let it sit more than I think I should.

STAY CONSTANT Use a constant retrieve while nymphing for bass. It's almost impossible to discern a bass eating underwater with a nymph, even with an indicator. A constant retrieve of your bug, slow or fast, will help you feel the eat and catch more fish.

FIND FISH IN BIG WATER Learn one lake and fish it consistently. Fish with a local and ask a ton of questions. Find the structures, such as old creek channels, dropoffs, old buildings, roads, and so forth, and you will eventually find the fish.

TIME YOUR TRIP Of course you can catch fish throughout the day, but if I put in time at night or early in the morning with topwater bugs, I've found fish are far more receptive.

TRY PLASTIC Don't be afraid to toss soft plastics on the fly rod. At night, when it's tough to see vegetation, nothing works better than a light weedless rigged lizard or a four inch worm. Heck, half of all bass fishing "flies" are basically lures to begin with. Why not try what works when the going gets tough? You're still doing it on a fly rod.

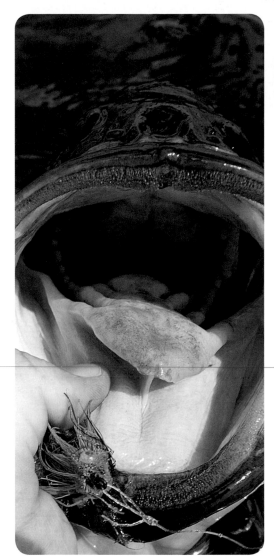

ESSENTIAL FLIES: DEAD DRIFT CRAYFISH

TYPE: Streamer/Wet Fly
PRIMARY SPECIES: Bass, Trout, Carp

There is no shortage of crayfish-imitating flies on the market, but I have yet to find one as effective as the Dead Drift Crayfish. Unlike other patterns that require stripping on the bottom to make them work, the Dead Drift is meant to free-float downstream. I like to hang this pattern under a large strike indicator and let it lazily drift through riffles and eddies. The rabbit-strip claws pulse in the current, and heavy smallmouths are quick to commit to a take. It's equally effective on large brown trout, especially in fall. Likewise, if you find carp feeding mid-column in deeper water, they'll gladly suck it up.

301 CATCH SMALLIES WITH SALTY FLIES

When rivers heat up in late summer, smallmouths can get downright lazy. The same fish that charged fast-moving streamers and poppers earlier in the season often take to feeding at night, and if your river is loaded with late-summer shad or herring fry, getting bass to eat fur and feathers becomes even harder.

Smallmouth guide Joe Demalderis gets around this by leaning on a bug tied with synthetic fur and fiber for the salt, such as a Mushmouth. Flies tied with Angel Hair or Puglisi Fiber retain more buoyancy and a wider profile when wet compared with flies using feathers, bucktail,

and rabbit fur, which take on water and sink faster.

Demalderis casts these flies on the outside of bait schools or in the deeper, slower runs that summer smallmouths frequent, and lets them fall broadside with the current. Where a Zonker or Clouser would sink away quickly, these synthetic baitfish imitators flutter down slowly, presenting a more accurate representation of a dying baitfish—and an easier target for lazy bass. Even if you don't want to use saltwater flies, incorporating some synthetic fur geared for the salt into your favorite smallmouth patterns can up your dog-day catch rate.

302 PICK A PRIME STEEL SPOT

When choosing a steelhead run, there's more to think about than just the number of chromers in the hole. As these fish often make screaming runs as soon as you stick them, a true "A spot" will also have water downstream that's more conducive to getting the fish in the net.

If a steelhead hole has a quarter mile of whitewater below it, you'll have a much tougher time keeping up with the fish as you chase it downcurrent. In fact, water below a hole that's too gnarly might make it impossible or dangerous to give chase. Whenever you can, fish runs with pockets of soft water 25 to 50 yards downstream and minimal root snarls or logjams. This will help you avoid getting tangled by fish running for line-popping structure, and will offer a calmer area you can steer the fish into for easier netting after that first hard run.

ESSENTIAL FLIES: GURGLER

TYPE: Popper
PRIMARY SPECIES: Saltwater, Bass, Pike, Muskies

Originally developed as a shrimp imitation, and most commonly associated with tarpon fishing, the Gurgler has proven a great crossover fly in other fisheries with tweaks to size and color. Thanks to its unique foam back and wide, cupped head, this pattern gurgles across the surface when stripped steadily, creating a bubble trail fish can follow. That action still accounts for a lot of big tarpon, redfish, snook, and seatrout gorging on shrimp when it's tied in pink, purple, or white. But tied in all black, it makes an excellent mouse pattern. Tied in green, it becomes a frog. With the addition of a monofilament weed guard, a Gurgler can pull bass, pike, and muskies out of pretty heavy vegetation.

303 RATTLE A SPECK

Some gamefish have keen eyesight or sense of smell. Speckled seatrout, on the other hand, can hear a shrimp clicking as it swims from a mile away. Given that these fish hunt in large part by sound, it's never a bad idea to use shrimp and baitfish flies with an internal glass rattle when hunting for specks. The click a tiny rattle produces can dramatically increase the number of seatrout you fool. Likewise, don't stamp around on the boat deck or slam the cooler loudly when you approach a likely spot. They'll hear that too...and bolt.

304 PLOT A DIY BONEFISH ATTACK

Sure, catching a bonefish from the bow of your guide's skiff is a thrill. But stalking the flats and landing one on your own is a true flyfishing feat. If you're fishing in south Florida or the Caribbean, make time to hit the flats and try to catch a bonefish the best way—on your own. As for flies, stick with the classics: Small Clousers, Gotchas, and Crazy Charlies in pink, white, and tan.

SEARCH FOR SIGNS Focus on the water 40 to 60 feet around you in all directions, and move very slowly. You're more likely to see the shadow below the fish than the fish itself. Look for the flash of a tail sticking out of the water or a color change on the bottom that's moving or irregular. Don't expect to see the whole fish.

CHANGE CHANNELS Schools of bonefish like to travel through channels on the flats with a bit more depth. Depressions also offer a quick escape route as the tide falls. If you find a channel close to a vast muddy flat, it's worth standing and waiting a while. Often, bones will come to you as the tide drops and they return to the channel to head to deep water.

TAKE THE LEAD If you drop a fly directly into a school of fish, or on a loner fish's head, it'll spook. Make every effort to lead the fish by 8 or 10 feet. Bonefish like moving targets, so, as the fish gets closer, make short strips to hop the fly. When you get hit, strip-strike hard before you lift your rod to fight. Lift too early and you'll pull the fly.

305 ANNOY A KING

Once king salmon migrate from the ocean into coastal rivers to spawn, they stop feeding. Yet they still crush flies. How's that possible? While salmon may no longer eat once they enter a freshwater, they still get mad. Imagine a bumblebee buzzing around your face. Your instinct is to swat it away. King salmon don't have hands, so when a fly gets in front of their faces and annoys them, they swat with their mouths. To increase your odds of angering a king into a crushing blow, cast full-bodied, gaudy streamers full of bright or neon colors and lots of flash. The more visually stimulating the pattern—the more obnoxious—the more often it'll get smoked. Small patterns in dull colors might swing right by a king without so much as raising its blood pressure a blip.

ESSENTIAL FLIES: PERMIT CRAB

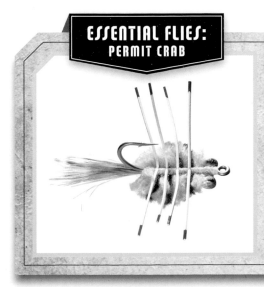

TYPE: Streamer

PRIMARY SPECIES: Saltwater

Created by legendary saltwater flyfisherman Del Brown, the Permit Crab (otherwise known as Del's Merkin), is one of the most effective flats flies ever tied. The combination of yarn, feathers, dumbbell eyes, and rubber legs is not complicated, yet it routinely fools permit—one of the most difficult fish to hook in saltwater. With a keen sense of smell, the uncanny ability to tell a natural offering from a fake, and a propensity to spook over the slightest misstep from the angler, even bait fisherman tossing live crabs at cruising permit end up pulling their hair out in frustration. The Permit Crab splashes down gently, sinks fast, and it only takes an ever-so-slight twitch to get its legs fluttering. Subtlety in your presentation counts when targeting permit, and even if you have more modern offerings, go with this one first.

306 SNEAK UP ON A CARP

Flyfishing for carp continues to rise in popularity, and by now everyone who wants to do it has found a lake or river with plenty of targets. But big carp don't need big water to thrive. I love the challenge of catching these fish on small streams. It's much like trout fishing, and with the right berry fly, you can even score surface strikes. But presentation is everything, and fighting a carp in tight quarters requires serious skill. Catching these spooky brutes spring through fall requires silent, patient stalking.

WAIT GAINS Because carp scare so easily, you may only get one cast at them. Take plenty of time to sit still and watch the fish before you cast. If they're rising, note any timing patterns. If they're grubbing the bottom, are they doing so in a circular course that brings them back to a starting point? These observations will help you figure out where and when to place that first cast. Pay particular attention to blowdowns that block the

current, as carp love to stack up and feed behind them (A). Gravel bars (B) that form in the dead water on the inside of hard turns are also great spots to find a few grubbing fish.

MUD WRESTLE Any small coves or indentations off the main current that silt up are usually carp magnets. You'll often find fish swimming a loop in these areas as they grub the soft bottom and sip in the surface film. Belly-crawl to the edge of the bank (C) and dapple your fly.

SOFT SELLS Ideally, your fly line should never hit the water during a presentation—especially if the stream is clear. This is where a long leader comes into play. Assume brush and branches along the stream will make false casting tricky. Roll casting may cause too much commotion and force you to stand or kneel and cast a shadow. The whole game revolves around the carp never knowing you're there.

307 WRANGLE OLD RUBBERLIPS

Carp might plod along very slowly, but these big-shouldered fish have serious speed and power once you set that hook. And they fight dirty. These four tricks will up your chances of getting a bruiser suckermouth into the landing net.

BE GENTLE Since carp eat small flies and can be very line shy, you'll likely need a light tippet to score a take. When you first set the hook, the fish will often not move instantly, which feels like pulling against a cinder block, or it will take off like a jet fighter the second it feels the sting. In either case, if you swing with all your might, you're going to break the tippet. A gentle lift is all it takes to plant the hook in that gummy mouth.

RAISE THE ROD If there are lily pads, roots, rocks, or sunken shopping carts in close proximity, count on the carp running right for them. They'll do their best to wrap and snap the leader. The trick is to keep their heads up. A high rod angle will make it harder for a carp to dive or slide under structure.

RUN FOR THE MONEY A carp's first run is typically the most powerful. If you survive it, you've greatly increased your odds of landing the fish. However, that doesn't mean you should take it easy if the fish turns into deadweight. Keep the pressure on, because it doesn't take much slack to allow a tiny hook barely lodged in the skin of a carp's mouth to fall out.

PRE-WET THE NET Anglers lose many crap right at the net. That's because the angler assumes the fish's energy is zapped, but when the net splashes, it suddenly wakes up and thrashes or runs. When the battle is coming to an end, I'll lay the net hoop in the water at my feet, gently steer the fish over the top of the bag, and then raise the net in one quick swoop.

ESSENTIAL FLIES: GAME CHANGER

TYPE: Streamer
PRIMARY SPECIES: Trout, Bass, Pike, Muskies, Saltwater

Game Changer is a fitting name for this fly, as it is perhaps the best example of how modern tying materials and new-school innovation are working together to create the next generation of classic patterns. Featuring three body segments linked together, this jointed streamer moves in a tight snake-like S pattern when stripped. This fly frequently incorporates new-wave Laser Dub—a lightweight, synthetic body material that gives flies a full look. With nearly endless possibilities for color combinations and sizes, you can tie the Game Changer to match just about anything: an 8-inch rainbow trout for trophy largemouths, a 6-inch mullet for striped bass and snook, or a 3-inch alewife herring for brown trout and smallmouth bass.

INDEX

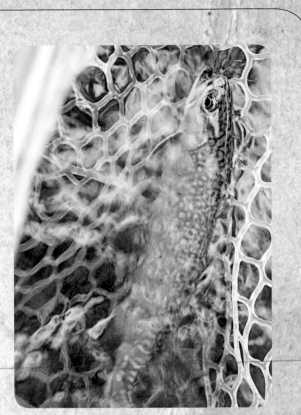

ABOUT THE AUTHOR

Joe Cermele started his career in outdoor journalism in 2004, covering fishing tournaments for a local magazine in his home state of New Jersey. In 2005, while attending Rider University, he became an intern at *Salt Water Sportsman* magazine, joining the editorial staff full time that same year after graduation. In 2008, he moved to sister publication *Field & Stream*, where he was named Fishing Editor in 2011. His writing appears monthly in the magazine, he blogs weekly on the magazine's website, and also hosts and produces *Field & Stream's Hook Shots*, an award-winning web-based fishing show with a punk-rock edge. He is also the author of *Field & Stream's Total Fishing Manual*. Cermele has fished all over the country and abroad, but when he's not traveling on assignment, you can find him casting flies to striped bass off the Jersey coast, smallmouth bass on the Delaware River, or trout in New York's Catskill Mountains.

ACKNOWLEDGMENTS

I would like to thank Mariah Bear, Allister Fein, Will Mack, and Conor Buckley from Weldon Owen first and foremost. Getting a book of this caliber together and on shelves is truly a team effort, and they are an exceptional team to work with. I would also like to thank all the amazing photographers who contributed to this project, especially my good friend Tim Romano who, in my opinion, is the best in the business. Finally, I'd be remiss if I didn't thank every contributor that shared his or her knowledge and passion for flyfishing on these pages, all in the hope that it will inspire someone else to fall in love with the sport.

ABOUT THE MAGAZINE

In every issue of *Field & Stream* you'll find beautiful artwork and photography, adventure stories, wild game recipes, humor, reviews, commentary, and more. That mix is what makes the magazine so great and what's helped it remain relevant since 1895. But at the heart of every issue are the skills. The tips that explain how to use the right lure for every situation, the tactics that help you catch that trophy bass, the lessons that you'll pass on to your kids about the joy of fishing—those are the stories that readers have come to expect from *Field & Stream*.

You'll find a ton of those skills in this book but there's not a book big enough to hold them all. Besides, whether you're new to fishing or an old pro, there's always more to learn. You can count on *Field & Stream* to teach you those essential skills in every issue. Plus, there's all that other stuff in the magazine, too, which is pretty great. To subscribe, visit www.fieldandstream.com/subscription.

When *Field & Stream* readers aren't hunting or fishing, they kill hours (and hours) on www.fieldandstream.com. And once you visit the site, you'll understand why.

On the site, you'll get to explore the world's largest online destination for hunters and anglers. Our blogs, written by the leading experts in the outdoors, cover every facet of hunting and fishing and provide constant content that instructs, enlightens, and always entertains.

Perhaps best of all is the community you'll find online at fieldandstream.com. It's where you can argue with other readers about the best trout fly or share photos of the fish you catch. And it's a place where you can spend a lot of time. Which is okay. Just make sure to reserve some hours for the outdoors, too.

CREDITS

All articles by Joe Cermele, with the following exceptions: *Gerald Almy:* 87, 89; *Steve Boyer:* 47; *Ed Cartier:* 79; *Kirk Deeter:* 1, 4, 7, 8, 11, 14, 16, 28, 31, 39, 61, 78, 80, 88, 91, 94, 104, 109–110, 120, 125–126, 131, 133, 139, 150, 159, 165, 193–195, 197–198, 221, 225, 227, 232, 240, 242–243, 246–247, 255, 258, 262, 267, 270, 278, 284, 290; *John Flambures:* 76; *John Frazier:* 187; *John Gierach:* 123, 166, 169–170, 213, 269; *Urban Giuliani:* 6; *Jeff Hull:* 241; *Mark E. Jackson:* 112; *Colin Kearns:* 15, 37, 41; *Tom Keer:* 43–44, 52, 58–61; *John Larison:* 157; *Ted Leeson:* 25–26, 180, 216, 244, 251, 273, 287, 295–296; *Anthony Licata:* 160; *James Masaoka:* 105; *Landon Mayer:* 143; *Craig Matthews:* 115; *Nate Matthews:* 75; *Keith McCafferty:* 124, 141; *Charlie Meyers:* 111; *John Merwin:* 3, 18, 21, 32–34, 38, 40, 42, 50–51, 119, 134, 136, 144, 149, 158, 164, 168, 171, 173–174, 184, 201–203, 204, 210–211, 215, 229, 259; *Stephen Miller:* 55; *T. Edward Nickens:* 2, 35, 54, 65, 67, 97, 113, 121–122, 128, 138, 148, 151, 156, 176, 185, 191, 220, 223, 252, 257; *Tim Romano:* 53, 172, 274; *Jerome Robinson:* 146, 288; *Will Ryan:* 19, 22, 207, 209, 212, 233–234, 237, 239, 245, 256; *Dave Scroppo:* 254; *Bob Stearns:* 135; *Greg Thomas:* 64; *Slaton L. White:* 206, 250; *Don Wirth:* 276, 277, 280–281, 289

Photography courtesy of: *A&R Allied Enterprise:* 31; *Rick Adair:* 261; *Jeffrey B. Banke / Shutterstock.com Barry & Cathy Beck:* 18, 19 (Brown Drake), 121–122, 133, 279, 281–282, 297 (snow); *Tosh Brown:* 73, 292–294, 299–301, 303, 305; *Denver Bryan/Images on the Wild Side:* 146, 291; *Bill Buckley:* 35 (lanyard); *Cabela's:* 175; *Louis Cahill Photography:* 36; *Joe Cermele:* Anthony Licata intro, Joe Cermele intro, Tools intro, 8, 9, 10, 12 ,13, 17, 20, 23, 24, 28, 30, 34, 35 (fisherman), 51, 64, 83, 90, 92 (flies), 95, 98, 101, 103, 106–107, 130, Techniques intro, 114, 116, 120, 123, 140, 145, 152–153, 156, 163, 166, 173, 182, 186, 188–189, 193, 196, 199, 207, 212–214, Tactics intro (fish), 218, 226, 228, 230–231, 235, 248, 251, 253, 255, 265, 268–269, 272, 274, 283, 286, 296, 297 (fly), 302, Index page 2; *Nigel Cox:* 102; *Ted Fauceglia:* 2 (nymphs), 112 (insects); *Pat Ford:* 285; *Michael H. Francis:* 19 (Hex); *Cliff Gardiner & John Keller:* 2 (Squirrel Nymph), 37, 41, 59, 62, 93, 105; *Peter Gathercole:* 136 (lower), 176, 229, 232; *Gehrke's Gink:* 113; *Jim Golden:* 19 (flies), 237–238; *Gorman Studio:* 4; *Brian Grossenbacher:* 19 (Giant Salmonfly, Golden Stone), 50, 142, 183, 205, 215, 223, 256, 263, 290, 304; *Matt Guymon:* 19 (Green Drake); *Alexander Ivanov:* 49, 56; *Mark Johnson/Images on the Wild Side:* 169; *Spencer Jones:* 38, 58, 180; *John Juracek/Images on the Wild Side:* 292; *Sam Kaplan:* 260; *Korkers Products:* 48; *Lon Lauber:* 191; *John Lawton:* 75 (tree); *Bill Lindner:* 209; *Loon Outdoors:* 35 (floatant, forceps, nippers); *Macomber Inc:* 136 (upper); *Tom Martineau / www.therawspirit.com:* 252, 278; *Midland Radio Corporation:* 42; *Ted Morrison:* 75 (fly-tying materials), 94, 112 (flies); *Jens Mortensen:* 15; *Luke Nilsson:* 27, 65; *Orvis:* Essential Flies (March Brown, Zug Bug, March Brown Wet, Mickey Finn, Black Stonefly, Krystal Spinner, Sneaky Pete, Gurgler); *Travis Rathbone:* 1, 7(large fly), 21, 22, 29, 77, 85, 89; *RIO Products:* 35 (tippet); *Tim Romano:* half title, title page, 39, 53, 68, 69, Tying intro, 71, 76, 87, 100, 111, 124, 125, 127, 132, 138, 150, 155, 159, 161, 177, 178, 184, 210, Tactics intro (tattoo), 217, 220, 221, 227, 246, 249, 259, 307, Credits; *Dan Saelinger:* 2 (flies except Squirrel Nymph), 3, 32–33, 35, 44, 54, 104, 79 202, 289; *SF Digital Studio:* 70, 71 (hooks), 84; *Shutterstock:* Chapter openers (background), 19 (reel), 40, 72, 74, 80, 82, 92 (basket), 96–97, 147, 192, 254, 266, 287; *Jan Siman:* 243; *William Styer:* 99; *Tenkara Pyrénées www.tenkara.fr/english/:* 67; *Kyle Thompson:* 7 (small flies); *Tidal Roots www.TidalRoots.com:* 171; *John Toolan:* 135; *Umpqua Feather Merchants:* Essential Flies (Parachute Adams, Woolly Bugger, Hare's Ear, Stimulator, Copper John, Elk Hair Caddis, Flashback Pheasant Tail, Blue Winged Olive, Prince Nymph, Zonker, San Juan Worm, Muddler Minnow, Clouser Minnow, Dave's Hopper, Deceiver, Royal Wulff, Zebra Midge, Salmon Egg, Foam Bass Bug, Epoxy Scud, Foam Beetle, Griffith's Gnat, Crazy Charlie, Inchworm, Chernobyl Ant, Flesh Fly, Banger, Foam Ant, Adult Damsel, Flashtail Whistler, Mouse Rat, Tarpon Bunny, Dead Drift Crayfish, Permit Crab, Game Changer), 179, 194–195, 219; *Pasi Visakivi:* 298; *WestWater Products:* 86

Illustrations courtesy of: *Conor Buckley:* 28, 47, 52, 60, 126, 143, 149, 151, 187, 197, 200, 206, 233–234, 236, 244–245, 250, 257, 260, 273, 295, 306; *Dogo:* 190; *Dan Marsiglio:* 134, 157, 160, 165; *Christine Meighan:* 43, 102, 167, 203–204, 222; *Hayden Foell:* 88, 104, 115, 141, 170, 184, 198, 225, 240, 242, 247, 258, 267; *Jason Lee :* 131, 137; *Samuel A. Minick:* 162, 239; *Chris Philpot:* 264; *Robert L. Prince:* 4, 15, 185, 208, 216, 284; *Jason Schneider:* 139, 148; *Mike Sudal:* 108, 118, 281; *Lauren Towner:* 57, 119, 125, 158, 164, 172–174, 201, 275, 277, 280

weldon**owen**

CEO Raoul Goff
VP PUBLISHER Roger Shaw
EDITORIAL DIRECTOR Katie Killebrew
VP CREATIVE Chrissy Kwasnik
ART DIRECTOR Allister Fein
VP MANUFACTURING Alix Nicholaeff
PRODUCTION MANAGER Sam Taylor

Copyright © 2022 by Weldon Owen
an imprint of Insight Editions
P.O. Box 3088
San Rafael, CA 94912
www.weldonowen.com

No part of this book may be reproduced in any form without
written permission from the publisher.

ISBN: 978-1-68188-822-4

Printed in China

Flexibound edition first printed in 2015

2022 2023 2024 2025 • 10 9 8 7 6 5 4 3 2 1

FIELD & STREAM

EXECUTIVE VICE PRESIDENT Eric Zinczenko
EDITOR-IN-CHIEF Anthony Licata
EXECUTIVE EDITOR Mike Toth
MANAGING EDITOR Jean McKenna
DEPUTY EDITORS Dave Hurteau, Colin Kearns,
Slaton L. White
COPY CHIEF Donna L. Ng
SENIOR EDITOR Joe Cermele
ASSISTANT EDITOR Kristyn Brady
DESIGN DIRECTOR Sean Johnston
PHOTOGRAPHY DIRECTOR John Toolan
DEPUTY ART DIRECTOR Pete Sucheski
ASSOCIATE ART DIRECTORS Russ Smith,
James A. Walsh
PRODUCTION MANAGER Judith Weber
DIGITAL DIRECTOR Nate Matthews
ONLINE CONTENT EDITOR Alex Robinson
ONLINE PRODUCER Kurt Shulitz

2 Park Avenue
New York, NY 10016
www.fieldandstream.com